AMERICAN CICHLIDS I · DWARF CICHLIDS

Horst Linke · Wolfgang Staeck

Horst Linke · Wolfgang Staeck

AMERICAN CICHLIDS I

DWARF
CICHLIDS

A Handbook for their
Identification, Care,
and Breeding

Cover photographs:
Above left: *Laetacara dorsigera*
Above right: *Papiliochromis ramirezi*
Below left: *Apistogramma cacatuoides*
Below right: *Dicrossus maculatus*
Rear: *Laetacara curviceps*

Photo insertions:
front: Locality of *Apistogramma linkei* (Rio Yucapani in Bolivia)

back: Rio Chinipo in Peru; such waters are biotopes of rheophile cichlids.

The American Cichlids are presented in 2 volumes:

Cichlids I: Dwarf Cichlids
Cichlids II: Large Cichlids

© 1994 Tetra-Press
Tetra-Werke Dr. rer nat. Ulrich Baensch GmbH
Herrenteich 78, D-49324 Melle, Germany

Distributed in U.S.A. by
Tetra Sales U.S.A.
3001 Commerce Street
Blacksburg, VA 24060

Distributed in UK by
Tetra Sales, Lambert Court,
Chestnut Avenue, Eastleigh Hampshire S05 3ZQ

Translation from German: HERPRINT INTERNATIONAL cc,
P.O. Box 14117, Bredell 1623, South Africa
Typesetting: Fotosatz Hoffmann, Hennef
Lithos: Flotho Reprotechnik, Osnabrück
Printed in Germany

WL-Code: 16757
ISBN 1-56465-168-1

CONTENTS

PREFACE

This translated edition is based on the fourth revised and updated German edition about South American Dwarf Cichlids which was first published in 1984. Comparing this book with the first edition it becomes obvious that our knowledge about these fishes has been greatly expanded by ichthyological collecting trips and the work on ichthyological collections in zoological museums. This increase in information is visible in the numerous descriptions of new species and the imports of species which have not been available before.

Within the eight years from the publication of the first edition more than twenty new species and even three new genera have been scientifically described.

We would like to express our thanks to Messrs. Bernd KILIAN, Ingo KOSLOWSKI, Rüdiger SCHÄFER, Rainer STAWIKOWSKI, Frank WARZEL, and Wolfgang WINDISCH especially who granted us support by photographs and information.

Horst LINKE   Wolfgang STAECK

THE CICHLIDS

Cichlids today range amongst the most popular fishes for the aquarium. Not only that they are extremely interesting to observe and to study, their usually very splendid colourations have also made them desired inhabitants of the underwater world behind glass. The opinion that these fishes would be aggressive and vicious predators which would destroy plants was caused by improper husbandry conditions and could be eliminated in the meantime. The species portrayed in this book without exception belong to the peaceful Cichlids tolerating plants — and even require large numbers of aquatic plants. They are usually fairly shy by nature and use the thickets of vegetation to hide and live.

Small Cichlids with a maximum length of 10 cm, in exceptional cases of up to 12 cm, are usually referred to as Dwarf Cichlids amongst aquarists. This group includes species of different origin and systematic position. The South American Dwarf Cichlids also do not form a homogenous and closed organization and originate from various cladistic groups. Containing approximately 50 described and more than 20 undescribed species and many more yet to be discovered, the genus *Apistogramma* is by far the largest genus of Dwarf Cichlids.

Taeniacara and *Apistogrammoides* on the other hand are monotypical, i.e. contain only a single species each. A few Dwarf Cichlids are also assigned to a genus which otherwise exclusively contains species of moderate to large size, i.e. the genus *Crenicichla*.

Dwarf Cichlids are found in not less than 12 genera of South American Cichlids. All of

With their ruby to purplish red colours, the small *Laetacara dorsigera* undoubtedly belong to the most beautiful Cichlids of South America.

9

them are peace-loving and most of them are brilliantly coloured. Only amongst members of their own species they may temporarily become quite aggressive. The defence of the living-area, the "territory" as it is referred to in the science of behavioural biology, plays an important role during courtship periods. Since these are very small fishes, their tanks accordingly do also not need to be very large. Notwithstanding this, one should take into consideration that it is of advantage for all biological processes as well as for the fishes themselves to have tanks available which are as large as possible. The larger the aquarium is the better is its biological stability. As is the case in all Cichlids, the small Cichlids are bottom-dwellers thus the available ground-space is significant, whereas the height is not. One should therefore preferably chose long and deep aquaria for the husbandry of these fishes. The height of the tank is however of secondary interest.

Another remark appears to be appropriate to be made right here in the beginning. Most of these small South American fish originate from the tropics. Only a few species inhabit the subtropics. It is therefore crucial to constantly monitor that the temperatures are high enough.

Furthermore, one should be aware of the fact that most of these fishes originate from very soft, partly even very acidic waters. The modern aquarium technology however offers the necessary equipment to create the required "environment" also in captivity. Desalting filters and the fortification of aquarium-water with humin acid by filtration through peat are on the other hand no new inventions, but have belonged to the "tools" of the aquarists for a long time.

Before the husbandry of these Dwarf Cichlids is looked at in detail, some remarks on their systematic positions, the naming, their special features, and their body-patterns cannot to be avoided. Cichlids are distinguished not only by their behaviour, distribution, and reproductive mode, but also by their body-shape and other morphological traits. A system for arranging the organisms in an order is necessary for proper differentiation. This system was suggested by the Swedish botanist Carl VON LINNÉ in the year 1758.

Despite of vast new knowledge gathered during the course of the centuries, this system is still in use. It arranges the variety of forms of plants and animals and also shows the systematic position of the Cichlids.

In the class Osteichthys, the bone-fishes, one finds in the order Perciformes, the perch-like fishes, and the suborder Percoidea, the perch-fishes, the family of Cichlidae, the Cichlids which contains more than 100 genera. This view into the systematics is not unnecessary for the aquarists. In the 10th edition of his book "Systema naturae", LINNÉ combined the systematic order with the binary nomenclature. This means the double naming for the scientific arrangement. Even with this system some aquarists experience problems and frustrations due to the unfamiliar scientific designations.

Therefore the common names are very much in use which however differ and do not permit a clear and exact determination. Only the scientific names allow an unmistakable identification worldwide. This may be illustrated by an example. Many aquarists have kept the small slender Cichlid from South America which is often referred to as Agassiz' Dwarf Cichlid. Despite this widely used name, confusion often occurs.

If the scientific name *Apistogramma agassizii* is used instead, confusion is eliminated. For the informed aquarist this name however means much more. Staying with this example and writing it in full, one gets *Apistogramma agassizii* (STEINDACHNER, 1875). The first name *"Apistogramma"* indicates the genus. It is always capitalized. One may recognize the relationship provided one is able to assign it to the family. The second name, *"agassizii"* in this case, refers to the species and is never capitalized. It has priority, which means that even if the generic name changes, the fish still keeps the species name introduced by the first describer. Since both generic and specific name are Latin or Latinized and the species name has to be of the same sex as the genus name, only the last syllable of the species name may change to fit the new generic name. The third part of the name (STEINDACHNER, 1875) indicates that this fish was described by the Austrian scientist STEINDACHNER in the year 1875.

Since the name is indicated in brackets, it is obvious that the generic name has been changed at a later date for at least once.

STEINDACHNER described this species in 1875 as *Geophagus agassizii*.

As important as the name is for the formal identification of the fish, the knowledge about the morphology of its body is just as important. If one wants to understand the description of a species one has to know how the body of a Cichlid is organized. "Head" refers to the zone from the tip of the snout to the hind edge of the gill-cover, to the gill opening. The part from there to the anus is considered the "body". The remaining part from there to the base of the tail where the caudal fin begins is referred to as the "tail".

The "caudal peduncle" on the other hand ranges from the hind edge of the anal-fin to the base of the caudal fin. Cichlids have a dorsal fin on the back, a pectoral fin on either side of the anterior body, and two often extended ventral fins usually at the level of the pectoral fins. In the posterior part of the lower body there is an anal fin.

At the end of the body, the caudal peduncle carries the caudal fin.

This has an impact on the measuring system applied. The total or over-all length, often referred to just as length, is measured from the tip of the snout to the end of the caudal fin. The body-length, sometimes also named standard length, indicates the distance from the tip of the snout to the end of the body, i.e. up to the caudal peduncle. The caudal fin is thus not taken into consideration.

The colour-pattern plays an important role in distinguishing between the various species of small South American Cichlids and especially between the many forms of *Apistogramma*. A brief look at these features therefore appears to be appropriate here. Running from the eye to the nape, there is a superorbital stripe (1). The preorbital stripe (2) connects the tip of the snout with the eye, and a suborbital (3) runs from the eye to the lower hind edge of the gill-cover. The lateral band (4) begins right behind the eye. It crosses over the body and usually ends on the caudal peduncle. On the base of the tail there is a caudal spot (5). The back is marked with dorsal blotches (6) which

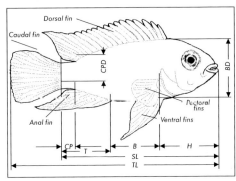

TL = Total length   SL = Standard length
H = Head length   B = Body
T = Tail   CP = Caudal peduncle
CPD = Depth of CP   BD = Body depth

often extend up to the base of the dorsal fin. The anterior body is patterned with seven transversal bars (7) which run arching up to the tail ending at the caudal peduncle. On the lateral band, usually at the height of the third transversal bar, there is a lateral spot (8). Below the lateral band, there are horizontal abdominal stripes (9) which extend up to the tail. If these are not arranged horizontally but obliquely or vertically, they are referred to as abdominal streaks (10). If a black marking is present at the base of the pectoral fins or in its immediate vicinity, it is named the pectoral spot (11). The edge of the belly is often marked with a different colour and this stripe is then referred to as an midventral stripe (12). If there is a dark or even black marking present at the anus, it is named an anal spot (13). All these terms are significant when it comes to the identification of a species of *Apistogramma* and will consequently be used very frequently in the following.

The body-shape of the species of *Apistogramma* is often described as high-backed or slender and elongate. The different shapes of the caudal fins are also important factors for the determination of the species. They are indicated as being either rounded, oval, truncate, lanceolate, or lyreate.

The small Cichlids of South America have been enjoying an increasing popularity during the past years. There was however a considerable amount of confusion regarding their proper names. During the 1930' it was primarily Dr. Ernst AHL who intensely worked on the genus *Apistogramma*. Then, during the fifties and sixties, Dr. Hermann MEINKEN was

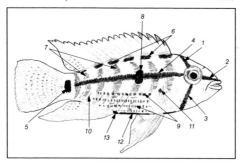

1 = Superorbital stripe
2 = Preorbital stripe
3 = Suborbital stripe
4 = Lateral band
5 = Caudal spot
6 = Dorsal blotches
7 = Transversal bars
8 = Lateral spot
9 = Abdominal stripes
10 = Abdominal streaks
11 = Pectoral spot
12 = Midventral stripe
13 = Anal spot

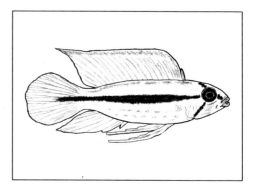

Elongated body-shape

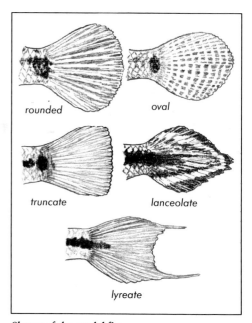

Shapes of the caudal fin

especially interested in this genus and described several new species. Unfortunately both happened to err on several occasions, and the genus was considered incomprehensible and in urgent need for a revision for decades. It then was the merit of the Swedish ichthyologist Sven O. KULLANDER who took over this task in the seventies and rapidly went ahead with it so that there are presently only a few unanswered questions left the genus *Apisto-*

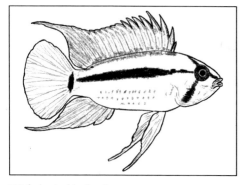

High-backed body-shape

gramma and the mix-up of synonyms and mis-identifications is sorted out. Thanks is how-ever also due to some German aquarists who committed themselves to research in the new and scientifically still undescribed species.

Their almost complete documentation in this sector has largely clarified the situation. In this connection Messrs. Werner SCHMETTKAMP and Ingo KOSLOWSKI must especially be

mentioned. They have kept the aquarists informed about new imports and discoveries.

With these explanations the introductional part may be considered completed. The fol-lowing first part of this work deals compre-hensively with the Dwarf Cichlids of South America. The large Cichlids of South and Cen-tral America will be introduced in the second volume.

Palmtree oasis in the dry steppes of the Llanos in eastern Columbia, the habitat of *Apistogramma viejita* Colour-morph III

SOUTH AMERICA

Caracas

Atlantic Ocean

Magdalena
Cauca
Orinoco
Meta
Bogotá
Guaviare
Orinoco
Rio Negro
Rio Branco
Esequibo
Georgetown
Paramaribo

Quito
Japurá
Manaus
Maraca
Belém
Fortaleza

Marañón
Amazonas
Juruá
Madeira
Tapajós
Xingu
Tocantins
Parnaíba
Teresina

Ucayali
Madre de Dios
Guaporé
Jurueña
Recife

Lima
Beni
Xingu
São Francisco
Salvador

Titicacasee
Araguaia
Brasilia

La Paz
Poopósee
Belo Horizonte
Vitória

Pacific
Ocean
Paraguay
Paraná
Rio de Janeiro
São Paulo

Pilcomayo

R. Salado
Uruguay
Porto Alegre

Paraná

Santiago de Chile
Buenos Aires
Montevideo

Rio Colorado

Rio Negro
Atlantic
Ocean

Chubut

Las Heras
1000 km

DWARF CICHLIDS FROM SOUTH AMERICA

Although the term Dwarf Cichlid is commonly and frequently used by the aquarists, it is not properly defined. Most authors regard species with a maximum length of 10, sometimes up to 12 centimetres, to be Dwarf Cichlids. Despite that this seems to be a clear criterion, experience shows that it is still a problem since many species do not exceed these lengths in the wild, but grow considerably larger in the home aquarium. Another problem is caused by the fact that the females of several species do not exceed the drawn borderline, but the males reach sizes clearly above it.

Since the term Dwarf Cichlid is neither of ecological relevance nor has a systematic impact, its usage does not make any statement on the ecological requirements or the systematic position of a particular species. The first model of a hypothetical genealogical tree of the South American Cichlids was developed by the English ichthyologist REGAN in 1906. His theories about the cladistic relationships of the various Cichlid genera were widely accepted for decades. It was not before the 1980' when numerous new species and further genera were described that an increasing number of details of this model were questioned and subsequently amended (KULLANDER 1980, 1983, 1986, 1988, 1989, 1990). The most important perception of the past years was the fact that the modern South American Cichlids cannot be traced back to a single common ancestral form, but that there were probably several progenitors.

Nearly 80 species have been described from South America, whose small body-size enables them to classify for the title Dwarf Cichlids.

These are added by approximately another 30 species which are known in the hobby or from the collection of zoological museums, but which have not been scientifically described yet.

The South American Dwarf Cichlids belong to twelve genera and form a very heterogenous group systematically with the individual members belonging to different cladistic groups. Due to the large number of species, *Apistogramma* is the most important genus. Together with the genera *Apistogrammoides*, *Taeniacara*, and *Papiliochromis*, which are poor in species, it is placed in the clade of the Geophagines. The three genera *Dicrossus*, *Crenicara*, and *Mazarunia* which do not contain more than seven species altogether, form the group of the Crenicarines.

Their cladistic relationships are presently unclear (KULLANDER 1990).

The species of the genus *Teleocichla* are closely related to those of the genus *Crenicichla* (KULLANDER 1988) which also contains a number of Dwarf Cichlids. Both are consolidated in the group of the Crenicichlines.

According to new information the *Laetacara*-species, previously referred to as *Aequidens*, show corresponding features with the Cichlasomine Cichlids (KULLANDER 1983), and the same apparently applies to the representatives of the genus *Nannacara* which are quite similar to the *Apistogramma*-species. The cladistic relationship of the two species of *Biotoecus* is unclear (KULLANDER 1989).

Since the increasing number of species caused the genus *Apistogramma* to become quite incomprehensible, attempts have been made in the past few years to consolidate similar forms in groups in this cladistic unit (KULLANDER 1980, KOSLOWSKI 1985) which are however not always especially closely related to one another or even monophyletic in every case. Only if the term species-complex is used, it is to be supposed that the relevant forms have derived from a common ancestor.

Especially rich in species is the regani-group which may obviously be further divided into several species-complexes. Most of the fishes assigned to this group are characterized by a relatively high back and a generally well recognizable pattern of dark transversal bars. Another typical feature is that the sexual dimorphism is comparatively weakly developed in most these species making it difficult to distinguish the sexes of subadult specimens. The regani-group consolidated the species A. caetei, A. cruzi, A. eunotus, A. geisleri, A. gossei, A. moae, A. ortmanni, A. pleurotaenia, A. regani, A. resticulosa, A. taeniata, A. urteagai, and probably A. piauiensis.

The distribution of the species mentioned before concentrates in the north of the South American subcontinent. In the southern parts, the commbrae-complex forms the counterpart to the regani-group. The typical character of these species is a large, almost quadrangular caudal spot which results from the spot of the caudal-base being fused with the seventh transversal bar. The group consists of the three species A. commbrae, A. inconspicua, and A. linkei.

Typical traits for the males of the cacatuoides-complex are large mouths, thick lips, enlarged dorsal fins, and zigzag-shaped abdominal stripes. During periods of reproduction, the lateral band is reduced to a lateral spot in the female. This complex consolidates the species A. cacatuoides, A. juruensis, A. luelingi, and A. norberti.

The forms A. payaminonis and A. nijsseni are closely related to this group.

The members of the agassizi-group are the species A. agassizii, A. bitaeniata, A. gephyra, A. elizabethae, A. pulchra, and possibly also A. paucisquamis. These are quite slender fishes which are characterized by a broad lateral band, a distinct lateral spot, and rudimentary transversal bars.

The macmasteri-group unites A. guttata, A. hoignei, A. hongsloi, A. macmasteri, and A. viejita. All these species are high-backed and the males have enlarged dorsal fins. During

periods of parental care, the females show a black zone around the base of the pectoral fins, i.e. a so-called pectoral spot.

The gibbiceps-group consists of fairly slender species, all of them having a lyreate caudal fin and abdominal bands. It consolidates the forms A. gibbiceps and probably A. roraimae and A. personata.

Another small assembly is the steindachneri-group with also only three species, i.e. A. hippolytae, A. steindachneri, and A. rupununi.

These fishes are characterized by a comparatively narrow lateral band and a conspicuously large lateral blotch. During the breeding phase, the females show only the caudal and the lateral spot.

The pertensis-group contains quite elongate fishes which are characterized by a distinct lateral spot, reduced transversal bars, and — in the male sex — by a conspicuously enlarged dorsal fin in which the membranes are at least partly fused. This may cause the dorsal fin to become sail-like in shape. Besides several undescribed species, A. iniridae, A. meinkeni, and A. pertensis are assigned to this group.

Apart from the species of Apistogramma mentioned before which can be assigned to one or another group — though with varying certainty — there are a couple of other fishes whose cladistic relationships have to be considered unclear as there is too little information available until today. In some of these cases an assignment is complicated because they assume isolated positions due to morphological or anatomical factors or have features of two groups.

A quite isolated species is for example A. borelli from the catchment area of the Rio Paraguay. The males of these quite high-backed fish have membranes in the dorsal fin which greatly exceed the length of the spines and which are fused. In the females, on the other hand, the black pattern on the flanks is almost entirely reduced. Further species whose cladistic relationships cannot be identified and which can therefore not be assigned to one of the groups with some degree of certainty are A. brevis, A. diplotaenia, A. staecki, and A. trifasciata.

The South American Fish-regions

(after GERY [1969] in LOWE-MCCONNELL [1975])

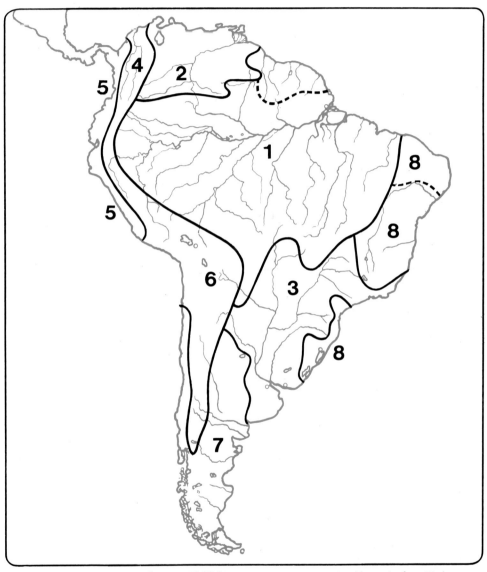

1 = Guyana — Amazon (more than 150 Cichlids)
2 = Orinoco — Venezuela
3 = Paraguay — Uruguay — Paraná
4 = Magdalena Region
5 = Trans-Andean Region
6 = Andean Region
7 = Patagonian Region
8 = Eastern Brazil

The distribution of the Dwarf Cichlids is mainly restricted to the regions 1 to 3 and parts of 6 and 8.

THE SUITABLE TANK FOR DWARF CICHLIDS FROM SOUTH AMERICA

The most important precondition for the husbandry and breeding of fishes in the long run is an aquarium appropriately set up for a species. Before one starts to prepare a tank for the keeping of Dwarf Cichlids it is therefore recommendable to obtain fundamental information on their natural ecology and the conditions under which they live in the wild. Only the sound knowledge about all environmental factors which influence the life of the fishes in their natural habitats enables us to emulate conditions in captivity which resemble those as closely as possible. Nothing but a suitable set-up of the aquarium meeting the requirements of the fishes as widely as possible provides some sort of guarantee that the animals will stay in good health long-term and may even start breeding one day. In contrast to the larger growing Cichlids whose numerous species also inhabit Central America, the distribution of the Dwarf Cichlids dealt with in this book is restricted to South America. The majority of species known so far originates from the Guyana-Amazon fish-region.

Important centres of the distribution of Dwarf Cichlids are however also the Orinoco-Venezuela region and the Paraguay-Uruguay-Paraná region. A small number of species is found in the eastern parts of the Trans-Andean region whereas the occurrence of Dwarf Cichlids in the Eastern Brazilian fish-region is exclusive to the northwestern regions.

The major part of the vast distribution range of these fishes is covered by tropical rainforest and the majority of Cichlids portrayed here therefore inhabits this type of landscape. It is however to be taken into consideration that the areas of tropical rainforest are constantly shrinking due to the destructive activities of man. In the areas of villages and inter-city roads of Brazil and Peru especially there are vast regions today which were covered by rainforest ten or twenty years ago, but which are nothing but meadows and arable land today. However, quite a number of species were obviously able to adapt to the changing environment and still occur in these cultured areas. Apart from these, there are Dwarf Cichlids which naturally inhabit regions outside the rainforests. This group in others include species in the Orinoco-Venezuela fish-region whose natural habitats lie in tree-less, steppe-like plains in the east of Colombia which are referred to as the Llanos. Their biotopes are the small water-bodies in the oasis-like vegetation-islands which are scattered over the steppes.

Within the vast distribution range of Dwarf Cichlids in South America, there are obviously very different kinds of water-bodies. It may therefore be amazing that, at the first glance, the natural biotopes of these species are all relatively similar. It has however to be taken into consideration that the Dwarf Cichlids are a favourite prey of all sorts of larger fishes and thus are under constant threat. Their major predators are less the ill-famed Piranhas which actually prefer other types of waters but more the predatory Characines of the genera *Hoplias* and *Erythrinus,* predatory Cichlids such as the genus *Crenicichla,* Knife-fish, and numerous Catfishes. The typical habitats of *Apistogramma*-species and their allies are therefore rarely the larger rivers and lakes but more the streams, ponds, pools, and remainders of water-bodies which are always under threat to dry up completely during the dry seasons.

Dwarf Cichlids generally avoid zones of free water. Their favourite places are near the banks in extremely shallow water, i.e. a depth of just a few centimetres. It is characteristic for all *Apistogramma*-biotopes that they provide a lot of hiding-places, are well covered, and enable the fishes to lead a secretive and concealed life. Only in rare exceptional cases is this requirement for cover of the Dwarf Cichlids met by aquatic plants since the South American waters are generally poor in submerse vegetation. In water-courses crossing the rainforests, a thick layer of leaf-litter on the ground provides the required cover. Additional hiding-places are supplied by roots and dead branches and twigs. In the open terrains the fishes usually find cover amongst the flooded or overhanging terrestrial vegetation, i.e. between grass and emerse bank-vegetation. It is remarkable, especially as it has never been reported before, that the species of *Apistogramma* are not necessarily bottom-dwellers. In water-bodies which lack a definite zone of shallow water, but have a dense canopy of floating plants, mainly such as *Eichhornia* and *Salvinia*, instead, the Dwarf Cichlids may also live, as the author was repeatedly able to observe in Bolivia, amongst the leaves and roots of these plants immediately below the water-surface! Three types of South American

waters are distinguished by their degree of murkiness and colour. In every case their development results from very specific geological, environmental, and climatic factors. A high percentage of anorganic suspended matter is responsible for the so-called white-water rivers to which the Rio Solimoes and the Ucayali belong. This causes the water to be cloudy and loamy yellow in colour reducing the visibility often to only a few centimetres. In contrast to these are the water-courses of the second group which are referred to as clearwater rivers. Rivers such as the Rio Xingu and the Rio Tapajoz carry clean and transparent water which is poor in sediments and has a green to yellowish green colour. The water of the third type, the so-called black-water rivers, to which the Rio Negro and the Rio Cururu belong, also have a clear transparent water, which is however tinted deep dark brown having the colour of tea. This colouration is caused by vast masses of plant decay-matters which are flushed into the rivers during the rainy seasons whilst the surrounding

Most Cichlids require densely planted aquaria like this one. Low plants (*Anubias barteri* var. *nana*) decorate the foreground whilst moderately sized *Echinodorus*-species, *Hygrophila polysperma*, and *Alternanthera reineckii* grow in the central parts. The back ground is vegetated by large stem-plants.

rainforest is flooded for months. Obviously there are a lot of intergradual forms between these three types of water. A general feature of all Amazonian waters is that they have pH-values which are clearly in the acidic regions and that they are extremely poor in dissolved minerals which means that their total and carbonate hardness are extremely low. This applies to black-water especially and is also the reason for the fact that Dwarf Cichlids from this type of water are often problematic species in the aquarium.

Since there are very few publications on this subject so far, it appears to be of special importance to point out that many water-courses in Peru and Bolivia which are inhabited by Dwarf Cichlids and other aquarium-fishes do not correspond with this picture of South American water which is so widely considered a fact to be accepted by the aquarists. Surveys conducted by the authors in these areas revealed that there are numerous white- and clear-water rivers which have to be considered already moderately hard and which have pH-values which are clearly in the neutral to slightly alkaline levels.

Despite of the widely accepted opinion that South American Dwarf Cichlid would exclusively originate from acidic and soft waters, the information about the natural habitats supplied for each species in the species accounts should therefore be given special attention.

It is noteworthy that almost all specimens of Dwarf Cichlids represented in the scientific collection of museums are juveniles.

This corresponds to the fact that the fishes imported for the pet-shop trade usually are also only sub-adult. It also corresponds with the experiences made by the authors in the wild, i.e. that during times of low water-levels, the only time when it is possible to catch these fishes, usually no adult specimens are found. The only surmise of this is that the small Cichlids do not have a high life-expectation in their natural habitats in many cases and that the succession of generations is amazingly short. It is to be supposed that the reproductive period corresponds with the rainy season and thus

Table 1. An example of white-water in Peru

pH		7,1
Conductivity	µS	154
Total hardness	°dH	2,9
Ca	°dH	2,9
Mg	°dH	0
Carbonate hardness	°dH	3,9
Na	mg/l	9,0
K	mg/l	1,8
NO_3	mg/l	0,8
PO_4	mg/l	0,7
Cl	mg/l	<5
SO_4	mg/l	n.n.
Zn	g/l	7
Pb	g/l	n.n.
Cd	g/l	n.n.
Cu	g/l	13
CO_2	mg/l	10

This sample of water was taken by the authors from the Paca Cocha near Pucallpa in the catchment of the central Rio Ucayali and analyzed by the laboratory of the company Tetra.

A high content of anorganic material is characteristic for the so-called white-water rivers and responsible for their murky, yellowish ochre appearance.

with the floodings. It appears that the majority of adult fishes then die and the juveniles only survive the time of low water. With the beginning of the next rainy season they then reproduce and thus ensure the survival of the species. This would furthermore mean that *Apistogramma* rarely reach a higher age than one year in nature.

Due to the small adult size of the Dwarf Cichlids one may presume that fairly small aquaria would be appropriate for keeping them.

This surmise is however only relatively correct. Though it is possible to breed these fishes in a tank of 70 cm in length, a considerably larger aquarium is required if one wants to study their partly highly complex social behaviour in all details. A length of one meter should therefore be considered the minimum requirement.

From the information supplied about the natural biotopes it becomes obvious that the size of the available ground space is important and the height of the tank is of secondary

interest. The latter should however not fall short of a minimum of 25 cm.

Specific particulars regarding an optimal decoration of the aquarium may be gathered from the individual descriptions of the natural habitats. Since Dwarf cichlids definitely require sufficient cover for their well being the tank should be furnished with several dense groups of aquatic plants between which however should be unobstructed interspaces which allow free swimming. Low-growing plants covering the ground are especially important. They replace the layer of leaf-litter which is found in most the natural water-bodies. It is therefore recommendable to utilize Java fern (*Microsorum pteropus*), Java moss (*Vesicularia dubyana,*) and the small Spear-leaf (*Anubias nana*) for decoration. Additional hiding places are provided by pieces of bog-oak, halved shells of coconuts, bamboo-tubes, and rock constructions.

It is of particular importance to create a number of cavities when decorating the aquarium as most of the species prefer to spawn

Table 2. An example of clear-water in Peru

pH		7,2
Conductivity	µS	142
Total hardness	°dH	4,9
Ca	°dH	3,6
Mg	°dH	1,3
Carbonate hardness	°dH	4,7
Na	mg/l	3,9
K	mg/l	0,5
NO_3	mg/l	0,8
PO_4	mg/l	<0,7
Cl	mg/l	<5
SO_4	mg/l	n.n.
Zn	g/l	11
Pb	g/l	n.n.
Cd	g/l	n.n.
Cu	g/l	27
CO_2	mg/l	10

This sample of water was taken by the authors from the Rio Chinipo in the catchment of the upper Rio Ucayali.

Clear-water rivers carry clean and transparent water which is poor in sediments and has a greenish to yellowish green colour.

inside caves. Additional comfort is provided by some floating plants such as *Ceratopteris cornuta* or *C. pteridoides* since they also provide a feeling of safety. Floating plants may furthermore be important by another reason. Most Dwarf Cichlids greatly prefer dimmed light and are shy with faded colours if the illumination is too bright. This applies to species originating from largely shaded water-courses in the tropical rainforests especially where the colouration of the water additionally reduces the light-intensity. This is the reason why one should also use dark coloured sand or fine gravel as substrate and paint the rear wall in a dark colour too.

Despite paying attention to all factors mentioned before, some Dwarf Cichlids occasionally nevertheless tend to be shy and nervous. In these cases it is advisable to not keep them on their own but together with some other fishes. For this purpose peaceful species of comparable size are adequate; numerous options are found amongst the Tetras.

For a long-term husbandry, the species dealt with in the following are happy with temperatures between 25 and 27 °C. An increase up to 28 °C may be recommendable for breeding attempts since this speeds up the development of the eggs and the embryos. A permanent movement of the water-surface which ensures adequate oxygenation of the water is ideally devised by an appropriate filter-system. Attention must be paid to the quality of the water as Dwarf Cichlids are usually sensitive towards increasing nitrite- and nitrate-contents. One precondition for their successful keeping is therefore a regular exchange of approximately one third of the water-volume every fortnight during which the harmful metabolism byproducts are reduced.

By applying the technical aids available from the pet-shop trade correctly and consequently it is no problem today to emulate the water-values established in the wild in the aquarium. Desalting devices allow one to reduce the hardness of water to any desired

Table 3.
An example of black-water in Peru

pH		6,0
Conductivity	µS	17
Total hardness	°dH	0,12
Ca	°dH	0,07
Mg	°dH	0,05
Carbonate hardness	°dH	0
Na	mg/l	1,9
K	mg/l	1,1
NO_3	mg/l	1,6
PO_4	mg/l	<0,1
Cl	mg/l	<7
SO_4	mg/l	n.n.
Zn	g/l	5
Pb	g/l	n.n.
Cd	g/l	n.n.
Cu	g/l	7
CO_2	mg/l	~1

This sample of water was taken by the authors from a stream near Jenaro Herrero in the catchment of the lower Rio Ucayali and analyzed by the laboratory of the company Tetra.

Although black-water rivers also have clear transparent water, it has the dark brown colour of strong tea.

A green carpet, the rain forest from above

findings of captive observations show that the captive husbandry of these fishes is a method appropriate to clarify the one or the other question regarding their biology.

The Genus Apistogramma
REGAN, 1913

Of the one dozen of taxonomic groups in which Dwarf Cichlids are arranged the genus *Apistogramma* is no doubt the most popular one. An explanation for this may be the fact that most *Apistogramma*-species are ideal fishes for the aquarium. Some of their pros are certainly the very attractive colourations, a relatively small requirement of space, the usually easy husbandry and breeding, their interesting social and parental care behaviour, and their absolute tolerance towards plants.

Although most of the species have a very limited range, this genus, endemic to South America, has a vast over-all distribution. Its representatives do not only inhabit the Guyanas, the Orinoco, and the Amazon regions, but also occur in the catchment of the Rio Paraguay and the Paraná. So far, 48 species of *Apistogramma* have been described. Since however round about another 20 are known to await description one could estimate that approximately 70 species are included in this genus. A typical feature of all species is a distinct sexual dimorphism which is directly linked to the reproductive biology of these fishes.

All *Apistogramma*-species are secretive or cave brooders which rear their offspring in a male-mother-family in which a worksharing system exists. Whilst the fry is taken care of by the female exclusively, the male only defends the breeding territory. Some species however show a tendency towards a mother-father-family structure with the male showing intentions to also guide the fry after it swims free. A tendency towards harem polygyny is often seen in the genus, i.e. a single male spawns with the same group of females over an extended period.

level and filtration through peat may alter the pH-value from an alkaline or neutral level to acidic regions. Although it has been found out that some black-water Cichlids can be kept in moderately hard water with an alkaline reaction as well, it is known that most Dwarf Cichlid are much less susceptible to diseases and have a higher longevity in soft water. Surprisingly enough they also show brighter colours and a grow clearly larger fins under those conditions.

The water-values are however to be given special attention also for other reasons when it comes to breeding attempts. Observations made by the authors have repeatedly revealed that a reduction of the conductivity of the water is very often the release mechanism for courtship and breeding activities. This could be explained by the fact that the heavy downpours of the early rainy season also considerably reduce the hardness of the remains of the water-bodies which often form the biotopes of these fishes. In several species it has furthermore been demonstrated that the sex of the offspring largely depends on the pH of the water in the breeding tank.

An increase of the pH towards neutral levels obviously increases the percentage of female specimens in the fry whereas an alteration towards strongly acidic results in an increased number of male offspring. These

▶ *Apistogramma agassizii*
(STEINDACHNER, 1875)

This small species described more than hundred years ago in honour of Prof. Jean Louis Rodolphe AGASSIZ, definitely ranks amongst the most popular fishes for the aquarium. They are slender fish with only a moderately high back lacking produced membranes of the dorsal fin. The males may reach a length of approximately 9 cm and have a lanceolate caudal fin. In contrast, the female specimens are fully grown at 5 cm and their caudal fins are rounded. This species has a dark lateral band which extends up onto the caudal fin.

The ventral fins are weakly developed. Aquarists differentiate between several colour-morphs and recognize a blue-white, a yellow, and a red colour-variety. According to SCHMETTKAMP the yellow colour-morph slightly differs in its body-shape from both the other forms.

Distribution of *Apistogramma agassizii*

The determination of sex is easy and possible at an early stage due to the different shapes of the caudal fins.

Apistogramma agassizii ♂, blueish white colour-variety

Specific traits

are the lanceolate shape of the caudal fin and the conspicuous dark lateral band which extends up onto the caudal fin. This fish lacks abdominal stripes and a caudal spot.

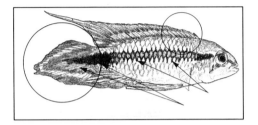

Similar species

Apistogramma gephyra is a similar species which however has only a slightly lanceolate caudal fin with spots and speckles in the top section. The males furthermore have a fire-red bordering of the dorsal fin. These fish also have a slightly different colouration.

The males of *Apistogramma elizabethae* have a lanceolate caudal fin, but on the other hand have greatly produced membranes in the anterior portion of the dorsal fin. As far as is known so far, these fish have a completely different colouration.

Apistogramma agassizii ♂, yellow colour-variety

The

natural habitat

respectively the distribution, is, according to the present state of knowledge, spread over a vast area. Accordingly various colour-varieties are known. It appears that the blue-white morph is preferably caught in the region between west of Manaus and Santarem on the central Amazon River. The red colour-morph probably originates from northern Peru, i.e. from north and especially from southeast of Iquitos. Data on the distribution of the yellow form have to be considered uncertain at present and require confirmation by new imports and collecting records. The biotopes known so far are soft to very soft, acidic to very acidic waters almost with exception.

Accordingly, the

care

requires a usage of soft and acidic water as well. A pH of 6 is recommendable for an optimal environment. To live to its full potential, *A. agassizii* requires a large tank thus aquaria exceeding one metre in length are adequate. Fine dark gravel with a grain-size of 1 to 2 mm is suitable. Large densely planted groups of plants covering the ground with heaps of rocks in between and small caves formed by coconut-shells and bamboo-tubes should be an obligatory part of the decoration. A high quality of the water is a crucial factor to keep the fish healthy. The males tend to collect a harem which means that the space of ground available to the male determines the number of

Apistogramma agassizii ♂, red colour-variety

females which may share his tank. A varying diet should be obligatory. Optimal temperatures range around 27 °C.

Once the fish have reached maturity they easily start

breeding.

In this species of *Apistogramma,* as is the case in many others, the specimens live together in a male-mother-family structure. The pair spawns inside a cave and the female takes care of the fry and defends the spawning territory driving the male out of it.

When breeding with this species several aspects have to be taken into consideration. If the breeding tank is too small, the female becomes highly aggressive after spawning. Her continuous attacks may severely threaten the male. If the female is however not willing to spawn, the situation changes and the male becomes a tyrant which obviously results in danger for the female. A large enough tank on the other hand enables the male to commit himself to the defence of the entire territory after spawning. It is not extraordinary that he even spawns with other females. The latter then claim subterritories within the borders of the general territory. For the successful development of the offspring soft acidic water is an important precondition and the pH may even drop to 5. The fry is devotedly taken care of by the female. The juveniles start swimming approximately nine days after spawning and immediately accept freshly hatched nauplii of the Brine Shrimp. MikroMin dust-food is highly recommendable as supplement.

This species may be quite productive. In addition to the high quality of the water feeding the fry for several times a day is important for the rapid growth of the juveniles.

Apistogramma agassizii ♀ in breeding colouration

▶ *Apistogramma bitaeniata*
PELLEGRIN, 1936

is a colourful, slender, only moderately high-backed species reaching up to 8 cm in length in the male and 5 cm in the female sex. These fish were temporarily also referred to as

Apistogramma sweglesi
Apistogramma kleei and
Apistogramma klausewitzi

whilst they were originally described as *Apistogramma pertense* var. bitaeniata. All these names are however to be considered synonyms today. The species shows a distinct sexual dimorphism. Already at a length of some 4 cm, the caudal fin of the male assumes a truncate shape before it eventually transforms into a lyreate shape. The third to seventh membrane in the spinous zone of the male's dorsal fin is greatly produced in adult specimens and they have longer ventral fins. Depending on the mood of the fish, a second parallel lateral band may become visible below the first one. It is however indistinct and feebly dark coloured. Although a lateral spot is present, there is no such one on the caudal base. A broad lateral band begins immediately behind the eye and extends up onto the base of the caudal fin.

Female specimens basically show the same pattern, but have a less high dorsal fin without produced membranes. They retain the rounded shape of the caudal fin even when adult. The shock-colouration of this species consists of a feebly grey chequered body pattern.

Specific traits

are that the third to seventh membrane of the dorsal fin are conspicuously produced in larger males. Their caudal fins are distinctly lyreate in shape. Depending on the mood an often only faintly visible second parallel lateral band may appear below the first one. This species has a lateral spot incorporated in the lateral band. The body is slender and not very high. Abdominal strips are absent. Adult males

Apistogramma bitaeniata ♂

usually have a conspicuous striped pattern in their anal fins.

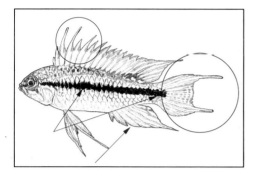

Similar species

Apistogramma paucisquamis grows smaller with the males lacking produced membranes in the anterior dorsal fin.

Apistogramma cacatuoides is more high-backed and less elongate, has a bigger head, and comparatively thicker lips. The most

important point of distinction is however the three to four wave-like abdominal stripes. Furthermore, these fish differ in their colouration and individual colour-forms may have red spots in the dorsal and anal fins which are bordered black.

Apistogramma gibbiceps has less produced membranes in the dorsal fins and obliquely arranged abdominal lines. This species grows smaller in comparison and differs in colouration.

The

natural habitat

of *Apistogramma bitaeniata* lies in the upper and central regions of the Amazon River. Records have been made in the Lago Tefé and the Igarapé Preto in Brazil, in the vicinity of the town of Leticia (Colombia), and especially the town of Iquitos (Peru). It appears that these fish inhabit black-water biotopes exclusively where they live amongst the several centime-

Apistogramma bitaeniata ♀

tres thick layers of leaf-litter which are usually present near the banks of all rainforest water-courses. Measurements taken by one of the authors at one of those sites in the vicinity of Iquitos on July 28, 1990, a small stream flowing into the Rio Momon, revealed a water-temperature of 23 °C and a conductivity of 10 μS/cm. The pH established to be 5,8.

The total as well as the carbonate hardness were below the detectability-level of 1 °dH.

Care

Keeping these fish is easy. As is the case with all other Dwarf Cichlids of South America, this species should be regarded as shy. Their aquarium should therefore be densely planted and offer many hiding facilities. A partly dense canopy of floating plants is recommendable since it provides an additional feeling of safety to the fish and reduces their shyness. An appropriate number of other peaceful and not too large fishes is very important for the same reason. Soft, slightly acidic water-values are of advantage for the husbandry and a varying diet

should be given attention. Water-temperatures of 27 °C on average are suitable for this species' requirements.

For the

breeding

aquaria of 70 cm or more in length are advisable. The fish spawn inside small shelters, on the ceilings of caves, or below leaves. The family-structure is of the male-mother type with the female alone caring for and guiding the fry. The male meanwhile defends the territory. This species is not very productive with 50 juveniles being an average result. Freshly hatched nauplii of *Artemia salina* are to form the first food with MikroMin stirred up to a "milk" being a valuable supplement. Provided food several times a day and a high water-quality the juveniles grow rapidly. This necessitates that a third of the water-volume is to be regularly exchanged every two to five days. The female guides the juveniles for three to four weeks.

Headwaters of the Rio Magdalena in the south of Columbia

◆ *Apistogramma borellii*
(REGAN, 1906)

Distribution of *Apistogramma borellii*

is the species which was erroneously described by Dr. Ernst AHL as *A. reitzigi* in the year 1939 and which henceforth haunted through the aquarium-literature as "The Reitzigi" for decades. It was not before some new imports of wild-caught specimens in the 1970' that this situation was clarified. Simultaneously it became obvious that the picture one had about the fish previously referred to as *A. borellii* had to be revised. It turned out to be in fact the species *A. cacatuoides*. Subsequently the name *A. reitzigi* was dumped into the synonymy of *A. borellii*.

There are two different colour-varieties known of *A. borellii* which occur syntopically which means they occur together at the same locality. Males of the yellow colour-morph have a golden yellow head and chest region and a bright blue body. The blue variety is in contrast more or less uniformly blue, but has some signal-red spots and steaks in the lower head region and on the gill-covers. The maximum

Apistogramma borelli ♂, blue colour-variety

size of males ranges around 6 cm. Females are smaller and rarely exceed 4 cm in length.

Specific traits

are a high back and a less elongate body-shape. Beginning behind the eye, a lateral band runs zigzag up onto the caudal fin but is usually only visible in the tail region. The dorsal fin is high and much enlarged in the soft areas. The fin membranes do not stand free, but are fused in their tips. The shape of the caudal fin is rounded.

Similar species

A high dorsal fin with the membranes fused in their tips is also found in the members of the *pertensis*-group which are however considerably more slender.

The

natural habitat

is vast and covers the area between the Mato Grosso region in the south of Brazil through the lowlands of the Rio Paraguay, through the

Apistogramma borellii ♂, yellow variety

state of Paraguay up to the north of Argentina. Here, the species has been recorded from the vicinity of the town of Corrientes.

Care

Keeping these peace loving and unpretentious fish is easy and even possible in fairly small aquaria. Notwithstanding this, one should provide the basic requirements for a keeping of species of *Apistogramma*. This includes that parts of the ground are covered with thickets of low growing aquatic plants with small open spaces and rock constructions and small caves in between. Pieces of bog-oak are also usually readily accepted as places to hide under. This species is peaceful even towards its own kind, thus a large enough aquarium may house several pairs.

Though no specific requirements regarding the water-quality exist, moderately hard to soft water which is slightly alkaline or neutral is recommended. The cleanliness of the water is however as an important factor as in other species of *Apistogramma*. Furthermore, the diet should be varying; the species willingly accepts flake-food. The temperatures should range between 24 and 25 °C for long-term care.

Table 4

Location:	small tributary to the Rio Cuiabá near Porto Cercado (Pantanal, Brazil)
Clarity:	clear
Colour:	brownish
pH:	7,3
Total hardness:	<1 °dH
Carbonate hardness:	<1 °dH
Conductivity:	10 µS
Depth:	20 to 50 cm
Current:	none
Temperature:	25 °C
Date:	29.7.1987
Time:	15.00 hrs

For the

breeding

the temperatures are to be increased. *A. borellii* spawns in small caves with the female caring for the fry. If no "enemy-fishes" are kept with them, the male commits himself to the juveniles at a very early stage. In contrast to almost all other species of *Apistogramma* the female tolerates his behaviour. If dither fish are present, the almost exclusive priority for the male is to protect his territory. Only later, once the juveniles have grown a little, the male increasingly frequently joins the school of offspring The young fish willingly take newly hatched nauplii of the Brine Shrimp as first food.

The Campa-Indians belong to the natives of the South American continent.

33

▶ *Apistogramma brevis*
KULLANDER, 1980

This only recently described species was collected by King Leopold of Belgium and the Belgian ichthyologist J.P. GOSSE in northwestern Brazil in 1967. A male of only 29 mm in

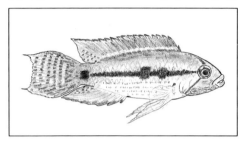

Probable appearance of *Apistogramma brevis* ♂

Distribution of *Apistogramma brevis*

length served a reference specimen (holotype). Based on the available material it is to be presumed that this is a small species. The males have a feebly lyreate caudal fin with up to five vertical dark small spots which give an appearance of transversal stripes. In comparison with other species occurring in this area, *Apistogramma brevis* has a more high-backed body-shape. A summary of the original description of the colouration may be of interest for the aquarist. Generally, the species shows a round-ish lateral spot which is slightly larger than the lateral band is in width. In fully grown males there is a second lateral spot on the second bar. The suborbital stripe is moderately wide and the superorbital stripe extends up onto the nape. The chin-region is sometimes darker and a pectoral spot is present. The abdominal stripes are often reduced to dark scale-rims. They extend approximately up to the beginning of the caudal peduncle. Altogether there are four abdominal stripes. Males have a faint spot in front of or behind the anus. The spot on the caudal peduncle is either square or broader than high; this especially applies to juveniles and females. Fully grown males show a dark zone on the base of the caudal peduncle. The dorsal fin is coloured dark with a narrow even darker zone on the base. The tips of the fin-membranes are translucent; the anterior

fin-membranes are slightly darker, but not black. The soft parts have one or up to three dotted lines. On its base, the anal fin is translucent with the tips of the membranes being dark and the soft parts being bordered dark. In its posterior portion there are also up to three dotted lines. The caudal fin is clear as well. It has three to five very irregularly arranged vertical dotted stripes. In very large males the fin is dark and the stripes are restricted to the top lobe of the caudal fin. The ventral fins are translucent to whitish and more or less dark in adult female specimens. Females are furthermore coloured dark in the anal region and have a short midventral stripe.

Specific traits

are that *Apistogramma brevis* is less long and elongate but more high-backed. The males have a feebly lyreate caudal fin with filamentous extensions on the top and bottom edge.

Similar species

Apistogramma gibbiceps lacks the lateral spot, the dotted stripes in the fins, the horizontal abdominal stripes, and the spot on the caudal peduncle, but has a lateral band extending up onto the caudal fin instead.

Apistogramma paucisquamis is distinguished from all other *Apistogramma* species by having 12 instead of 16 circumpeduncular scale rows. Males have an unusually large mouth, thick lips and skiny, brigd scales parallel to and above and below the lateral stripe.

Male *Apistogramma bitaeniata, A. cacatuoide, A. hoignei* and *A luelingi* have conspicuously produced anterior lappets in their dorsal fin. *Apistogramma staecki* has no abdominal stripes.

The

natural habitat

of the type specimens lies on the Rio Tiquie and Rio Uaupes (Rio Vaupes) in the vicinity of the villages of Trovao, Assai, and the Lago Penero in northwestern Brazil. The species *Apistogramma elizabethae, A. meinkeni,* and *A. uaupesi* have also been recorded from the area around Travo as is the case in *A. personata* from the vicinity of Assai.

The Rio Ucayali in the south of Peru during the dry season

◗ Apistogramma cacatuoides
HOEDEMAN, 1951

is one of the most popular fishes for the aqua-rium. Based upon erroneous determinations this species has been dealt with as *Apisto-gramma borellii* for many years. In the early 1960's several aquarists became however aware of the error and subsequently two names were used for these fish. Only upon new imports of wild-caught specimens of *A. borellii* this erro-neous name was eventually eliminated in the mid-seventies. It will however still take many years until the correct name is thoroughly established.

Since this species breeds willingly, it may be presumed that its existence in captivity is secured. The numerous captive breedings have also led to changes in the colouration. As to how far our fish resembles the wild form at all should be investigated. Aquarists distinguish between a grey and a yellowish brown colour-variety. Even specimens with pretty orange

Distribution of *Apistogramma cacatuoides*

coloured fins have been offered. The authors were able to record this species in Peru. The relevant specimens showed little of the colours known from the fish in the aquaria.

Apistogramma cacatuoides ♂, wild-caught specimen from southern Peru

Specific traits

Adult male have a slightly elongate, moderately high body, greatly produced fin-membranes between the second and eighth spine of the dorsal fin, a large mouth with thick lips, and a bifurcate caudal fin. The lateral band runs up onto the caudal fin. The ventral fins are short, but have one enlarged ray. The most distinct feature of this species is three to four wave-like abdominal stripes which are present in either sex. Adult females have no produced dorsal fin-membranes and develop a truncate or subtruncate caudal fin. Occasionally the males have a varying number of fire-red spots in the caudal fin which are bordered black. Males reach approximately 8 cm, females fully 5 cm.

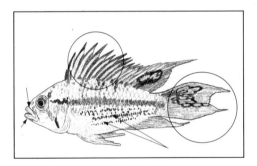

Similar species

Apistogramma bitaeniata is more slender and less high-backed, lacks the abdominal stripes, and may show a second dark stripe parallel to the lateral band depending on mood. Females of this species always have a rounded caudal fin.

Males of *Apistogramma norberti* differ in their colourations and have no bifurcate but a rounded caudal fin. This species never has black spots in the caudal fin.

In *Apistogramma luelingi* the abdominal stripes are less developed and never arranged in zigzag-shape. The dorsal fin of adult males is usually bordered orange-red posteriorly continuing on the caudal fin.

In *Apistogramma gibbiceps* the anterior membranes of the dorsal fin are only slightly produced. This species has abdominal stripes.

The

natural habitat

lies in Peru. The authors managed to record this species from the vicinity of the town of Pucallpa on the Rio Ucayali in 1983. The southernmost locality lies in the region Chicosa, only a few kilometres far from the site where the Rio Urubamba and Rio Tambo join to form the Rio Ucayali. The collecting sites were small shallow water-courses or lagoon-like water-bodies in the rainforests. The wild-caught male illustrated here was caught at this place by the authors in July 1983. The water-quality in the natural biotopes of *A. cacatuoides* is interesting. In the region of Chicosa as well as in the vicinity of Pucallpa it was always soft to moderately hard water with a pH between 7 and 8. The water-temperatures ranged around 25 °C. The fish live in zones of very shallow water with the ground covered by a thick layer of leaf-litter and partly much branchwork. The specimens were usually found amongst the leaves.

Rocks and strictly submerse growing plants are absent in almost every case. On the other hand, emerse vegetation stands in the water, at times of floodings especially, providing covered zones by branchwork or leaves hanging into the water.

Care

The aquarium should therefore be decorated with a partly dense vegetation and groups of bog-oak and rocks. The plants should especially form thickets near the ground. Dark coloured fine gravel or sand should be used as substrate.

The question of water-quality is of special interest. So far, the opinion was predominant that soft and acidic water would be advantageous for an optimal husbandry of these fish. Examination of their natural habitats however confirmed the presumption that soft to moderately hard, neutral to slightly

Apistogramma cacatuoides ♂, grey colour-variety

Apistogramma cacatuoides ♂, yellowish brown colour-variety

Table 5

Location:	Lagoon Aquajal, appr. 3 km northeast of the Farm Bella Vista on the eastern side of the Rio Ucayali. The Farm Bella Vista is situated some 10 km south of Chicosa in Peru.
Clarity:	slightly cloudy
Colour:	none
pH:	7,6
Total hardness:	12 °dH
Carbonate hardness:	14 °dH
Conductivity:	387 µS at 27 °C
Nitrite:	<0,1 mg/l
Depth:	not established
Current:	none
Temperature:	27 °C
Date:	24.6.1983
Time:	11.00 hrs

water are more suitable for a successful long-term keeping.

The temperatures should range between 25 and 26 °C. The males tend to collect a harem and thus may be kept together with several females if the size of the aquarium allows. Other peaceful fishes of not too large size should be kept in the same tank since these cause the *A. cacatuoides* to lose their natural shyness and thus offer better opportunities for studies. A high water-quality, i.e. regular exchanges of a quarter to a third of the water-volume every fortnight, and a varying diet are very important.

Provided these conditions the fish start

breeding

easily. A male-mother-family structure is formed. The female lays the eggs on the ceiling of a cave and solely cares for the fry. The embryos hatch from the eggs after approximately 48 hours and are placed on the ground by the mother then. Another 5 days later the larvae can swim. The female guides and protects the young fish. Newly hatched nauplii of the Brine Shrimp are a "palatable" first food for the small *A. cacatuoides*. Additionally, a "milk" made up of MikroMin dustfood and aquarium-water is recommendable. It is carefully injected into the school with a pipette. The same procedure may be applied with the nauplii of the Brine Shrimp. This kind of feeding ensures that the major part of the food reaches the juveniles. If several females are kept in the same tank, the male spawns with several partners. Due to this, several small spawning territories are claimed and the entire area is defended against invaders by the male.

In order to avoided losses by intraspecific quarrels, each female should have a ground-space of 30×40 cm available. The rearing of the juveniles is simple.

Species of *Apistogramma* live amongst branchwork and plants in the shallow bank-zones.

▶ *Apistogramma caetei*
KULLANDER, 1980

is a small and attractive species which has frequently been referred to as *Apistogramma taeniata*. It is very peaceful and easy to keep.

The males reach just under 6 cm in length whilst the females are fully grown at approximately 3,5 cm. Determination of sex is difficult and possible with some certainty only in larger specimens.

Mature female specimens have much more yellow as ground-colour on the head and belly. Their lateral bands are broken into spots in the mid-body region. The females do however not only grow smaller, they also have less pointed tips of the soft dorsal and anal fins. A distinct spotted pattern in the caudal fin is typical for the males; it is considerably more indistinct in the females. For the identification of the species the colour-pattern of the males is of interest. The fish shows a moderately elongate head and body. The fin-membranes of the

Distribution of *Apistogramma caetei*

dorsal fin increase in size from front to hind being approximately of same length from the fifth membrane on. The first two are darker in colour. A dark lateral band begins narrow

Apistogramma caetei ♂

behind the eye, increasing to approximately one scale in width on average towards the gill-cover, and ends on the seventh transversal band on the caudal peduncle. With the mood changing, it is partly weakly disrupted and may transform into the typical zigzag-band. The frontal and caudal stripes as well as the cheek-band are usually clearly visible. The seven transversal bars on the other hand are generally only recognizable in the upper half of the body and usually end just below the lateral band. The exception is the seventh band. The continuations of the third and fourth band are indicated by dark scale-edges on the lower body. They might also be referred to as oblique abdominal stripes. A small oval and very dark spot is found on the base of the caudal fin. The posterior sections of the dorsal and anal fins bears rows of dots. The caudal fin is rounded and all over marked with a feeble pattern of rows of dots. The tips of the ventral fins are yellow.

The ground-colour of the body is grey to brilliant blue in males. A golden yellow snout and a light ivory coloured throat and belly region are often observed though more common in female specimens. Their abdominal areas are however usually cadmium-yellow in these cases. Their body-colouration is mainly grey otherwise. This species belongs to the *A. regani*-group.

Specific traits

In addition to the brilliant blue colouration of the body in adult males, the zigzag-shaped lateral band, the obliquely arranged abdominal, stripes which may sometimes appear as a spotted pattern, and the only small oval spot on the base of the caudal fin are to be mentioned. The end of the lateral band at the seventh transversal band on the caudal peduncle should also be observed. This sort of a "lying T" in front of the caudal spot is another specific feature.

Similar species

Apistogramma resticulosa
In this species the lateral band ends freely in front of a larger oval caudal spot. Furthermore

it shows small dark spots on the posterior part of the gill-covers.

Similarities also exist with *Apistogramma geisleri* and *Apistogramma regani,* but these fishes show different colourations and patterns.

The

natural habitat

of this species lies in the Rio Caete and the Rio Apeu in the region of the villages of Castanhal and Braganca, east of the town of Belem in the coastal area of the Atlantic Ocean in northeastern Brazil.

Care

Small aquaria are sufficient for this species. Tanks of approximately 70×40 cm ground space and a height of 25 cm are suitably sized for a successful longterm keeping. It is self-explanatory that larger tanks are always recommendable. For decoration one should use fine gravel as substrate, extensive plant-groups, small rock constructions which form tight caves, and pieces of bog-oak and well soaked bamboo-tubes to provide additional hiding-places. Although the species does not require specifically conditioned water, a soft and slightly acidic quality is advantageous for a successful longterm keeping. The temperatures

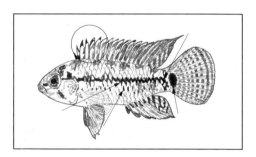

may range around 26 °C. A varying diet is important and the regular exchange of water, every week or two a quarter to a third of the total volume, mentioned so often, should be obligatory. In large tanks an adequate number of fishes may be kept together. If it is however the small aquarium described above, only a few company fishes with suitable ecologies should share the tank. This means that a pair or a male with two to three females of this species and some Tetras and a few South American Cat-fishes are an appropriate combination. This recommendation of course primarily applies if detailed studies of the behaviour of these small Cichlids are intended.

Only in a sparse population with aggressive fishes absent, will the fish start

breeding

one day and this is the beginning of an interes-ting time. The males of this species claim large territories and successively mate with several females. The latter occupy small territories around the spawning site and care for, i.e. guide and defend, the fry alone. The male meanwhile conducts territory defence on large scale, but is not permitted to participate in

parental care. Spawning takes place inside a cave which may be just below a stone or in a bamboo tube.

Once spawning is completed the male is driven away. At a water-temperature of 27,5 °C on average and water-values of just under 300 micro-Siemens at a pH of 6,5 the female leaves the spawning cave after approxi-mately 10 days guiding a school of some 60 juveniles. At this point of time the young fish measure 4,25 mm on average and readily feed on nauplii of *Artemia salina* and MikroMin as supplement.

The school stays closely together during the first few days and obediently follows the instructions of the mother. Run-aways are caught by her with the mouth and brought back to the school. Not before 20 days after spawning is the male allowed to come close to the school and participate in caring. If several females are present, the behaviour changes since the male has spawned with other females in the meantime.

Apistogramma caetei ♀

◆ *Apistogramma commbrae*
(EIGENMANN, 1906)

"A fish for the small aquarium" was the description used for this species already 70 years ago. Then and now it has been a popular fish although it is more and more pushed into the background today with the more colourful species taking over its place. *Apistogramma commbrae* belongs to the small fishes. The males reach approximately 5 cm in total length whilst the females are fully grown at some 3 cm.

This species does certainly not deserve the attribute to be especially colourful. On the other hand it is not without charm and has an interesting colour pattern. A lateral band runs from the tip of the snout through the eye up to an oval black spot in the seventh transversal bar which is fused with the large oval to round blotch of the caudal fin thus forming a double-blotch. The membranes of the dorsal fin are truncate and not produced. The caudal fin is rounded and has a pattern of spots which

Distribution of *Apistogramma commbrae*

are especially obvious in the top section. The tips in the soft parts of the dorsal and anal fins are only slightly produced. The fish have dorsal spots and usually two to three

Male of *Apistogramma commbrae* from the catchment of the Rio Cuiabá

43

three abdominal stripes. A suborbital and a superorbital stripe are distinctly developed.

Due to their inconspicuous appearance these fish are not frequently imported any more and are usually only found as company fish for *A. trifasciata* and *A. borellii*.

Specific traits

The fish shows a double-spot-like marking between the caudal peduncle and the base of the caudal fin. Depending on comfort two to three sound dark coloured abdominal stripes and dorsal spots may appear.

Similar species

Apistogramma linkei grows larger and is more high-backed. This species furthermore has a more sound blue body-colouration and frequently a yellow pectoral region. The abdominal stripes are less distinct.

In *Apistogramma inconspicua* the lateral band does not reach up to the seventh but only up to the sixth transversal band. Abdominal stripes are absent or are just visible as indications. Furthermore there are only 15 spines in the dorsal fin and three in the anal fin whereas *Apistogramma* commbrae may have up to 17 spines in the dorsal fin and sometimes four spines in the anal fin.

Table 6

Location:	side-arm of the Canal do Tamengo near Corumbá (catchment of the Rio Paraguay)
Clarity:	clear
Colour:	slightly brownish
pH:	7,2
Total hardness:	1,5 °dH
Carbonate hardness:	4 °dH
Conductivity:	100 µS
Depth:	max. 50 cm
Current:	none
Temperature:	25 °C
Date:	7.8.1991
Time:	10.00 hrs

The

natural habitats

of *Apistogramma commbrae* lie in the catchments of the Rio Paraguay and the Rio Paraná in the countries of Bolivia, Brazil, Paraguay, and Argentina between the towns of Cárceres in the north and Corrientes in the south. One of the authors had opportunity to repeatedly examine the natural biotopes in the catchment of the Rio Cuiabá, in the vicinity of the town of Corumbá and in the Rio Paraná drainage where the fish were always found living in zones of shallow water amongst thickets of aquatic and floating plants.

Care

Keeping these fish is easy and even possible in very small tanks. These should nevertheless still be richly structured. Partly dense growing plants, rock constructions and small caves on a fine dark substrate are important for a successful keeping. The fish make little demands on the quality of the water, and moderately hard, slightly alkaline water may be sufficient. Soft, neutral or slightly acidic water may however be given preference nevertheless. The husbandry in very soft and strongly acidic water on the other hand is not recommended.

This fish is incompatible with swift or aggressive species and should only be kept together with peace-loving fishes.

Provided the aforementioned conditions, the

breeding

can be expected to be successful. The specimens form a male-mother-family structure. The female spawns below a leaf or on the ceiling of a cave and cares for the fry. The male meanwhile patrols the frontiers of its territory. It may however be observed that the male is permitted to temporarily care for the fry as well. Even newly hatched nauplii of the Brine Shrimp may be too big as first food for the juveniles immediately after swimming free. Smaller live food and MikroMin made up as "food-milk" should therefore be offered. Besides several feedings a day, cleanliness of the water is important for a healthy growth of the juveniles.

◆ *Apistogramma diplotaenia*
KULLANDER, 1987

Distribution of *Apistogramma diplotaenia*

is a species known to aquarists since the early 1980's. It has however been imported in single specimens found only as side-catches in shipments of the "Red Neon" (*Paracheirodon axelrodi*). SCHMETTKAMP (1981) was the first author to introduce this fish aquaristically under the name "Double-banded *Apistogramma*", this description referring to the unusual shape of the lateral band of this species. With a maximum length of 50 millimetres, *Apistogramma diplotaenia* belongs to the smallest representatives of the genus.

This species has a slender elongate body and a comparatively low dorsal fin.

The rounded caudal fin is longer than high. The inconspicuously coloured fish show a beige shade of ground-colour on the flanks. The most important point of distinction in their colouration is the unusual shape of the lateral band which usually splits up into two separate branches except for both its ends thus

causing an appearance of a double-band. Depending on the disposition the two branches may however widen to form one very broad lateral stripe. Further dark components of the pattern are a well recognizable preorbital

Male of *Apistogramma diplotaenia*

45

and a suborbital stripe which widens downwards and extends onto the throat region. Male specimens show feebly yellow shades on the lower portion of the head and approximately six vertical rows of dark dots in the caudal fin. Their ventral, dorsal, and anal fins are distinctly longer if compared with the females. Female fish have unpatterned caudal fins in contrast and frequently have four or five dorsal spots. Instead of the double-band, they often have a broad lateral band.

Specific traits

of *Apistogramma diplotaenia* are the slender elongate body and especially the lateral band which is split into two branches with a light brown zone in between.

Similar species

The only species which might cause confusion is primarily *Taeniacara candidi* due to its similar body-shape. This Dwarf Cichlid however has a lanceolate caudal fin. The suborbital stripe is absent.

The

natural habitats

of *Apistogramma diplotaenia* lie in the north of South America in the frontier area between the countries of Venezuela and Brazil.

Localities are known from the upper as well as from the central and lower catchment of the Rio Negro. One of the authors was able to catch this Cichlid in the lower course of the Rio Negro in the vicinity of the Anavilhanas Island-groups in 1981 and again in 1986.

It is however fairly rare there. One collecting site was situated in the partially flooded bank-zone of a small islet on the right bank of the Rio Negro. There, the substrate consisted of almost white sand. Aquatic plants were absent, but the flooded bank-vegetation and many branches lying in the water provided profound opportunities for the fish to hide. The accompanying ichthyofauna included species such as *Apistogramma pertensis*, *Apistogramma gephyra*, *Acarichthys heckelii*, and *Mesonauta insignis*. Measurements taken at

this place revealed a pH of 4,7 and a water-temperature of 28 °C. The total as well as the carbonate hardness were below 1 °C.

Another collecting site was also on the right bank of the river, in a small brook. There, the fish stayed in the cover of a several centimetres thick layer of submerged leaf-litter. Other Cichlids caught in this biotope were *Apistogramma paucisquamis* and *A. pertensis*. The water at this locality was very acidic as well (pH 4,3) and soft, since a conductivity of 10 micro-Siemens was established at a water-temperature of 28 °C.

Care

Although *Apistogramma diplotaenia* is one of the smallest species, a moderately large aquarium should be chosen whose bottom is covered with sand and where a dense vegetation provides much cover for the fish.

A precondition for their

breeding

is certainly water of soft and acidic quality. Reports of a successful reproduction in captivity are still rare.

Table 7

Location:	right bank of the Rio Negro south of Novo Airão in the region of the Anavilhanas Islands
Clarity:	clear
Colour:	dark brown, tea-coloured
pH:	4,3
Total hardness:	<1 °dH
Carbonate hardness:	<1 °dH
Conductivity:	10 μS
Depth:	max. 50 cm
Current:	none
Water-temperature:	26 °C
Air-temperature:	29 °C
Date:	27.3.1986
Time:	11.00 hrs

► *Apistogramma elizabethae*
KULLANDER, 1980

is yet another species which has not been available to the aquaristic alive so far. It was collected in 1967 for the first time and resembles

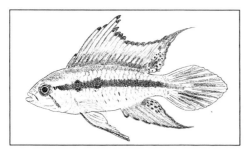

Probable appearance of *Apistogramma elizabethae* ♂

Distribution of *Apistogramma elizabethae*

Apistogramma agassizii to some extent. Sven O. KULLANDER, the author of this species, chose the name *elizabethae* in honour of the wife of Prof. AGASSIZ who accompanied her husband on his expeditions and worked as his assistant. The name is also to implicate that close affinity of this species with *A. agassizii.*

The largest male specimens known up to today are just under 6 cm in length, whilst females only measure approximately 3 cm. These are fish with a slender elongate body-shape. Distinguishing between the sexes is simple. The males grow larger and have elongate horizontally striped caudal fins whilst the females have rounded dotted caudal fins. Further points of recognition are summarized from the original description: The shapes of the head and body are slender and elongate. The spines in the dorsal fin of the male are unequal in length from the fourth or fifth spine on increasing in size posteriorly. The fin-membranes are produced between the second and sixth spine with the fourth being the longest by taking three or four times the length of the spine. It is however only of moderate length in females and juveniles. The soft section of the dorsal fin is pointed in the male and produced extending approximately over the central part of the caudal fin; the same applies to the anal fin. The caudal fin is lanceolate in shape and rounded in females and juveniles. Preserved specimens have a yellowish body-colouration turning into brown towards the back. Only below the lateral band are there some indications of transversal stripes. The nape and back regions are distinctly darker. The lateral band, which covers one and a half scales in width on average, begins immediately behind the eye and ends at the base of the caudal fin. This stripe runs above and on the lower lateral line. A spot on the caudal peduncle is absent, but is replaced by the dark extension of the lateral band which ranges up onto the caudal fin. Two lateral blotches are present on the often visible second and third transversal bar. They are roundish and just slightly exceed the height of the lateral band. A frontal stripe is absent, and the cheek-band is of moderate breadth.

There is a spot in the dorsal fin. Although abdominal stripes are missing some specimens show dark-edged scales in the belly-region.

The dorsal fin is dark, its membranes are slightly darker at the base becoming lighter distantly; a dark edge is visible on their base. The soft part bears two or three rows of dots with the tip of the fin being slightly darker. The anal fin is dark with an even darker border and has also up to three rows of dots in the rayed area. The caudal fin bears longitudinal brownish stripes in the membranes. The females have up to four irregular transversal rows of speckles which are entirely absent in the males. The pectoral fins look dark whilst the ventral fins are translucent and dark on the edges.

Specific traits

are the large, produced membranes in the dorsal fin with the fourth membrane being the largest. The lanceolate shape of the caudal fin in the slender males should also be noted.

Similar species

Apistogramma agassizii
The males of this species have no produced dorsal fin lappets, and the females lack the rows of spots in the caudal fin.

Apistogramma gephyra
The males of this species lack produced dorsal fin lappets.

The

natural habitat

So far, specimens of this species were only recorded from a tributary to the Rio Uaupes in the vicinity of the village of Trovao near the Rio Negro, and from the Lago Penera in northwest Brazil. From the same areas records exist for *Apistogramma brevis*, *Apistogramma meinkeni*, and *Apistogramma uaupesi*.

Vegetated waterholes are favourite biotopes for small fishes.

◆ *Apistogramma eunotus*
KULLANDER, 1981

was discovered by Dr. K.H. LÜLING and certainly does not belong to the most colourful representatives of the genus *Apistogramma*. The males reach a total length of approximately 8 cm and the females just under 5,5 cm. These fish are relatively high-backed and less elongate. Male specimens carry a moderately high dorsal fin whose pointed membranes are of equal length from the third spine on and which lack enlargements. The soft parts of the dorsal and anal fins show two to four rows of spots. The soft dorsal fin is produced and extends up to the middle of the caudal fin. The ventral fins are slightly enlarged in adult males. The dark pattern is visible only occasionally.

Distribution of *Apistogramma eunotus*

Apistogramma eunotus ♂

A narrow lateral band of little contrast begins right behind the eye and ends in front of the upright rectangular caudal spot. The transversal bars are only recognizable as slightly darker blotches on the back. The cheek-band and the frontal stripe are indistinct. The first two dorsal fin lappets are coloured black. Abdominal stripes are absent, and the rounded caudal fin has a faint orange hue.

The few

Specific traits

for the determination of this species are the high-backed body-shape, the dorsal fin without enlarged membranes, and the pale, only occasionally visible lateral band which ends in front of a upright rectangular caudal blotch. This fish does not have abdominal stripes.

Similar species

are the Parallel-striped *Apistogramma (Apistogramma* sp.) from Peru which however has sound abdominal stripes and which may be identical with *Apistogramma cruzi* from the catchment-area of the Rio Napo. The latter species also has distinct abdominal stripes. It furthermore differs from *Apistogramma eunotus* by having undivided transversal bands, a fairly broad lateral band, and an unpatterned caudal fin.

Apistogramma moae also differs by a distinctly broader lateral band and undivided transversal bands. This species furthermore lacks a pectoral spot and there is no indication of abdominal stripes whatsoever.

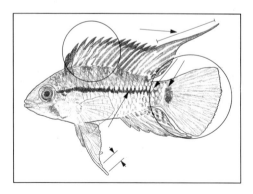

The

natural habitats

of *Apistogramma eunotus* are spread over the catchment-areas of the Rio Ucayali and the upper Amazon River in the countries of Peru, Colombia, and Brazil. The distribution ranges from the Rio Shahuaya in the southwest up to the Rio Japur in the northeast. Collecting sites are furthermore known from the lower course of the Rio Yavar and from the Rio Tigre.

Apistogramma eunotus is a species with a surprising potential to adapt when compared with other representatives of the genus. Although it seems that these fish prefer biotopes of the white-water type, they have also been collected in black-water, where they occurred together with *Apistogramma nijsseni* and *A. norberti,* and in clear-water. It is furthermore noteworthy that they even tolerate a quite strong current and not only inhabit lakes, swamps, and remaining water-bodies but also torrential streams and small rivers where they however appear to be confined to the calmer zones. Preferred places to stay are the shallow areas immediately on the banks where either a several centimetres thick layer of leaf-litter provides the necessary cover or the land-vegetation reaches into the water.

Measurements taken by the authors over a period of ten years at widely separated collecting sites of *Apistogramma eunotus* revealed the following data: total hardness 1 to 11 °dH, carbonate hardness 1 to 11 °dH, conductivity 10 to 404 µS/cm at water-temperatures between 24 and 27 °C. The pH varied at levels from 5,9 to 8. These water-values indicate that keeping these fish is easy.

Care

Accordingly, moderately hard, slightly alkaline water has been proven to be fully adequate. Small to medium-sized, well decorated, and sufficiently planted, aquaria providing numerous hiding-places are important for a successful longterm husbandry. Water-temperatures around 27 °C, a varying diet, and regular partial exchanges of the water are recommendable. As these fish are as shy as many other small South American Cichlids, some

Rainforest ponds in the area of Pucallpa in Peru are the habitats of *A. cacatuoides* and *A. eunotus*

company fishes should be provided. Adequate species are found amongst the Live-bearing Toothcarps or the Tetras.

Apistogramma eunotus is polygamous which means that several females should be given to a male. The available space in the tank has however to be taken into consideration as every female should be enabled to claim a territory of approximately 30x30 cm.

Semi-adult specimens grow rapidly under these conditions and start

breeding.

Despite positive experiences with moderately hard and slightly alkaline water, soft, slightly acidic value should be preferred for the optimal development of the fry. The species is not especially productive which means that adult specimens produce approximately 80 descendants at a time. Once the juveniles swim free they can easily be fed freshly hatched nauplii of the Brine Shrimp. The females cares for the juveniles for approximately four weeks. Provided clean water and feeding them several

times a day they grow rapidly and measure some 4 cm after four months.

Table 8

Location:	Stream in the catchment of the upper Amazon River south of Iquitos near the town of Santa Ana
Clarity:	very clear
Colour:	none
pH:	6,7
Total hardness:	5 °dH
Carbonate hardness:	7 °dH
Conductivity:	280 µS
Depth:	max. 75 cm
Current:	strong
Temperature:	24 °C
Date:	31.7.1990
Time:	17.00 hrs

Apistogramma geisleri
MEINKEN, 1971

The description of this species is based on three specimens being one male and two females. The type material was collected by Prof. Dr. Rolf GEISLER in December 1967. This species is of average size with the males reaching approximately 7 cm and the females 5 cm in total length.

Determination of the sexes is not without problems as the species does not show a distinct sexual dimorphism. Adult females grow smaller in comparison with the males and usually have rounded fins in the soft areas of the dorsal and anal fins. The species is assigned to the regani species-group and has a moderate high body.

Distribution of *Apistogramma geisleri*

Apistogramma geisleri ♂

The head also appears to be relatively high. The spines of the dorsal fin increase in length posteriorly and are of almost equal length from the fifth spine on. The tips of the fin-membranes are short. The soft section of the dorsal fin is pointed, but lacks a distinct enlargement, thus reaching only up to the first quarter of the caudal fin. A similar situation is found in the case of the anal fin which is however even shorter. The caudal fin is rounded. The colour-pattern is furthermore of interest for identification purposes.

Reference is made here to the features of the preserved specimens indicated in the original description respectively to their citation by Sven KULLANDER. The transversal bars on the body of these fish are feebly developed. The first ones extend up to just below the lateral line whilst the fifth an sixth band reach up to the base of the ventral fin. The most dense pigmentation is found in the top zones of each bar right at the base of the dorsal fin and partially even extending onto the same. The lateral band, which begins immediately behind the eye, is often incompletely developed and ranges up to the seventh transversal bar. The spot on the base of the caudal appears oval in shape. Except for the first two fin-membranes which are black, the dorsal fin is colourless. Two rows of spots mark the soft section. The same applies to the anal fin except that the anterior lappets are bordered dark. The caudal fin is also colourless, but bears five vertical rows of spots forming stripes in the centre of the fin with the posteriormost stripe marking the hind edge. The anterior section of the ventral fins are shaded black whilst the rest is colourless. The colours displayed in life are not especially conspicuous. The body-colouration is ivory turning into brown towards the back and slightly yellowish on the throat and chest regions. The lateral band is not constantly visible varying in its intensity with the disposition of the fish. The frontal and snout stripes are weakly developed whereas the cheek band is permanently recognizable. The rows of spots in the soft sections of the dorsal and anal fins as well as in the centre of the caudal fin are usually pale or may be absent entirely in many cases. Above the lateral band and in the lower hind parts, the body may temporarily assume a light blue tinge. Narrow dark transversal stripes may occasionally appear on the abdominal parts during courtship and as impressive behaviour.

Specific traits

It is very difficult to indicate single features which characterize this species and it is rather the combination of traits which identifies it. This includes the low dorsal fin of almost levelled height, the rounded caudal fin, the small oval caudal spot, the lateral band which ends on the seventh transversal band, and moderately high and little elongate body-shape. This species lacks a lateral blotch.

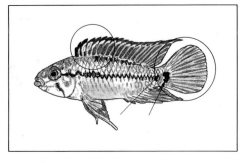

Similar species

Apistogramma regani has a different colour-pattern, usually seven very distinct and sound dark transversal bars, and a very high narrow oval caudal spot which covers almost the entire height of caudal peduncle.

Apistogramma ortmanni has a more elongate habitus in comparison, temporarily shows very broad transversal bars, and a lateral spot above the lateral band.

Apistogramma taeniata differs regarding its colour-pattern and the shape of the snout.

The

natural habitat

lies in the region of the Rio Curucamba near the village of Obidos on the Rio Amazonas, northwest of the town of Santarem in Brazil.

Care

Keeping these small South American Cichlids is not connected to specific problems. Well structured aquaria with rich vegetation and sand used as substrate are recommendable. The water-temperatures should range around 27 °C. Soft, slightly acidic water is required for a successful longterm keeping.

Attention should be given to a varying diet. The fish are peaceful and tolerate plants. They may only be kept together with other equally peace-loving species of approximately the same size.

For the

breeding

the abovementioned husbandry conditions apply. Small caves formed by halved coconut-shells or bamboo-tubes or cavities between rocks are the favourite spawning-sites. As is the case in all other species of *Apistogramma*, *Apistogramma geisleri* is also a cave brooder with a male-mother-family structure which means that the female alone takes care of the fry whilst the male is only allowed to defend the borders of claimed territory. Once the juveniles have reached two or three weeks of age the male is tolerated to come close to the young fish temporarily or even join the school.

The rearing is easy as freshly hatched nauplii are of palatable size for the juveniles. Clean water is of extreme importance during this time so that regular exchanges of a quarter to a third of the water-volume every two to five days is strongly recommended. These conditions are important factors for an optimal growth of the small *Apistogramma geisleri*.

Small aeroplanes are an important means of transport in rainforest regions.

▶ *Apistogramma gephyra*
KULLANDER, 1980

Distribution of *Apistogramma gephyra*

is a species known to the aquarists for only a short time. It has been imported only sporadically as side-catch of *Apistogramma pertensis*. The fish were usually not recognized and considered to be *Apistogramma agassizii* which they closely resemble. In direct comparison, this species is however smaller with the males reaching total lengths of only 6 cm and the females 4,5 to 5 cm. The colouration is not very conspicuous consisting mainly of dark grey to brown shades. Males have an oval to lanceolate caudal fin. Their lateral band runs up onto the caudal fin with its intensity slightly decreasing. This fin has a spotted and speckled pattern in the upper section whilst the lower section is coloured uniformly yellowish to brownish. The dorsal fin is bordered with red and the first lappets lack a dark colouration. When assuming courtship or impressing poses the body-pattern changes. The lateral band shows two blotches in the front portion of the body then whilst the posterior part simulta- neously fades. This feature is a well recogniz- able point of distinction also in the females. They however show these two blotches alter- natingly with the dark lateral band only during phases of parental care.

Male of *Apistogramma gephyra*

Table 9

Location:	Lago Arará on the left bank of the lower Rio Negro
Clarity:	clear
Colour:	brown, tea-coloured
pH:	4,3
Total hardness:	<1°dH
Carbonate hardness:	<1°dH
Conductivity:	10 µS
Depth:	10–50 cm
Current:	none
Water-temperature:	28°C
Air-temperature:	26°C
Date:	21.3.1987
Time:	09.00 hrs

Specific traits

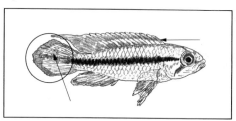

of male specimens of *Apistogramma gephyra* are the lack of dark colours in the first membranes of the dorsal fin and the red edge over the entire length of the same. They have a feebly lanceolate caudal fin with a spotted and speckled pattern in its upper section.

Similar species

Apistogramma agassizii grows larger in the male sex and has a distinctly lanceolate caudal fin with a different pattern, lacks the red edge of the dorsal fin, and is generally more brilliantly coloured.

Apistogramma elizabethae has greatly produced membranes of the dorsal fin and brown longitudinal stripes in the lanceolate caudal fin in the male sex.

The

natural habitat

of this species are the zones of the banks of the Anavilhanas Island-group which lie near the left bank of the Rio Negro approximately 100 km northwest of the city of Manaus. Specimens of *Apistogramma regani* and *Apistogramma pertensis* have also been recorded from this region.

Another locality is known to exist in the Lago Jurucui, some 600 km farther to the east, near the town of Santarem on the lower Amazon River. This is a small clear-water lake. All records known so far lie in Brazil.

Care

Small to medium-sized aquaria are sufficient which however have to be adequately planted and offer several hiding-places in the form of caves amongst rocks or bamboo-tubes. No specific requirements exist regarding the quality of the water as long as it is free of nitrite and rich in oxygen. The species is peaceful and adequate for a community aquarium. Live food is preferably accepted.

If one however intends

breeding

with this species, certain factors should be given attention. The most important criterion for the development of the fry is obviously the water. Soft acidic water with a total and carbonate hardness below 5, a pH below 6, and temperatures around 28°C only ensure a successful development of the eggs. The juveniles swim free after approximately 7 days. Forming a male-mother-family, the female alone takes care of the fry whilst the male is only permitted to protect the territory.

Powdered food is useful as first food and should be mixed into a liquid and carefully sprayed into the shoal of fry with a pipette. Freshly hatched nauplii of the Brine Shrimp are also suitalbe.

◆ Apistogramma gibbiceps
MEINKEN, 1969

In the original description Dr. Hermann MEINKEN suggested the common name "Ram-headed Cichlid" because of a conspicuous bulge on the frontal head of adult males. Since this turned however out to be no specific feature of the species, SCHMETTKAMP (1978) introduced the name "Black-stripe *Apistogramma*". The males of this species reach just under 8 cm in length whilst females are fully grown at approximately 5,5 cm. Not before the sexes are grown to some 5 cm is the determination of sex without problems. Male specimens then show slightly enlarged membranes from the second to the fourth spine of the dorsal fin and a lyreate caudal fin. Female specimens on the other hand lack the enlarged membranes of the dorsal fin and the caudal fin remains rounded, but may however also be truncate in larger specimens. The species is very peaceful and ideal for a community aquarium.

Specific traits

of these fish are a broad black lateral band which ends in the caudal fin and a sound coloured cheek-band which is almost permanently visible. Male specimens have the second to fourth membrane of the dorsal fin slightly produced and a lyreate caudal fin. The spot on the base of the tail is absent. Obliquely arranged abdominal lines are typical for the species although they may transform into spots in a certain mood. They are especially sound on the lower caudal peduncle.

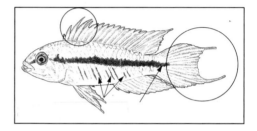

Apistogramma gibbiceps ♂

Similar species

Apistogramma bitaeniata is more elongate with the head being more slender. It also differs in its colouration and lacks abdominal lines. Adult males have longer membranes in the dorsal fin in comparison. Specimens of this species have a distinct lateral spot.

Apistogramma cacatuoides are more high-backed, have a different colouration, a higher dorsal fin, and show wave-like abdominal stripes.

Apistogramma brevis has a similar habitus, but show a distinct lateral blotch on the third transversal bar and another one on the base of the tail. Furthermore, there are four abdominal stripes.

Fully grown males have an additional lateral spot on the second transversal bar.

Numerous clear-water rivers cross the rand zones of the Andes.

The

natural habitat

was indicated by MEINKEN as being "Brazil, probably the area of the Rio Negro".

Care

Keeping this species is easy in an aquarium decorated for a small Cichlid.

Fine gravel of dark colour, a dense vegetation, and a sufficient number of hiding-places in the form of rock constructions and small caves should make out the decoration. Soft acidic water with values around 5 °dH total and carbonate hardness, approximately 6 pH, and a temperature of 28 °C on average are very important for an optimal longterm husbandry. This obviously also includes a high cleanliness of the water with regular exchanges of a quarter to a third of the volume every week or two. A varying diet is of extreme importance.

The

breeding

has not always been successful in the past. It appears that a right pH is responsible for the development of the fry and it is to be presumed that breeding is possible in very soft, very acidic water with a pH around 5,5. Reproduction may take place in the community aquarium or in a separate breeding tank. However, the recommendations made with regard to the care apply in either case.

The females prefer caves with a very small entrance as spawning sites. Coconut-shells or pieces of bamboo-tubes whose entrances are partially blocked with sand are appropriately meeting this requirement. Even in a breeding tank some other peaceful fishes should provide company. The species forms a male-mother-family. The female cares for the fry and the male defends the borders of the territory against the company fishes. Once the juveniles begin to swim, freshly hatched nauplii of the Brine Shrimp are adequate as first food. A "milk" made up of the powder-food MikroMin and water should additionally be given. The juveniles grow very slowly.

◆ *Apistogramma gossei*
KULLANDER, 1982

Distribution of *Apistogramma gossei*

The type specimens of this species were amongst others collected by the Belgian Dr. Jean-Pierre GOSSE in 1962 and the Frenchman F. D'AUBENTON in 1976. First live specimens were imported in 1988. As far as is known so far, the males reach approximately 6 cm and the females just under 4 cm in total length. For a proper identification of the species reference is made to the description by KULLANDER. The patterns of the body and the fins are especially relevant in this respect. The species has a moderately elongate and laterally little compressed body. The membranes of the dorsal fin hardly exceed the spines in height. The soft section of this fin is produced with the second ray extending up to the centre of the caudal fin. A similar situation is found in the soft section of the anal fin where the second and third ray form a streamer reaching approximately up into the first third of the caudal fin. The spines of the dorsal fin are of equal length from the fourth spine on. The species has a rounded, more rarely a slightly truncate caudal fin.

Male of *Apistogramma gossei*

For a long time, only the colour of preserved specimens was known.

The ground-colour of these fish is yellowish to white distinctly darkening towards the back. The areas of the cheeks and the gill-covers are brownish grey whilst the lips and the lower jaw are grey.

The snout and the nape are coloured dark grey. The snout and frontal stripes are predominant with the latter reaching almost up to the central nape area. The suborbital stripe is conspicuous having approximately a breadth equal to the pupil's diameter running obliquely backwards.

It is however interrupted on the anterior part of the gill-cover. The flanks are marked with seven distinct transversal bars which are slightly broader than the interspaces between. They are slightly more intense in colour on the back and extend up to the base of the dorsal fin. The seventh transversal bar crosses over the caudal peduncle.

Furthermore, there is a dark lateral band which begins immediately behind the eye and ends on the seventh transversal bar. It is approximately one scale in breadth.

A characteristic feature for this species is the presence of three abdominal stripes which are however often only faintly visible and rather consist of small dark spots on the bases of the scales. The first stripe begins at the height of the upper insertion of the pectoral fin and ends approximately above the insertion point of the anal fin. The second runs from the lower insertion point of the pectoral fin to above the anal fin. The third eventually begins between the pectoral fin and the base of the ventral fins ranging approximately up to the central section of anal fin. The first two fin-membranes of the dorsal fin are coloured black whilst the rest of the fin is grey with darker zones on its base. This is especially conspicuous above the transversal bands. On the base of this fin's soft parts, there are three rows of light dots. The anal fin looks smoky grey and the membranes in the soft section have light spots which especially concentrate on the base. The outer edges of the ventral fins are blackish and the caudal fin appears in some sort of smoky grey without any spotted pattern except for a very clear rectangular blotch on the base of the fin which is bordered with light brown on the top as well as on the bottom.

Specific traits

Besides the characteristic broad transversal banded pattern *Apistogramma gossei* shows a very distinct rectangular blotch on the base of the caudal fin which has a light brown edge on the top and on the bottom sides. A specific feature of this species is furthermore the presence of three abdominal stripes which are however indistinctly developed.

The

natural habitat

and the distribution is restricted to parts of French Guyana and the bordering area in Brazil. The localities known so far belong to the river systems of the Oyapock and Approuague. Imported alive for the first time in 1988, these specimens originated from one of the headwaters of the Creque Macouria in French Guyana.

There, the depth of the water ranged from 0,2 to 1 metre. At a temperature of 26 °C the water flowed calmly and had a colour of brownish amber. Examination of the water-quality revealed a total and carbonate hardness of 0,14 °dh each, a conductivity of 20 µS, and a pH of 5,6 (MAYLAND 1990).

South American women are interested in and often experts on fishes.

▶ *Apistogramma guttata*
ANTONIO, KULLANDER & LASSO, 1989

Distribution of *Apistogramma guttata*

is one of the species which have become known only very recently occurring naturally in the northeast of Venezuela. These fish belong to the *Apistogramma macmasteri* species-group and are medium-sized representatives of the genus. The maximal total length of the males should range between five and six centimetres whilst the females should measure approximately three centimetres when fully adult. Adult males have sandy brown ground-colouration on the body with the lower parts of the head and the area behind the pectoral fins often being yellow. The fins are more or less translucent and greyish yellow in colour except for the pectoral and caudal fin which are yellowish.

The truncate caudal fin is bordered with shades of light red which however appear very indistinct. The ventral may also show faint inconspicuous shades of reddish with the anterior edges often being black whilst the pointed tips on the other hand are whitish. The presence or absence of the lateral band, an oval shaped spot on the base of the tail, the cheek-band, and the frontal-, snout-, and postocular stripes depend on the disposition and are therefore displayed only in certain stages of excitement. Dominating males willing to spawn show a very regular pattern of small black speckles on a uniform ground-colouration which form five longitudinal rows on the flanks between the gill-cover and the base of the tail. Similar speckles also appear in the head

Male of *Apistogramma guttata*

region. Males and females have a midventral stripe each. Female specimens lack the black speckles on the head and the speckled pattern on the flanks is reduced to an indication of three longitudinal rows. During periods of parental care they show a sound yellowish orange ground-colour and a large black pectoral spot between the pectoral fins.

Specific traits

of A. guttata are the lateral black speckles which are arranged in several longitudinal rows.

Of the

similar species

the representatives of the macmasteri-group are to be mentioned especially which however all have different colour patterns. A similar speckled pattern is found in *Apistogramma* sp. "Tucurui" which is however even more regularly arranged in this species.

The

natural habitats

are simultaneously the northernmost distribution records of this genus. The range of this species seems to be confined to the catchment of the Rio Morichal Largo which cuts through the Caño Mánamo and flows into the northern delta of the Orinoco. In its central sections, this river has a fairly strong current whose speed was established by us to be 0,5 m/sec. The ground of the water-course consists of light sand whilst a thick layer of mud and silt is often deposited on the banks. The water is clear and slightly brownish in colour. In areas of slight current, the river has a rich growth of numerous species of aquatic and swamp plants including amongst others *Nymphaea* sp., *Cabomba aquatica*, *Chara* sp., and several species of *Echinodorus*. Frequently, there is furthermore a belt of floating plants consisting of *Eichhornia crassipes*, *E. azurea*, and *Paspalum repens*. Measurements taken by us at two localities revealed the following data:

Approximately 2 km down the river from the road Temblador — Maturin, on 18.4.92 at approximately 13.00 hrs, water-temperature 31 °C, conductivity 50 μS/cm, and a pH of 5,2.

Further measurements were taken on the following day at 12.30 hrs in the village of El Salto and revealed an air-temperature of 34 °C, a water-temperature of 30 °C, a conductivity 30 μS/cm, a carbonate and total hardness below the detectability-level of 1 °dH, and a pH of 5,6.

ANTONIO et al. (1989) caught this species exclusively in floating fields whereas we could find it in the immediate vicinity of the banks only where the specimens stayed in the cover of the bank-vegetation or amongst branches and leaf-litter which had fallen into the water. There depth of the water measured approximately only 10 to 30 cm at these places. Biotopes like these were also the home for Schomburgk's Leaffish (*Polycentrus schomburgkii*), a species of *Nannacara*, and a representative of the genus *Rivulus*, presumably *R. deltaphilus*.

Care

Keeping *Apistogramma guttata* in an aquarium has revealed that this species is an adaptable hardy fish which readily accepts all sorts of conventional fish-food. Attention should however be spent to the fact that this Cichlid has a much higher degree of aggression towards specimens of its own kind than other species of the *macmasteri-group*.

Therefore, A. guttata should only be kept in comparatively large-sized tanks in which a dense vegetation provides sufficient cover for subordinate fishes.

For

breeding

this fish the natural water-quality should be taken into consideration as water poor in salts and with an acidic reaction provides better preconditions for a normal development of the eggs and embryos.

◆ *Apistogramma hippolytae*
KULLANDER, 1982

The identification of this species used to be difficult in the past years. Before its scientific description in the year 1982, it was usually referred to as "Double-spotted *Apisto-gramma*".

The males of *Apistogramma hippolytae* reach total-lengths around 6 cm and the females are only a smaller. The distinction of the sexes is easy in adult specimens. The rays in the soft section of dorsal and anal fins are then longer in the males. The anterior spines of the ventral fins are also longer and reach up to the caudal peduncle when pressed against the body. During periods of parental care the female is coloured golden yellow on the body.

In order to simplify the identification of this fairly new species, reference is made to the original description by KULLANDER who stated that this is a moderately elongate species with a

Distribution of *Apistogramma hippolytae*

narrow lateral band and a distinct black spot in the third transversal bar which extends from the lateral band up to the dorsal fin. The hind

Apistogramma hippolytae ♂

edge of the caudal fin is rounded to slightly cut in shape with a third of the fin being scaled. The spines of the dorsal fin are almost equal in size from the fifth spine on. The membranes exceed the spines only minorly, are rounded to slightly truncate, and do not differ in length or shape in both sexes. The soft section of the dorsal fin is pointed. The third spine is the longest extending up to shortly behind the caudal fin base. The soft section of the anal fin is also long and pointed with the fourth spines being the longest also reaching up to shortly behind the tail-fin base. The ventral fin is pointed with the inner edge being rounded and the first spine slightly enlarged reaching up into the anal fin. The lateral band begins narrow behind the eye and extends up to the seventh transversal bar. The third transversal bar is very dark between the dorsal fin and the lateral band however continuing very faintly below the lateral band though clearly recognizable. All transversal bars are much broader than the interspaces and darker in the vicinity of the dorsal fin. The anterior membranes of the dorsal fin are black and there are five rows of dots in the soft section. The anal fin is lighter and has four indistinct rows of dots. The large dark blotch on the base of the tail covers almost the entire caudal base. The caudal fin is transparent and has six grey transversal stripes whose widths equal their interspaces and which extend over almost the complete fin. The light abdominal stripes are of varying intensity, but never conspicuous. The species belongs to the *steindachneri*-group.

Specific traits

of *Apistogramma hippolytae* are the lateral band ending in the upper part of the seventh

transversal bar and the large oval blotch on the base of the caudal fin. Depending on the mood the tail also assumes a pattern of approximately seven transversal stripes. Besides the aforesaid, the rounded to slightly truncate shape of the caudal fin is another characteristic feature.

Similar species

Apistogramma rupununi resembles *Apistogramma hippolytae* very closely and its males also have a rounded caudal fin. It however has a lateral blotch which ranges up to the upper lateral line.

Apistogramma steindachneri males have a subtruncate caudal fin already when subadult. These fish furthermore have a caudal blotch with a different shape. The third transversal bar is different above the lateral band, i. e. the central blotch is not connected with the lateral band and is triangular in shape with one tip in direction of the dorsal fin. There are however specimens which lack this blotch entirely or where it is reduced to small size. Adult males of this species never have filamentous extensions of the ventral fins.

Apistogramma ortmanni and its possible relationship to *A. hippolytae* still have to be investigated. The illustrations published so far cannot be considered typical. According to the original description this species is said to have a rounded caudal fin and two to four abdominal stripes. The lateral band should furthermore extend up onto the centre of the caudal fin.

The

natural habitat

of *Apistogramma hippolytae* was indicated as the vicinity of the Lago Manacapura in the Rio Solimoes River-system. The paratypes originated from the Rio Negro River-system, i. e. a lake on the Ilha de Buiuacu near the Rio Urubaxi and a central lake on an island in the Rio Daraá. Besides *Apistogramma hippolytae, Apistogramma diplotaenia, Biotoecus, Dicrossus filamentosus,* and *Taeniacara candidi* were also recorded from the Rio Negro area.

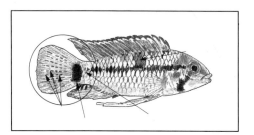

Care

Keeping these fish is generally not difficult since normal moderately hard neutral water is adequate. Soft and slightly acidic water should however be given preference if a long-term husbandry is intended. As is the case in all small South American Cichlids, densely vegetated aquaria with small caves should be made available.

Regular exchanges of water are highly recommendable and special attention should be paid to a varying diet. Company fishes should not be too large in size or in numbers.
Provided these conditions, the fish will soon start

breeding.

Courtship behaviour can be observed already approximately two days prior to spawning.

The females deposits the blood-red coloured eggs in a small cave where they usually hang down from the ceiling on small and very short stems. They measure 1,4 mm in length. A few hours after fertilization light caps appear on their lower ends. The female has not yet assumed the typical breeding colouration at this time. At a temperature of 27 °C, the embryos break through the egg-shells after approximately 40 hours.

The female now assumes a golden yellow colouration and approximately four days later the development of the larvae is complete.

This species is very productive and 200 juveniles are nothing exceptional in fully grown specimens. Soft and slightly acidic water-values are a definite must for successful reproduction. In moderately hard, slightly alkaline water only a very low number of juveniles is to be expected.

Apistogramma hippolytae ♀ in breeding-colours

◗ Apistogramma hoignei
MEINKEN, 1965

The description of *Apistogramma hoignei* by
MEINKEN was based on just two specimens
with lengths of 44 and 23 mm respectively.
Both specimens were kept in a an aquarium for
some time before they were preserved. The
larger animal, which MEINKEN thought to be
the male, had died — probably on Hexamitosis
— unnoticed and been dead for quite some
time before it was transferred into preserva-
tives and is therefore in a bad state (KULLAN-
DER 1979, MEINKEN 1965). Almost 15 years
after their description, KULLANDER (1979)
again intensely studied both type specimens of
A. hoignei. Since he stumbled over a couple of
disagreements he published his findings as a
revision of the original description.

Due to the insufficiency of the available
material the description of *A. hoignei* was
however now as before far from satisfactory.

Distribution of *Apistogramma hoignei*

Apistogramma hoignei belongs to the
moderately sized representatives of the genus.
Even under aquarium conditions the males

Male of *Apistogramma hopignei* from the catchment area of the Rio Portuguesa

reach just under 6,5 cm in total length and the females 4,5 cm. The body is high-backed. The morphological features of adult males include a subtruncate caudal fin, which becomes bifurcate with age, and greatly produced membranes in the dorsal fin which gives the latter a conspicuously high shape. Its anterior portion may be as high as the body or even slightly higher. The most important fact which was discovered during the examination of new material however is that *Apistogramma hoignei* has not three but three to four spines in the anal fin — a feature very unusual in this genus.

As is the case in many species of *Apistogramma,* the colour-patterns of the males not only vary geographically but also very much individually. The body-colourations of adult males is creamy white to slightly greenish blue shining metallically under certain light-conditions. The head and chest area, sometimes also the entire belly region, are coloured deep yellow. The extension of the yellow zones is however subject to a large amount of individual variability. Even members of the same population may have a lot of yellow or entirely lack it.

The snout-stripe is bordered with shining blueish green stripes on either side and the lips also gleam in blueish green. The anterior parts of the dorsal and anal fins are slightly blueish to translucent whereas the posterior portion is yellowish especially in the soft section. The pectoral fins are colourless and the ventral fins are blueish or yellowish in specimens with a lot of yellow components respectively. The caudal fin is yellowish in the central areas and either sound red or black in the outer regions, i. e. in the area of the distant four or five rays.

As is the case in other *Apistogramma-*species which have similar patterns of black in the caudal fin, the presence and intensity of this feature is subject to great individual variability. Specimens of *A. hoignei* from one and the same population may thus be considerably different.

Furthermore, there are geographical colour-varieties. Specimens from the catchment areas of the Caño Biruaca have black bordered caudal fins in almost every case whereas the black in those from the catchment of the lower Rio Portuguesa is usually replaced by deep red. The black body-patterns typical for species of *Apistogramma* consist of six largely and very irregularly blotches of different size being the remains of a disintegrated lateral band, a blotch on the tail base, a cheek-band, a snout-stripe, distinct dorsal spots which extend onto the base of the dorsal fin, and seven very broad transversal bars which may cover up to three scales in width. The significance of all these markings however depends very much on the mood. They may even completely vanish in dominant specimens in a neutral calm disposition. The transversal bars are especially rarely observed.

In addition to the black elements of the pattern listed above, adult males of *A. hoignei* show characteristic black speckles between the eye and the gill-cover which a typical for the species and thus an accurate point to observe for determination.

Outside periods of parental care, the most important features of the females are a creamy to dirty yellowish brown ground-colouration and a dark lateral band which is however often more or less disintegrated into lateral spots. Whilst engaged in parental care they assume a sound lemon-yellow body-colouration. The anterior edges of the ventral fins and the fin-membranes of the first two or three spines of the dorsal fin are coloured black. The lower fringe of the anal fin is also black. The dark elements of the body-pattern consist of the snout- and frontal-stripe, the vertically enlarged blotch on the tail base, the six lateral blotches which decreases in intensity from the rear to the front, and the dorsal blotches which extend onto the basal parts of the dorsal fin. The lateral spot is conspicuous only in exceptional cases. The lower part of the body is marked with a black midventral stripe which may range from the lower lip to the anal fin.

Specific traits

of *A. hoignei* are that this species has four, in rare cases three, spines in the anal fin. A breeding female shows a midventral stripe, a pectoral blotch, and usually a black throat. Adult males on the other hand have subtruncate to bifurcate caudal fins, greatly produced membranes in the dorsal fin, and a specific pattern of black speckles in the head region. The caudal fin is furthermore conspicuously coloured.

Similar species

Confusion appears to be possible best of all with *A. macmasteri* and *A. viejita*. Both species however have always only three spines in the anal fin and the males have a rounded caudal fin. They furthermore lack the pattern of black speckles in the head region.

Natural habitats

Apistogramma hoignei is distributed in the catchment of the lower Rio Apuré in central Venezuela. The species belongs, as most the other representatives of the genus do, to the inhabitants of the extremely shallow zones of water-courses and appears to prefer areas up to 40 cm in depth. There, the fish lead a very seclusive life in the cover of submerged leaf-litter or plants which usually belong to the embanking emerse vegetation and which are flooded during times of high-water.

One of the localities in the catchment of the Rio Portuguesa is a larger lake whose shores are vegetated by reed and high grass and which partially has a canopy of floating plants of the species *Eichhornia crassipes*. The syntopic ichthyofauna includes the Cichlids *Caquetaia kraussii*, *Cichlasoma orinocense*, and representatives of the *"Aequidens" pulcher*-complex.

Another collecting site is a swampy flood area on the Caño Biruaca which is mostly covered with a dense layer of the floating plants *Eichhornia azurea* and *Pistia stratiotes*. Round about 12 o'clock the temperature of the air there measured 31 °C with the water being 28 °C.

The conductivity was established to be approximately 100 micro-Siemens/cm, the pH 6,6. The total hardness was 2 °dH whilst the carbonate hardness was 4 °dH. This biotope was shared by the *Apistogramma* with the Killi-fish *Rachovia maculipinnis*.

Care

If you keep this species in captivity, it is good to know that the males claim relatively large territories not only amongst themselves but also from males of other species of *Apistogramma*. Intraspecific fights very quickly result in mouth-dragging. On the other hand, males and females are relatively tolerant towards their sexual partners thus it is even possible to initiate

breeding

in a densely planted tank of only 50 cm in length. Kept in much larger tanks it was observed that males are polygamous and congregate several females in their territories with whom they alternatingly spawn. It has been experienced that hiding-places underneath pieces of bog-oak were preferred sites for spawning. As is the case in all other species of *Apistogramma*, the juveniles are reared in a male-mother-family structure. The male's only task is to defend the spawning-territory. Although *A. hoignei* originates from relatively soft waters, breeding has repeatedly been successful in moderately hard water with an electrical conductivity of approximately 700 micro-Siemens, and total hardness of 12 °dH, a carbonate hardness of 14 °dH, and a pH of 7,6.

Table 10

Location:	Larger lake in the catchment of the Rio Portuguesa, appr. 10 km north of San Fernando de Apuré
Clarity:	poor, very murky
Colour:	loamy yellow
pH:	7,3
Total hardness:	3 °dH
Carbonate hardness:	5 °dH
Conductivity:	250 µS
Depth:	max. 40 cm
Current:	none
Water-temperature:	33 °C
Air-temperature:	34 °C
Date:	3.8.1989
Time:	10.30 hrs

◆ *Apistogramma hongsloi*
KULLANDER, 1979

Distribution of *Apistogramma hongsloi*

is yet another Dwarf-cichlid well known to aquarists which has been imported for the first time as an undescribed species as early as in the early seventies. Temporarily it was referred to under the name of "Red-lines *Apistogramma*". In the genus these fish are included in the mac-masteri species-group. They are popular aquarium-fish, which are however rarely available since they are neither frequently imported nor easily bred in captivity.

This species belongs to the moderately sized representatives of the genus *Apistogramma* with the males reaching just under seven centimetres in total length under optimal husbandry conditions.

Female specimens on the other hand grow to a maximum length of 45 millimetres. The morphological features of a male include a moderately high-backed body, a rounded caudal fin, and long pointed soft sections of the dorsal and anal fins whose tips may extend up to the hind edge of the caudal fin. The mem-branes of the anterior spines of the dorsal fin are produced and exceed the height of the rest of the fin.

According to our present state of knowledge *Apistogramma hongsloi* is a exceptionally

Male of the blue-yellow variety of *Apistogramma hongsloi* from Columbia

69

variable species. This fact has led to the recognition of several distinct geographical varieties, races, or even separate species in past times when the available information was sparser than today.

Males of the blue-yellow morph originating from Colombia have the head and the anterior portion of the body up to behind the ventral fins coloured sound lemon-yellow. The central and posterior part of the body in contrast is bright light blue. A narrow bright red zone marks the hind and lower edge of the body. It begins on the base of the caudal fin and runs along the lower edge of the caudal peduncle over the base of the anal fin up to about the anus. The same colour is shown on the inner and outer edge of the iris. The ventral, dorsal, and anal fins are more or less uniformly light blue whilst the membranes of the dorsal fin show feebly red shades. The caudal fin is largely colourless and translucent.

The colour-pattern shown by males which are caught in the Rio Cataniapo in Venezuela is fairly sleek in comparison. Their ground-colour is some sort of beige which turns into grey towards the back and into whitish towards the belly. The bases of the caudal and pectoral fins are orange. A few greenish shining speckles or lines are found on the orange brownish coloured lower part of the head.

Dominant males in neutral mood may completely lack the black pattern which is otherwise so typical for the genus *Apistogramma*. The lateral band is however mostly visible which is actually an extension of the narrow postocular stripe covering more than one scale in width. It has a typical chain-like shape in males and females which results from only the edges of the scales being coloured black whilst the centres remain light. In addition, the males usually have distinct abdominal stripes which are arranged in two longitudinal rows. The number, size, and colour intensity of these lines can increase in courting males so much that almost the entire belly region becomes black.

The females have a yellow ground-colour. The lateral band, the cheek-bands, and a small

Male of *Apistogramma hongsloi* from the Rio Cataniapo in Venezuela

usually round spot on the tail-base are always clearly recognizable. In addition, they show the dorsal spots typical for the macmasteri species-group which extend onto the dorsal fin.

The first two or three membranes of the dorsal fin, the front edges of the ventral fins, and the edge of the anal fin are also black in colour. During phases of parental care the lateral band disintegrates into irregular black spots. The females then show a pitch black midventral stripe and an extensive pectoral blotch.

The

specific traits

include the chain-like pattern of the lateral band and the abdominal stripes in the male sex which may fuse to a black area during courtship.

Similar species

are found amongst other members of the *macmasteri*-group which however have completely different colourations in the male sex.

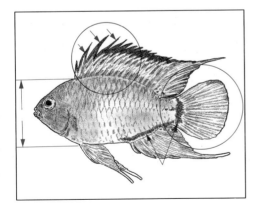

The

natural habitats

of this Dwarf Cichlid lie in the catchment of the upper and central Orinoco in the countries of Colombia and Venezuela. One of the auth-

ors managed to catch these fish in July 1989 in a small river of five to ten metres in width with a strong current being a tributary to the lower Rio Cataniapo which, in its further course, flows into the Orinoco approximately seven kilometres south of Pto. Ayacucho.

The depth of this clear and colourless water-course ranged between 50 cm and one metre. Its ground was sandy. An analysis of the water conducted at approximately 11.00 hrs revealed that whilst the air-temperature was 32 °C, the water-temperature measured only 25,5 °C. The conductivity was established to be 10 micro-Siemens/cm and total and carbonate hardness were below the detectability-level of 1 °dH of the available equipment. The pH was 5,5. The fish were recorded from the shallow zones near the banks where the current was slow and where cover was provided by emerse vegetation reaching up into the water and partially profuse thickets of aquatic plants (amongst others *Tonia fluviatilis*). No other fishes could be recorded from these sites.

Care

Keeping these fish is quite easy since it is a hardy and adaptable species. Soft water and pH-values in the acidic zone however contribute as positively to the well-being of the animals as a richly vegetated aquarium does which provides cover and hiding-places.

The

breeding

of *A. hongsloi* and a normal development of the larvae require water-values which resemble those found in the natural habitats although eggs may also be laid in moderately hard water with a total hardness of 12 °dH, a carbonate hardness of 14 °dH, and a pH of 7,5. As is the case in the other species of this genus, this Cichlid is also a cave brooder which hides the clutch below roots or in other hiding-places. The eggs and larvae are exclusively cared for by the female, while the male defends the territory.

◆ Apistogramma inconspicua
KULLANDER, 1983

This species belongs to the *regani*-group and was introduced into science only in 1983 although the first specimens were collected as early as in 1909 by the American HASEMAN. The fish was however treated as *Heterogramma corumbae* and *Heterogramma taeniatum* in the scientific literature which are however today considered synonyms.

It was not before 1977 that the Belgian ichthyologist GOSSE collected new material and thus made a description possible. The largest male has a body length of 37,4 mm, but the total length of fully grown male specimens ranges around 8 cm. Since the species was available alive only on very rare occasions, the body- and fin-colourations and patterns are quoted here in summary from the original description by KULLANDER. The indications refer to preserved material.

Distribution of *Apistogramma inconspicua*

The head and body of *A. inconspicua* are moderately elongate. From approximately the sixth spine on, the spines of the dorsal fin are equal in length. The tips of the membranes are short and pointed in the males, but truncate in the females. The soft section of the dorsal fin is pointed with the third ray being the longest

extending approximately up to the centre of the caudal fin. In contrast, the soft section of the dorsal fin is more rounded in females, and the same applies to the soft parts of the anal fin with the tip also reaching up to about the centre of the caudal fin. Both sexes have a rounded caudal fin. Preserved specimens have a brownish yellow ground-colouration which lightens up towards the belly and darkens

Apistogramma inconspicua ♂

towards the back-regions. All elements of the pattern appear dark brown with the head-stripes, the lateral band, and the caudal spot being the most distinct components. The gill-covers, the area of the snout, the lips, and the frontal region are coloured grey. The width of the suborbital stripe almost equals the diameter of the pupil. Due to the brownish colouration of the nape it is not recognizable whether there is a superorbital stripe or not. The transversal bars are indistinct above the lateral band and are only visible as pale blotches along the base of the dorsal fin. They are much more distinct below the lateral band. The lateral band covers approximately one scale in width and runs from immediately behind the eye up to just before the sixth transversal bar.

At the point where the lateral band crosses the third transversal bar, its colouration slightly intensifies. The seventh transversal bar is fused with the more or less square caudal spot which is bordered with a whitish spot above and below. Said spot is narrowly bordered brownish anteriorly and posteriorly. Abdominal stripes are present as faint indications only with one running from the upper and another from the lower insertion point of the pectoral fins. Both extend approximately up to the base of the anal fin. There may be an indication of a third abdominal stripe in exceptional cases. The fins are smoky with the anterior two membranes of the dorsal fin being black. A dark spot is found in the membranes of the soft section. The anterior edge of the anal fin is bordered dark especially in female specimens. The caudal fin is marked with six vertical rows of light spots with black edges. These rows range over the entire height of the fin in males whereas they are confined to the central parts and only number five in females. The differences between males and females are not especially distinct and only clearly recognizable in adult specimens.

Specific traits

are the blotch on the tail which links the seventh transversal bar to the base of the caudal fin and the vertically arranged rows of light spots in the caudal fin which are bordered with

black. The lateral band ends on the sixth transversal bar in this species.

Similar species

are *Apistogramma commbrae* and *A. linkei*, the Yellow-chested *Apistogramma*. These

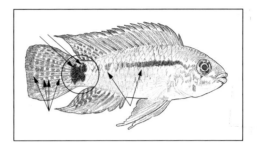

species are characterized by a black caudal blotch which includes the seventh transversal bar and the spot on the base of the caudal fin. The other members of the regani species-group all have a caudal spot which is restricted to the base of the caudal fin.

On the other hand, *A. commbrae* is smaller and has a pale spotted pattern restricted to the upper part of the caudal fin. Its abdominal stripes furthermore appear as distinct spots which form short stripes on the lower half of the body.

The Yellow-chested *Apistogramma A. linkei* in contrast has a sound though sometimes interrupted abdominal stripe and a slightly different body-shape. Its caudal fin is largely transparent without any pattern. The lateral band extends up to the caudal spot.

The

natural habitat

and the distribution of this species ranges from the headwaters of the Rio Paraguay and the Rio Guaporé, the frontier-river between Brazil and Bolivia. The type specimen was caught in a tributary to the Rio San Joaquin.

▶ *Apistogramma iniridae*
KULLANDER, 1979

is unfortunately a species not frequently kept. Its scientific name refers to its distribution area in Colombia. This is a slender elongate fish in which the males reach approximately 7 cm and the females up to 5,5 cm in length. The dorsal fin is high with the membranes fused together and the caudal fin is rounded. Adult male specimens have produced pointed ventral fins which extend up to the caudal peduncle. The species is peaceful, but not without problems in their captive husbandry.

Distribution of *Apistogramma iniridae*

Specific traits

are a high and large dorsal fin without free membranes anteriorly and long pointed ventral fins in the males. Both sexes have rounded caudal fins and lateral bands which extend up onto the caudal fin.

A caudal spot is absent. An especially distinctive feature is the presence of obliquely arranged abdominal stripes which may temporarily appear also as a sooty area on the poste-

Apistogramma iniridae ♂

rior belly area and on the tail. They are however not visible in every state of excitement.

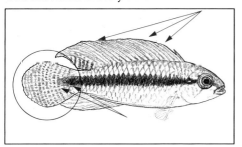

Similar species

are *Apistogramma pertensis* which however has a caudal spot, free fin-membranes in the anterior dorsal fin and lacks oblique abdominal stripes.

Apistogramma meinkeni is more high-backed, has a caudal spot, free fin-membranes in the dorsal fin, and lacks abdominal stripes.

The

natural habitat

known so far are sites in the rainforest areas around the village of Inirida (Puerto Inirida). The type series was collected in the Caño Bocón, i.e. a small water-course of the name of Bocón. There, this species lives together with *Dicrossus filamentosus* and Red Neon-tetra. The local water-values are very soft and very acidic.

Care

Aquaria of 100×40 cm in ground-size should be used for this species. Fine gravel or sand as substrate and small constructions of calcium-free rocks which form caves are highly recommendable. A rich vegetation should also be available.

Apistogramma iniridae loves very clean water which thus is a precondition for a successful healthy husbandry. To meet this requirement regular exchanges of a third of the water-volume every fortnight are necessary. For the normal keeping already it is advisable to have water with a total hardness of less than 5°dH. The concentration of hydrogen-ions

however appears to be even more important. One should therefore try to keep the pH below 6 or even better around 5 if a long-term husbandry is intended. Aquarists having soft water available from the tap obviously have an advantage.

According to experiences made so far, two pairs of this species can be kept together without problems in a tank of the indicated size.

Company in the form of a few *Dicrossus filamentosus* and a small school of other fish with the same water-requirements is very advisable. Provided a varying diet of live food — flake-food is also readily accepted if offered occasionally — the specimens will grow to splendid representatives of their species. Their pattern changes with increasing age with the sound dark lateral band being replaced by a spotted pattern from the belly to the tail. The females assume a loamy yellow colouration. Once they begin to "woo" their males with increasing frequency and "construction works" in a cave are observed, an interesting time is to be expected.

However, for successful

breeding

the keeper has to provide certain conditions. This does not only mean the very clean water mentioned above, but also a changed water-quality. Only very soft and very acidic water with a total hardness not exceeding 2°dH enables the development of the brood. Our experiments revealed that a hydrogen-ion concentration around 5,1 was insufficient for a development of the embryos resulting in the female eating the clutch after approximately 48 hours since there was no satisfying progress. Only by employing a filtration over peat which lowered the pH to 4,6 to 4,5 the requirements for an unproblematic growth were obviously met. An raised water-temperature is also important. Whilst temperatures of 27 to 28°C may be adequate for the normal keeping, the temperature should be raised by one or 2°C now.

Preceding the reproduction of *Apistogramma iniridae* is that a cave is claimed which is usually situated immediately on the ground. The female starts transporting sand out of the cave and blocking the entrance with it until a small opening remains. After an excessive and vigorous foreplay during which the male temporarily inspects the cave and helps to finish it, the partners spawn inside. The eggs are laid, better to say hung, on the ceiling since they have short stems of approximately 1 mm in length on which they hang down. Even without having fed *Cyclops* the eggs are red in colour and have light caps on the lower ends which will disappear after some 24 hours after spawning. The embryos hatch approximately three days after spawning.

They are drubbed out of their shells by the female which had already cleaned the eggs with her mouth all the time during their development. The larvae are then cared for by an alert female and may be transported by her to other depressions or hiding-places in case of unavoidable danger. The male is not tolerated inside the spawning territory. It protects a larger radius around the spawning site against co-inhabitants of the aquarium which is his indirect contribution to the parental care. During this time the female has lost the normal colouration with the lateral band on the body

and presents herself in loamy-yellow colours. The dark suborbital stripe is very conspicuous as is an almost square spot on the flanks, i.e. a lateral spot, of the body. The fins are feebly orange in colour.

Approximately four days later the development of the fry is complete and the female guides a small school of young fish through the territory around the breeding cave, always prepared to defend them against any antagonist whatsoever. Only a few days later the school spreads out to a larger formation and the individualism of the young fish makes it increasingly difficult for the females to defend them. The juveniles measure approximately 4,6 mm on the first day. Their described development took place at a water-temperature of 28 °C. The water had a conductivity of 160 micro-Siemens (at 28 °C) and a pH of 4,6. Approximately 130 eggs were originally laid and just under 60 juveniles were counted on the first day. Their first food consisted alternatingly of freshly hatched nauplii of *Artemia salina*, micro-worms, and MikroMin. If the quality of the water is constantly maintained, the rearing of the offspring is no problem.

A typical clear-water river near Atalaya in the south of Peru

◆ *Apistogramma linkei*
KOSLOWSKI, 1985

Distribution of *Apistogramma linkei*

This colourful yellow-chested *Apistogramma* was collected in larger numbers and brought back to Europe alive as well as preserved for the first time by the authors from an expedition in July 1983. This appears to be a species belonging to the *regani*-group in which the males reach approximately 6 cm and the females just under 4 cm in total-length. The fish has a high and moderately elongate head and body. In the male, the membranes of the dorsal fin increase in length from the first to the fourth spine and then continue at almost equal height. The produced rays in the soft section of the dorsal fin reach up to the centre of the caudal fin and the same applies to the rays of the anal fin. The caudal fin is rounded. The ventral fins end in short threads which extend up to the base of the caudal peduncle in the male when pressed against the body. An accurate determination of sex is only possible in larger specimens. In comparison, the females not only grow to a smaller size, they also have smaller and shorter fins in relation to their

Apistogramma linkei ♂; the "Yellow-chested *Apistogramma*"

bodies. When feeling well, different colourations are observed. The males may have brown frontal-, nape-, and back-region and a cadmium-yellow chest. Throat and belly appear in a light shade of ivory whilst the rest of the body is light blue.

The spotted and speckled markings of the head are also light blue. The fins usually have a light blue gleam which intensifies towards the outer edges. The females in contrast are coloured feebly umber-grey assuming a zinc-yellow colouration when willing to spawn.

The pattern is interesting. Male specimens usually show four dorsal spots at the height of the second to fourth transversal bar. A superorbital stripe is absent and the preorbital and suborbital are faintly visible. It is noteworthy that the suborbital is reduced to a spot marking its end on the edge of the gill-cover. A narrow lateral band begins immediately behind the eye and ends on the seventh transversal bar in a kind of oval blotch. The base of the caudal fin is marked with a spot which is often fused with the one on the seventh transversal bar thus forming a double-spot. Black edges of the scales below the lateral band form one or two abdominal stripes of varying intensity. A lateral spot is absent.

In display-pattern, the fish show all seven transversal bars which are then very dark and range from the back to the belly. Simultaneously, the fins assume a smoky colouration which intensifies towards the edges. All black elements of the pattern may however disappear in dominant males.

The species can be considered peace-loving.

The

Specific traits

are the oval spot on the base of the caudal fin and the second also oval spot next to it on the seventh transversal bar which are often fused to form a double-blotch. Furthermore, the lateral band ends on the seventh transversal bar. The cheek-spot on the gill-cover, being the remains of the lower end of a suborbital stripe, should also be observed.

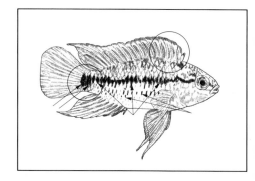

Similar species

Apistogramma inconspicua has a lateral band which ends on the sixth transversal bar already. Furthermore, these fish have vertically arranged rows of light spots in the caudal fin which are bordered with black.

Apistogramma commbrae grows to a smaller adult-size and shows a pale spotted pattern in the upper part of the caudal fin. The abdominal stripes are transformed into sound spots which may form short longitudinal stripes on the lower half of the body.

Table 11

Location:	Small water-course crossing the road and remains of water along the road between the villages of Portachuelo and Bella Vista, northwest of Santa Cruz in Bolivia
Clarity:	murky (after rain)
Colour:	brownish
pH:	7,8
Total hardness:	6°dH
Carbonate hardness:	6°dH
Conductivity:	198 µS at 24°C
Nitrite:	—
Depth:	2 to 100 cm
Current:	slow
Water-temperature:	24°C
Date:	6.7.1983
Time:	11.00 hrs

According to the present state of knowledge the

natural habitats

of his species are apparently exclusive to Bolivia. The biotopes are primarily rest-waters and small shallow water-courses in the vast cattle-breeding farm-areas of the lowlands. The easternmost collecting sites during our expedition in 1983 were near Santa Cruz where the examined places were approximately 50 km northeast and northwest of the city. This species was present everywhere with varying commonness. In every case the water-bodies and a slight to almost no current and were shallow. The fish could on the other hand not be recorded in other small rivers with a stronger current. An interesting collecting locality for example was on either side of the road between the villages of Portachuelo and Bella Vista. Since the flat meadows for the cattle are often flooded during heavy rainfalls, soil was moved from either side of the road and used to raise the road-level in order to protect it against being flooded.

The remaining dips along the dirt-roads are quickly filled with water during the rainy season and today form water-bodies which are often vegetated and are partly connected to the many small natural water-courses which cross the road. The Yellow-chested Apistogramma occur in large numbers in these shallow, i.e. only 2 to 10 cm deep lagoons with a partly very dense canopy of water-hyacinths. They however also occur amongst the grass, leaves, mud, and silt of the flooded meadows where the water-level often is only 2 or 3 cm deep. In depressions where the water may be up to 50 cm deep, they are on the other hand only found where cover is provided from the banks. Free swimming-space is clearly avoided and is dominated by larger, often predatory fishes. Although these waters are exposed to direct sunlight and the air-temperature ranges around 30 °C, the water-temperature was quite low at 25 °C.

At these collecting localities on the road from Montero through Portachuelo to the Rio Yacapani, the population density was high.

Beside the Yellow-chested Apistogramma the species Apistogramma luelingi was recorded at the same sites during this excursion. The very shallow zones were also inhabited by Pyrrhulina vittata whilst the deeper zones were suitable habitats for Characins, including predatory species, and Characidium fasciatum and Moenkhausia sanctaefilomenae.

The Catfish Hoplosternum littorale was also recorded from here. Other Cichlids of this area were Cichlasoma boliviense and Crenicichla lepidota.

A second large examination locality lies approximately 250 km farther to the northwest in the vicinity of the town of Trinidad.

Apistogramma linkei was also recorded from here and interesting data could be compiled. It was observed that this species was especially common when the hardness of the water was not too low, i.e. when the pH measured more than 7. In slightly acidic water the species was less frequent or was replaced by another species which was unknown at this time. A balanced ratio was obviously given when the hydrogen-ion concentration measured 6. At collecting sites where the pH-value was 5,7 the catches contained Apistogramma staecki only whereas the Yellow-chested Apistogramma was absent.

Table 12

Location:	West of the town of Trinidad on the road to Pto. Amacen near the Rio Mamoré (Bolivia)
Clarity:	very murky
Colour:	greyish brown
pH:	6,6
Total hardness:	1,5 °dH
Carbonate hardness:	1 °dH
Conductivity:	37 µS at 29 °C
Nitrite:	—
Depth:	max. 40 cm
Current:	none
Water-temperature:	29 °C
Date:	11.7.1983
Time:	15.00 hrs

Does the degree of acidity dictate the development and distribution of the species? Although this is hypothetical its possibility should not be ignored.

The most interesting collecting site of *Apistogramma linkei* was however found west of the town of Trinidad on either side of the road to Pto. Amacen approximately 1 km before one reaches the large Rio Mamoré. Here the fish lived also depressions created when the road was built and a small water-course which crossed the road. As described above, the water was partly very shallow, very murky, with no current whatsoever, and fully exposed to the sun. This resulted in light-values of 50 000 Lux at the water-surface, 1500 Lux at a depth of 10 cm, and only 100 Lux 20 cm below the surface. Submerse plants were absent and the air-temperature was 31 °C in the afternoon. On some occasions brush and grass creept into the water. The ground was sandy and muddy. The table summarizes the water-quality. This biotope furthermore was home to *Cichlasoma boliviense, Crenicichla lepidota, Chaetobranchopsis australis, Characidium fasciatum, Pyrrhulina vittata* and several other Tetras, *Paraucheniopterus galeatus, Hoplosternum littorale, Gymnotus carapo*, a species of *Hypostomus*, and *Eigenmannia* sp. aff. *virescens*. On yet another collecting side not far from there the Yellow-chested *Apistogramma* was recorded to occur together with *Cichlasoma boliviense, Aequidens vittatus*, and *Laetacara dorsigera*.

Apistogramma linkei ♀

Care

Keeping this fairly new species is possible in moderately hard, neutral to slightly alkaline water. Aquaria with a rich growth of plants, many hiding-facilities, and a fine substrate are an ideal environment. Regardless of the observations made in the field, attention should be spend on a high quality of the water. The fish are peaceful amongst themselves and may even be kept in larger numbers in appropriately sized tanks.

Their

breeding

is no problem at all and happens almost automatically once maturity is reached. The pairs form a male-mother-family structure where the female alone directly cares for the fry and the male viciously defends the breeding territory.

In large aquaria a tendency towards the formation of a harem can be observed. It is noteworthy that this species preferably chooses the underside of leaves of *Anubias* as spawning sites and ignored available caves. This *Apistogramma* is modestly productive and 100 descendants are an average result.

Swimming juveniles immediately accept newly hatched nauplii of the Brine Shrimp as first food.

A "milk" made out of MikroMin and aquarium-water has proven a valuable addition to the diet. Breeding was successful already a few weeks after the first import.

Collecting site of *Apistogramma linkei* in the vicinity of Trinidad in northern Bolivia. Here, this species occurs syntopically with Apistogramma staecki.

◗ *Apistogramma luelingi*
KULLANDER, 1976

Distribution of *Apistogramma luelingi*

Although the original description of *Apistogramma luelingi* was only published in the year 1976, the history of this species dates back to the year 1966. At this time, K.H. LÜLING, who worked at the Zoologisches Forschungsinstitut und Museum Alexander Koenig in Bonn, Germany, until his death in 1985, conducted an ichthyological collecting trip to Bolivia during which he caught amongst many others 15 semi-adult Cichlids in the catchment of the Rio Chaparé. Neither he nor Herbert MEINKEN, to whom he later passed on the preserved specimens for determination and further studies, recognized that this was a species new to science. MEINKEN instead was of the opinion that LÜLING had caught *Apistogramma cacatuoides*, a species which was erroneously dealt with at this time under the name of *A. borellii*.

It was only many years later when the Swedish ichthyologist S.O. KULLANDER examined these fish again that he recognized that this was an undescribed Cichlid species differing from other species of *Apistogramma* by the

Male of *Apistogramma luelingi* from the catchment region of the Rio Yacapani in Bolivia

possession of additional spines in the anal fin while all other forms generally have only three spines. Although MEINKEN had overlooked this point of distinction his misdetermination was not all that out of the blue since *Apistogramma luelingi* is in fact quite closely related to *A. cacatuoides* and both species share a few features regarding body-shape and colouration. At high age, males of either species have a deeply forked bifurcate caudal fin whose upper and lower tips from long streamers. Furthermore, the males of *A. cacatuoides* may have small orange-red spots with a black bordering in the upper and even in the lower half of the caudal fin.

Apistogramma luelingi is also known for this feature. Finally, *A. cacatuoides* has the reputation that old male specimens have the membranes of their dorsal fins so much produced that they compare to the plume-crown of a Cockatoo or the feathered head-dress of an Indian Chief. Fully grown males of *A. luelingi* also show conspicuously produced dorsal fin-membranes although these are not as extremely enlarged.

Specific traits

are the distinct pattern of seven to nine dark transversal stripes in the caudal fin and that the head is often coloured yellow. Another point of distinction separating this species from other forms and which is therefore important for the identification is the fact that the outer section of the soft part of the dorsal fin and the upper edge of the caudal fin show reddish orange to reddish shades. In females the black lateral bands disappears entirely during periods of parental care. It is then replaced with a small black lateral spot on a orange-yellow ground-colour. This breeding colouration distinguishes them from the females of *A. cacatuoides* which keep the lateral band even when caring for their young. The females of *A. luelingi* are fully grown at 3,5 cm whilst the males reach round about 7 cm in total length.

The

natural habitat

of *A. luelingi* lie in the catchment regions of the Rio Madre de Dios, the Rio Chaparé, and the Rio Yacapani, both the latter mentioned being headwaters of the Rio Mamoré which in turn is connected to the Amazon River through the Madeira River. During a study-trip in 1985, the authors managed to record this Dwarf Cichlid from a wetland vegetated with numerous swamp and aquatic plants. During periods of low water this area was meandered by several stream-like water-courses. Strong specimens of Amazon Sword-plants (*Echinodorus*) were especially frequently found which not only grew submerged but also entirely emersed on the banks of the streams. The ground of the water-courses consisted of yellow sand exclusively and it was noteworthy that there were not any stones or a sign of wood in the water. This means that nothing else but plant material is available to the Cichlids as breeding substrate. The *Apistogramma* exclusively lived in the shallow water covered by dense groups of plants. An analysis of the clear brownish water at the collecting site revealed that the total and carbonate hardness was below 1 °dH. Its conductivity measured 14 micro-Siemens and the pH was establish to be 6. The nitrite-content was below 0,1 mg/l and the thermometer showed the temperature to be 22 °C in the water and 25 °C air-temperature. These results largely correspond with the data collected by LÜLING at three other localities of *A. luelingi*. It therefore appears that this Dwarf Cichlid prefers water-bodies with extremely soft water and a pH which clearly ranges in the acidic zone.

Apistogramma-biotope in Bolivia

This presumption is supported by our observation that this fish was absent from other water-courses with different chemical qualities in the immediate vicinity of the examined site. These biotopes were instead inhabited by *A. linkei,* a species which is obviously adapted to harder water with an alkaline reaction.

Care

Despite the findings regarding the ecology of *Apistogramma luelingi* it has meanwhile turned out that this Dwarf Cichlid is fairly hardy and adaptable and could be successfully kept and even bred in moderately hard water at pH-values in the neutral zone.

Breeding

The fish usually chose a depression of a root as spawning site.

Even after hatching the larvae remain at the site where the mother had attached them to the substrate by means of their sticky glands on their heads. The actual breeding care is performed by the female alone. At a water-temperature of 25 °C the juveniles fish had completed their larval development one week after spawning. From that time on they were taken through the aquarium in a school by the mother.

Even in a small aquarium of only 50 cm in length no aggressive behaviour was observed to take place amongst the parental specimens and the fry was successfully reared in the presence of the male. The young fish can easily be fed the nauplii of the Brine Shrimp. Provided with sufficient quantities of food and a regular supply of fresh water, the juveniles grow fairly rapidly. They may have reached a length of 3 cm after only four months. The sexes can then be distinguished without problems.

Female of *Apistogramma luelingi*

◗ *Apistogramma macmasteri*
KULLANDER, 1979

is a quite intensely coloured and patterned fish which has been known to aquarists under names such as *Apistogramma taeniata* or *Apistogramma ornatipinnis* long before its formal scientific description.

These names are however regarded as synonyms today. The term "Villavicencio-*Apistogramma*" was also commonly in use when reference was made to this species.

These fish are placid reaching 8 to 9 cm in length in the males and up to 6 cm in the females. Reports of males of more than 10 cm in length should be noted with care since these sizes are certainly exceptions.

This species is closely allied to *Apistogramma viejita* and *Apistogramma hongsloi* and especially difficult to distinguish from the first mentioned species. *Apistogramma macmasteri* has a high-backed body shape with the head being fairly bulky in large male speci-

Distribution of *Apistogramma macmasteri*

mens. The fin-membranes do not increase much between the fourth and sixth spine of the dorsal fin or are even of almost same height.

Apistogramma macmasteri ♂

Adult males have the dorsal fin-membranes greatly produced between spines three to five. These enlargements are at least as long as the respective spine, but often longer. The second and the sixth to ninth membrane may also be fairly long whereas the following ones are described as being only of moderate length. The soft section of the dorsal has a long produced tip which may exceed over the caudal fin. A similar situation is found in the anal fin which may even reach the same length. According to the original description the caudal fin has a rounded shape, but various authors also described it as being truncate or even subtruncate.

The colour in life is generally known, but the indications made for the colour pattern of reference specimens may be helpful for a clear identification of the species.

The transversal bars are only indicated by dark spots along the base of the dorsal fin. The bars three to seven may however extend as indications down to approximately the height of the lower edge of the caudal peduncle. The transversal bars almost equal the interspaces in width. The blotches in the back region extend onto the base of the dorsal fin. A lateral band is absent, but is replaced by a row of blotches above the lower lateral line. The blotch at the height of the third transversal bar is the most prominent one and may be referred to as the lateral spot. These blotches are approximately one and a half scales in width with the last two often being fused.

The cheek band is broad tapering downwards. The frontal stripe extends up to the nape. The caudal spot is oval in shape. The anterior two membranes of the dorsal fin are coloured black. The remaining fin is unpatterned except for two to four rows of spots in the soft posterior portion. The anal fin is almost colourless with three rows of spots in the posterior part. The caudal fin is transparent without any speckles.

Apistogramma macmasteri ♀

Observations made in wild-caught specimens showed that the transversal bands may appear all over the body in great contrast depending on the mood. The black spots on the body which form an interrupted lateral band end on the seventh transversal bar in front of the large caudal spot. They are situated in the cutting points of the transversal and lateral bands. The red top and bottom bordering of the caudal fin is very intense and usually present in both sexes. Abdominal stripes are generally absent although individual specimens may have indications of two very pale stripes.

Adult males appear to be very bulky. Females lack a black throat and have a golden yellow chest colouration.

Specific traits

are the black spotted pattern forming a lateral band and the frequently observed intense broad transversally barred pattern.

Furthermore, the shape and size of the caudal blotch is an important feature for this species. As to how far a variable shape of the caudal fin may be a specific character is questionable at the moment and may also be dependant on age and size of the individual specimen.

The red pattern of the caudal fin is an important point of distinction in adult live specimens.

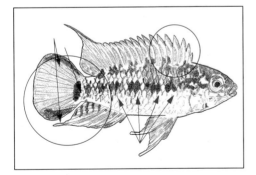

Similar species

Apistogramma viejita lacks a lateral band broken up into blotches, has a smaller caudal spot, and partly a higher number of abdominal stripes. Furthermore, these fish are slightly smaller in adult size. The transversal bars are seldom shown and are only partially visible then.

Apistogramma hongsloi differs in its colouration, often displays an uninterrupted broad lattice like lateral band, and a smaller caudal spot. The entire body pattern sometimes appears without contrast and "faded".

The

natural habitat

lies in the vicinity of the town of Villavicencio on the edge of the eastern Andes in Columbia. On occasion of a collecting trip we could record this fish from the headwaters of the Rio Ocoa only approximately 7 km southeast of Villavicencio in March 1983. It was a small, i.e. up to three metres broad and partly up to 10 cm deep stream whose ground was partly covered with numerous large stones of up to 30 cm in diameter. In between there were stone-free intersections which were richly vegetated with emerse and submerse plants and accumulations of leaf-litter in some places. These green areas usually had a water-level of only five centimetres.

Whilst the zones between the large round stones were inhabited mainly by a species of *Loricaria* and *Corydoras metae* in large numbers, the *Apistogramma macmasteri* were exclusively found in the vegetated zones. They were especially frequently observed amongst the leaf-litter and grass where the water was only one or two centimetres deep. There, they lived in surprisingly dense populations of almost exclusively semi-adult specimens with total-lengths between three and five centimetres.

The observations were made during a time of low-water although slight showers had fallen frequently during the preceding days. The air-temperature at the site was measured at 30 °C at approximately 16.00 h with the sky being overcast with temporary clearings. At the first glance the location appeared that no fishes would live amongst the slightly flooded heaps of leaf-litter and patches of grass. Only when carefully observing these zones for a longer time one could occasionally see the small Cichlids amongst the leaves and in the one to two centimetres deep dips between the grass.

In this extremely shallow micro-biotope they were fairly safe from larger predatory fishes and at the same time were duly separated from each other. Thus they had formed smallest territories underneath flat lying leaves which also provided cover against discovery from above.

These shallow water-bodies are frequently visited by birds which obviously represent another potential threat to the small Apistogramma. It was highly interesting to observe a larger predatory Characin which had sneaked into the milieu of this community and laid motionless, only half-covered by water, on the leaves successfully waiting for prey. The unsuspecting small Cichlids usually swam directly in front of its mouth.

From this sort of ecology of *Apistogramma macmasteri*, which is generally typical for all other *Apistogramma*-species as well, the following consequences are to be drawn.

Care

This small Cichlid is a shy fish which requires a partly very densely vegetated aquarium for a nearly optimal keeping. Caves, stone constructions, and other places providing hiding facilities are essential. Furthermore, very soft, slightly acidic water should be used for its husbandry. The cleanliness of the water obviously plays an important role. Only peaceful fishes with a timid temperament are appropriate as company fishes. Tanks of 70 cm in length are the minimum requirement although enhanced possibilities for observations are provided in larger aquaria. This would also be space enough to house several species of small Cichlids together.

Provided a varying diet, the specimens grow quickly and start

breeding

easily. The species reproduces in a male-mother-family structure with the male defending the breeding territory and the female dedicating herself to the care for the offspring.

Table 13

Location:	South of the town of Villavicencio, appr. 6 km east towards Puerto Lopez and then 2 km south in the headwaters area of the Rio Ocoa (Columbia)
Clarity:	clear
Colour:	none
pH:	5,5
Total hardness:	<1°dH
Carbonate hardness:	<1°dH
Conductivity:	5 µS at 27°C
Nitrite:	below 0,1 mg/l
Depth:	usually less than 10 cm
Current:	almost none
Water-temperature:	27°C
Date:	16.3.1983
Time:	16.00 hrs

During such periods both partners may become highly aggressive towards other fishes. Depending on the available space and the number of company fishes, they may claim territories of varying sizes for their fry. If many other fishes are around, it is obvious that only a small breeding territory can be maintained. However, a surface area of approximately 40 by 40 cm is usually occupied in its full height. Spawning takes places inside small caves below stones or in small cavities which leave enough space to just fit the female in. The fertilization of the eggs happens when the male moves sperm-laden water with the caudal fin in the direction of the eggs. The male thus need not glide closely over the eggs for fertilizing them as is the case in the substratum or cave brooders of West Africa. These observations also apply to the majority of *Apistogramma*-species observed in captivity so far.

A successful breeding of *Apistogramma macmasteri* requires soft, acidic water. Water-temperatures of around 27°C are recommendable.

That spawning has taken place is often only realized by the suddenly changed body-colouration of the female. Its breeding colour consists of a deep golden yellow with a black pattern. Fully grown specimens may have clutches of 130 eggs on average which individually measure 1,55 mm and are usually attached hanging from a solid substrate. The embryos hatch after approximately 72 hours, and their development is completed after altogether 7 days, i. e. 168 hours. The young fish then swim free and are guided by their mother. At this point of time they measure 3,8 mm in body length and 4,3 mm in total length. The juveniles immediately accept newly hatched nauplii of *Artemia salina* as first food. The above observations on the development were made at temperatures around 26 °C. The water had a conductivity of approximately 200 micro-Siemens and a pH of 6,7. Under these circumstances, circa 10 % of the eggs were lost due to fungal infection. However, no further losses were experienced during the larval development and malformations could not be observed. This shows that water of a soft, almost neutral quality is even adequate for successfully breeding wild-caught specimens.

A small water-course on the road from Villavicencio to Restrepo in Columbia is the habitat of *A. macmasteri* and *A. viejita* Colour-morph I.

▶ *Apistogramma meinkeni*
KULLANDER, 1980

is yet another species which was collected by King Leopold of Belgium and the Belgian ichthyologist GOSSE and described by KULLANDER in 1980. Fortunately, these fish were not fully unknown to aquarists since specimens had occasionally been imported before. It is another species which is difficult to distinguish from its allies and shows great similarities to *A. pertensis* which it usually had been taken for. Further links exist with *Apistogramma iniridae* which however has a different colour pattern. In order to draw a picture of the body-shape and colour-pattern of *A. meinkeni*, a summary of the original description by KULLANDER is given here.

Distribution of *Apistogramma meinkeni*

Apistogramma meinkeni ♂

The head and body are fairly elongate. The spines of the dorsal fin are of almost equal length between the fifth and eighth spine increasing in height only slightly. The fin membranes are of moderate length and fused together from the fifth spine on. The soft section of the dorsal fin is pointed, but usually lacks a real enlargement.

Even if such is present, it seldom exceeds the centre of the caudal fin. The same situation is found in the soft section of the anal fin which is usually even shorter. The caudal fin is rounded in shape.

Large male specimens may have the upper lobe of the caudal fin enlarged so that it becomes asymmetrical. It is however always symmetrical in subadult and female specimens.

For an identification of the species the pattern is obviously interesting. Therefore, reference is made to the description of the type specimens by KULLANDER:

This species entirely lacks transversal bars or these are reduced to tracks. This, in turn, causes light zones in the lateral band which is however not as pronounced as in *A. bitaeniata*.

The back region lacks any spotted pattern. The mentioned lateral band covers one to one and a half scales in width and begins immediately behind the eye. It is not sharply edged. At the place where the second and third transversal bar would be expected, the lateral band incorporates more intensely coloured spots. A superorbital stripe is absent and the suborbital stripe is only of moderate width. Abdominal stripes are missing.

The spot on the base of the caudal fin is oval in shape. The dorsal fin is colourless with only the tips of the fin membranes being slightly dark.

The anterior membranes lack a dark pigmentation. The soft section shows seven rows of spots. The anal fin is also translucent becoming darker towards its edge.

Four rows of spots are visible in its soft section. The translucent caudal fin is marked with eight to ten rows of spots which extend over the entire height and length of the fin. The ventral fins are white with the outer spines being slightly darker.

Specific traits

are the slightly higher body shape in comparison to similar species, the oval caudal spot and the anterior four spines of the dorsal fin which stand free.

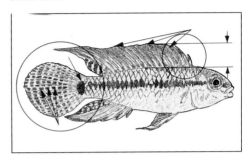

Similar species

Apistogramma iniridae corresponds with *A. meinkeni* regarding the body shape, the colour pattern, and the shape of the caudal fin, but is generally more slender and lacks a caudal spot. Its lateral band ranges up onto the caudal fin instead.

Apistogramma uaupesi has almost the same body shape, but shows a completely different colouration. The tips of the fin membranes in the dorsal fin are not fused in *A. uaupesi*.

Apistogramma pertensis is obviously the most similar species differing only in a few features. This species has a round caudal spot and its body is not as high. *A. pertensis* furthermore differs in its colour pattern and has a higher dorsal fin.

Little is known of the

natural habitat

and the distribution range of *Apistogramma meinkeni*. The type series was collected in a small right tributary to the Rio Uaupes in the vicinity of the village of Trovao. Approximately 20 km farther to the west, the Rio Uaupes flows into the Rio Negro. In this area, *A. elizabethae, A. brevis,* and *A. uaupesi* were also recorded. Further information on the ecology of this species are not available.

▶ *Apistogramma moae*
KULLANDER, 1980

this species has been described on the basis of two male specimens caught by the Belgian ichthyologist GOSSE and King Leopold of Belgium in November 1967. It shows great similarities to *Apistogramma eunotus*. In the meantime, only single specimens or very small numbers have been imported. According to experiences made so far, this species is easy to keep in captivity and has a very peaceful character. The males reach approximately 6 cm in total length and females are fully grown at some 3 cm. The body of *Apistogramma moae* appears relatively strong and little high-backed although the head is fairly high. The spines of the dorsal fin increase in height posteriorly.

The tips of the fin-membranes are elongate and pointed, but not produced. The section of the rays is enlarged to a point and ranges up to the end of the caudal fin. The soft part of anal fin is also enlarged, but shorter in comparison. The caudal fin is rounded. For the identification of this species, the pattern plays an important role. The following overview on the pattern is taken from KULLANDER and based on

Distribution of *Apistogramma moae*

preserved specimens. It cannot not always be accurately applied to the appearance of live fish, but provides a good basis for comparison. The anterior transversal bars range approximately down to the height of the insertions of the pectoral fin whilst the sixth and seventh bar extend to the lower edge of the caudal

Apistogramma moae ♂

peduncle. A row of indistinct spots marks the base of the dorsal fin which may feebly range onto the fin itself. The lateral band covers approximately one scale in width, begins right behind the eye, and extends up to the sixth transversal band. Where the lateral and transversal bands cross, there are conspicuous spots which are especially distinct on the second and third transversal bar. A real lateral spot is however absent. The suborbital stripe is broad whilst the stripe on the nape is more narrow. Abdominal stripes are missing. The spot on the caudal peduncle is indicated only and usually oval in shape. All fins are translucent to whitish with the anterior two membranes of the dorsal fin being black. The tips of the fin membranes have a dark tinge. Indistinct rows of spots may be present in the posterior section of the dorsal fin and the anal fin has up to three of those rows. The caudal fin has two to five vertical rows of spots.

The colours of live specimens are far from being conspicuous or even spectacular. Nevertheless, this species is not unattractive although the displayed body-pattern always appears slightly pale and lacks contrasts. This is typical for the species. The gill cover usually has a slightly greenish shade which is especially conspicuous due to two sound coloured stripes below the eye. The body is coloured ivory white or brownish on its lower parts becoming dark brown towards the back. These colours may darken with the mood changing and the pattern may fade until it becomes invisible.

The caudal fin is often coloured slightly yellowish. The ventral fins are short and slightly enlarged.

Care

Keeping this species is easy. Moderately hard and slightly alkaline water is adequate for keeping and breeding. The fish should only be kept together with other placid species of comparable size and temperament. A varying diet and clean water with water-exchanges every week or two of a quarter to a third of the total volume should be obligatory. The species does not damage aquatic plants.

Specific traits

The slightly pale indistinct body-pattern, the short ventral fins, the green almost horizontal lines on the gill-covers, the high oval caudal spot, and the sometimes recognizable two to five faint vertical rows of spots are features characteristic for this species.

It lacks a lateral spot and abdominal stripes.

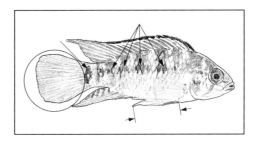

Similar species

Although *Apistogramma cruzi* species is often described as resembling A. moae, this is to be regarded with suspicion since A. cruzi has a more slender and elongate body shape. Its males furthermore have produced rays in the posterior parts of the dorsal and anal fins which exceed the caudal fin in length. The ventral fins are also very long and there are distinct abdominal stripes below the lateral band.

Apistogramma eunotus has a more rectangular caudal blotch, longer ventral fins, a slightly higher dorsal fin, and usually four rows of spots in the soft section of the anal fin. This species is generally more feebly coloured.

The

natural habitat

is only known from the type locality. The reference specimens were caught in the area of the Rio Moa, a tributary to the Rio Jurua in the vicinity of the village of Cruzeiro do Sul, Acre District, in eastern Brazil near the border to central Peru in 1967. No data on the ecology of this species are available.

◗ *Apistogramma nijsseni*
KULLANDER, 1979

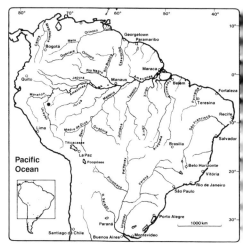

Distribution of *Apistogramma nijsseni*

was first collected by the Swiss Patrick de RHAM in 1979 and subsequently scientifically described by Sven O. KULLANDER. It is certainly one of the most pretty South American Cichlids which were discovered during the past years. For example, there is hardly any other female of an *Apistogramma* species which can match with the beauty of a mature *A. nijsseni*-female. The pitch black spot on the gill-cover, and also the large black lateral blotch may change into bright light green during various phases of courtship and in imposing behaviour. Adult female specimens reach 5 cm in total length whilst male may grow up to 8 cm and then look very bulky. They have a pretty yellow chest and belly region. The dorsal fin lacks produced fin membranes and the caudal fin is round with a semicircular fire-red fringe. The ventral fin are slightly enlarged and coloured cadmium-yellow. The rest of the body is light to gentian-blue.

Females of this species display a large black round to oval blotch on the base of the tail. This is only feebly visible in the males.

Apistogramma nijsseni ♂

An indistinct lateral band is recognizable in subadult specimens in certain moods. The differentiation of the sexes is difficult in subadult specimens, but possible by the females having a more pronounced black colouration in the anterior part of the ventral fins. When reaching maturity, the females usually assume a beautiful cadmium-yellow colouration which they always maintain. This distinguishes them from other species of *Apistogramma* where the display of such colours is restricted to the time after spawning and during parental care. It is only when the surroundings are drastically changed or the specimen is threatened that this colouration temporarily fades. According to unconfirmed communications the semi-circular band of the caudal fin may change its colour from fire-red to yellow within only a few generations.

Unfortunately, the few specimens imported in the late nineteen seventies had died out in the aquaria of the enthusiasts by 1983 already despite several successful breedings which however did not lead to a wider distribution amongst the aquarists. It was therefore a case of luck that the authors managed to collect some new specimens in their natural environment, import them in July 1983, and repeatedly breed them in the subsequent months.

Specific traits

A feature unique to these fish is — despite the striking body-pattern and -colouration — the semicircular red band on the outer edge of the caudal fin whose intensity is different between the sexes.

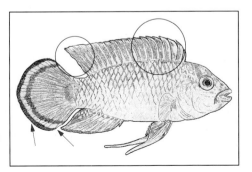

Similar species

Apistogramma nijsseni can hardly be mistaken for another species.

Superficially similar are
Apistogramma macmasteri,
Apistogramma viejita and
Apistogramma hongsloi,
but all these fishes have completely different colourations and patterns and usually different fin-shapes. No other species has a semi-circular bright red edge of the caudal fin.

The only known

natural habitat

lies in the area crossed by the road from Jenaro Herrero on the Rio Ucayali to Colonia Agamos, a frontier post between Peru and Brazil.

In the year 1983, the works on this road had proceeded for well over 20 km of the intended 100 km. Signs with indications of the kilometres had been erected every 500 m, starting with 0 on the limit of the town of Jenaro Herrero. This signs are important for the identification of the collecting site of Patrick de RHAM, the discoverer of this species, 14 kilometres outside Jenaro Herrero.

The landscape is slightly hilly in general. The area appears to function as a watershed since the species could not yet be recorded from the region in front of it to which the red colour-morph of *A. agassizii* is native as the only representative of the genus. It is not before the 13,5 kilometre sign that *A. nijsseni* is found, but then is more or less the only species. The specimens illustrated here were collected by the authors at this site in July 1983. The landscape is dominated by tropical rainforest which has however been chopped down partially along the road. All trees and shrubs have been removed there to avoid the forest to take repossession of the dirt-road within a short time. The bared ground almost exclusively consists of fine light yellow, partly loamy sand. Here and there the road is crossed by small narrow deep reddish brown coloured water-courses.

The collecting site is a stream of just under 2 metres in breadth on average with a depth of partly up to 80 cm. Due to the road works many branches and pieces of wood were lying in the water in the zones close to either side of the road. Furthermore, it was established that a thick layer of leaf-litter covered the ground.

The water of the stream was very clear, deep reddish brown in colour, and had a slight current. It was very soft and acidic with a temperature of 27,5 °C. In contrast to other information, *A. nijsseni* was present in large numbers and approximately 50 specimens could be collected within only an hour. They were found exclusively in the zone between the thick, loose, almost black layer of dead leaves and the branchwork above. Most specimens were subadult, but well coloured already and well fed. Due to the large numbers of shrimps the availability of food appeared to be excellent. Further Cichlids recorded from the same biotope were an undescribed species of *Aequidens* and *Laetacara flavilabris*. The water-courses of the region usually flow in the shady, semidark, dense forests. No submerse vegetation could be established.

Despite the following continuation of the trip through Peru and Bolivia for two weeks, the specimens were brought home safely and in good health. A few weeks later they were successfully bred under conditions emulating the natural biotope.

Care

The conditions for an optimal captive husbandry were subsequently tested. It was established that soft acidic water is recommendable although no problems were observed in moderately hard slightly alkaline water. The fish are less shy than many other species of the genus *Apistogramma*. Provided enough space and an appropriately decorated aquarium they might even be considered "tame". As is the case in the other members of the genus, *A. nijsseni* also requires well structured and densely decorated aquaria with a fine substrate and piles of stones, caves, and pieces of bog-oak. It is important that the vegetation forms extensive thickets above the ground thus a large ground space becomes necessary. The height of the tank is of secondary importance for the husbandry of these fish.

Table 14

Location:	Small black-water stream crossing the road from Jenaro Herrero to Colonia Agamos 13,5 km east of Jenaro Herrero (Peru)
Clarity:	clear
Colour:	dark brown
pH:	5,4
Total hardness:	<1 °dH
Carbonate hardness:	<1 °dH
Conductivity:	3 µS at 27,5 °C
Nitrite:	less than 0,1 mg/l
Depth:	up to 1 m
Current:	slight
Water-temperature:	27,5 °C
Date:	28.6.1983
Time:	17.00 hrs

Aquaria with a minimum length of 100 cm, a breadth of 40 cm, and a minimum height of 20 cm are recommendable. The cleanliness of the water is however of outstanding importance for *A. nijsseni* and a varying diet should be given special attention. The presence of company fishes is necessary.

Provided these conditions, the specimens will soon form pairs when reaching maturity. These partnerships are usually lasting ones, and a tendency of the males to accumulate harems could never be observed.

The breeding

turned out to be surprisingly easy. Very good breeding results could be achieved in very soft, very acidic water. Remarkable is however that it was also successful in moderately hard, slightly alkaline water from the tap. Although the results achieved are not optimal they are still satisfactory. Not fully adult specimens may show behavioural lapsi, but the third breeding attempt is eventually usually successful. This species also reproduces in a male-mother-family structure. The female alone cares for the fry, but also assists the male in defending the territory. The eggs are usually laid on the ceiling of a cave, but the fish also sometimes choose sites below strong leaves hanging immediately over the ground, branchwork, or pieces of bog-oak. The eggs are intensely cared for and often probed with the mouth. At a temperature of 27,5 °C on average, the embryos hatch after approximately 48 hours. Four days later, the young fish are completely developed and begin to swim. Feeding them newly hatched nauplii of the Brine Shrimp is no problem. In order to obtain large numbers of juveniles, very soft water with a pH of between 5 and 5,5 and a conductivity up to 80 micro-Siemens should be used. Conditioning the water by filtration over peat has a direct impact on the pH and is therefore advisable for the husbandry of this and many other species of *Apistogramma*. The deciding factor for courtship may be a partial exchange of the water with the most crucial point being a considerable decrease of the conductivity of the water. Provided an appropriate environment the species may be fairly productive and 60 juveniles may grow up from every clutch.

It is interesting to observe that with increasing age of the juveniles the male is more and more allowed to come close to the school or even to stay amongst the young fish for short periods. The growth-rate of the juveniles

Apistogramma nijsseni ♀ in breeding colouration

is surprising if sufficient quantities of food are provided in short intervals and the water-quality is kept at a high level. It appears that there is no other species in the genus where the young fish grow as rapidly. At three month of age they may already measure some 4 cm.

Where there is so much light there unfortunately is also some shade.

At the time of collecting this species in its natural habitat it was already noted that two thirds of all specimens were male. It could have been a coincident. In captivity however, in water of a conductivity of 120 micro-Siemens, a pH of 5,3, and a temperature of 27,6 °C at the time of spawning, 90 % of the fry were found to be males. This is a problem which is also known from other species of *Apistogramma* and especially from West African Dwarf Cichlids. Obviously, there is still much to investigate regarding the predetermination of balanced sex-ratios. The rearing of young *A. nijsseni* is otherwise easy and certainly will be enjoyed by every aquarist since this is one of the most beautiful Dwarf Cichlids in general. May the species achieve a wide distribution in the aquaria of the enthusiasts and not belong to those species which simply disappear after a short while. Presently, it is still a much sought after species. Hopefully this will remain so.

Apistogramma nijsseni ♀ in imposing colouration

▶ *Apistogramma norberti*
STAECK, 1990

When returning from an ichthyological collecting trip through the Peruvian Amazonas-
region in spring 1989, an aquarist discovered
four specimens of a representative of the genus
Apistogramma amongst the fishes brought
back alive which could not be assigned to any
of the known species. Initially, the exact collecting locality could not be reconstructed any
more, and it was only due to the assistance of
some local Peruvians that the site was found
again and further specimens could be collected
for the description of the new species.

This is a relatively high-backed species of
Apistogramma belonging to the *A. cacatuoides*
species-complex. It has a conspicuously large
mouth and a distinct sexual dichromatism and
fin dimorphism.

Apistogramma norberti is readily distinguished from all other species of the genus by a

Distribution of *Apistogramma norberti*

large dark blotch in the posterior portion of
the dorsal fin and the combination of three
zigzag-shaped abdominal stripes with a

Male of *Apistogramma norberti* from the type locality

99

rounded caudal fin. By reaching approximately 8 cm in total length, the males exceed the females by more than three centimetres.

At a length of some four centimetres the males can be distinguished from the females since they then begin growing enlarged fins.

The colouration of live specimens varies very much with the individual disposition. Males occupying a territory display a metallic blueish shine on the upper and hind parts of the body. The belly region is whitish, and the zone around the pectoral fins is usually coloured rosy to orange. The thick lips appear in sound rosy to reddish. The abdominal zigzag-stripes are very regularly arranged resulting from the outer areas of the scales of the lower body having black spots on their upper and lower edges only whilst the centres are always light. The dorsal fin shines blue and is bordered dark.

The fin membranes of the first three spines are coloured black whilst the tips of the produced membranes of the third to fifth spine are orange-red. A large black blotch with a faint bordering is found on the base of the fin between the 14th and 18th ray. It results from an extension of the fifth transversal bar. The posterior part of the fin carries three vertical rows of dark spots. The soft section of the dorsal fin, and also the caudal fin, have a dark edge and a light blue submarginal stripe. The blueish anal fin is marked with five or six vertical rows of dark spots in its posterior and upper parts and is bordered dark blue to black. The anterior edges of the light blue ventral fins are dark with the tips being whitish to slightly orange.

Males without a territory display a distinct lateral band. A large blotch on the flanks is usually clearly visible. It may extend up to the dorsal fin. The spot on the base of the caudal fin is variable in shape sometimes appearing as a roundish spot, sometimes as a vertical band, and may not always be displayed. The transversal bars are broader than their interspaces. They are however rarely shown and if so, only appear as indications.

During periods of parental care, the females are coloured deep yellow with exception of the slightly orange fringe of the dorsal fin and the black pattern. Females without a territory are usually beige and display a lateral band with the greenish lateral spot appearing lighter. They also show dorsal spots which range up onto the base of the dorsal fin. The colouration of suppressed females is more greyish brown, the lateral spot is large and dark, and there are distinct transversal bars.

Specific traits

One of the characteristic features is the large dark spot in the lower half of the soft section of the dorsal fin in adult male specimens. A comparable pattern may however also be found in females of species of the A. macmasteri-group. Males of A. norberti also differ from all other members of the genus by the combination of distinct zigzag-shaped abdominal stripes with a rounded caudal fin which lacks filamentous elongations.

Similar species

Apistogramma norberti is to be assigned to the A. cacatuoides species-group which presently holds the three species A. cacatuoides, A. luelingi, and A. juruensis. In contrast to the other members of the A. cacatuoides-complex males of A. norberti lack a bifurcate caudal fin, but have a rounded one. The red spots bordered with black which are typical for A. cacatuoides and A. luelingi are also missing. Furthermore, the posterior soft section of the anal and dorsal fins are only slightly produced.

The

natural habitat

lies in the Peruvian Amazon region in the Departemento Loreto. The type locality of A. norberti is a left tributary to the Quebrada Nuevo Horizonte which belongs to the catchment of the lower Rio Tahuayo. It is a small stream of one to two meters in breadth flowing in the shade of the rainforest with a considerable gradient draining the extremely hilly area. At the time of low-water, only the deeper parts of the stream carried water. These accumulations of rest water were disconnected from one another and usually covered not more than one square metre with a maximum depth of 30 to 60 centimetres. The entire stream-bed was covered with branches and twigs and a thick loose layer of leaf-litter in which the *Apistogramma* found hiding places. The clear, slightly yellowish water was soft and acidic. Its analysis revealed a water-temperature of 24 °C, a conductivity of 10 micro-Siemens, a carbonate hardness of 2 °dH, a total hardness below the detectability-level of 1 °dH, and a pH of 5,9. The syntopic ichthyofauna consisted of Knife-fishes (Gymnotidae), the predatory Characin *Erythrinus erythrinus*, the Top Minnow *Rivulus rectocaudatus*, and undetermined representatives of the Pyrrhulininae. It is especially worth to be noted that a single specimen of *Apistogramma eunotus* was also recorded.

Care

The maintanance of these conspicuous fish has unfortunately shown that they often are very fearful under captive conditions and preferably lead a very concealed life so that the possibilities for studies are limited. This experience corresponds with the observations made in their natural habitat where the fish stayed covered in the thick layer of submerged leaf-litter. If they are however kept in a community tank, the otherwise very shy fish become distinctly more active. Therefore dither fish are strongly recommended.

An aquarium for this species should be furnished with fine sand as substrate and a dense vegetation since this Cichlid only feels well if numerous hiding facilities are provided. The optimal water-temperature for the husbandry of *A. norberti* is supposedly ranging between 24 and 26 °C.

Although the

breeding

of *A. norberti* has repeatedly been successful, it is still a problem.

The embryos and larvae obviously require soft and acidic water for a normal development thus the water-values of the natural environment should be emulated closely in captivity. On the other hand, the rearing of the swimming juveniles by feeding them newly hatched Brine Shrimps is no problem at all.

Female of *Apistogramma norberti* in breeding colouration

▶ *Apistogramma ortmanni*
(EIGENMANN, 1912)

This species was originally described as *Heterogramma ortmanni* by EIGENMANN in 1912. The base was formed by approximately

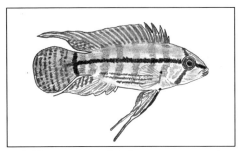

Probable appearance of *Apistogramma ormanni* ♂

Distribution of *Apistogramma ortmanni*

50 specimens which measured between 22 and 76 mm and which were collected at seven different localities.

According to the original description *Apistogramma ortmanni* has a moderately elongate body-shape. The caudal fin is rounded whilst the dorsal and anal fins are long drawn. The tip of the enlarged dorsal fin may exceed over the centre part of the caudal fin. The filamentous enlarged ventral fins reach up to the soft section of the anal fin if pressed against the body.

The colouration of preserved specimens was described by EIGENMANN as follows: the sides of the body are marked with approximately six transversal bars. The dark lateral band extends from the snout up to the centre of the caudal fin with two to four abdominal stripes below it. One, or even two, of the latter begin below the lower edge of the pectoral fins. A suborbital and a superorbital stripe are distinctly developed, and an obliquely running black blotch marks the base of the caudal fin. The anterior fin membranes of the dorsal fin are black whilst the following ones are uniformly dark. The posterior portions of the dorsal and anal fins are patterned with transversal stripes. Adult males carry seven dark bands on the caudal fin which may however decrease in intensity towards the edge. A black spot is found above the base of the upper rays of the pectoral fins. The spine of the ventral fin

is coloured black, and there is a spot of the same colour on its base.

This is an extract of the original description by EIGENMANN. The subspecies *Apistogramma ortmanni rupununi* is invalid today.

Specific traits

are the dark lateral band which extends from the snout up to the centre of the caudal fin and the two to four abdominal stripes below it. Furthermore, there is a black blotch running obliquely over the base of the caudal fin which is rounded in both sexes of this species.

Similar species

The only similar Cichlid is *Apistogramma regani* which however differs by having a larger blotch on the base of the caudal fin, which is especially enlarged vertically, and a distinct anal spot.

The

natural habitat

ranges from the Rio Cuyuni in eastern Venezuela through the Rio Potaro and the Rio Rupununi in the catchment region of the Rio Essequibo in British Guyana, up to the Corantijn area in Surinam.

▶ *Apistogramma paucisquamis*
KULLANDER & STAECK, 1988

Distribution of *Apistogramma paucisquamis*

is also known to aquarists under the common name of "Bright-banded *Apistogramma*" since the early 1980's. It however appears that the species was imported even earlier. With a maximum total length of below 50 mm, this fish ranks amongst the smallest representatives of the genus.

Apistogramma paucisquamis has a slender body, a relatively large mouth, and thick lips. The caudal fin is lyreate in males, and the fin membranes of the anterior part of the dorsal fin are not especially produced. The black pattern includes a suborbital stripe, a lateral band which extends up to the base of the caudal fin, and a lateral spot. Depending on the mood an additional abdominal band may become visible. The lateral band is bordered by a narrow blueish green line above and below to which the vernacular name "Bright-banded *Apistogramma*" refers.

Male of *Apistogramma paucisquamis*

103

Males of *Apistogramma paucisquamis* are subject to a noteworthy polychromatism, which means that individuals, even from the same locality, may have very different colourations. As far as the distribution of orange on the head, body, caudal, and dorsal fin is concerned one of the authors recorded not less than three different colour-types at one collecting site with some sort of intermediates in between.

In the most frequently found colourmorph the area of the lower head, the cheeks, the belly, and the zone around the lateral spot are bright orange. The dorsal fin is translucent grey with light yellowish shades being restricted to its base. The grey caudal fin is transparent except for a feeble pattern of speckles. In the second colour-morph the cheeks are greyish brown and the chest and belly regions are whitish. Laterally, a dark grey shade is predominant whilst the dorsal fin is coloured deep orange with a dark base and a narrow blueish submarginal edge. The cheeks of the third colour-variety are also grey, but the chest and belly regions are whitish and the flanks dark grey. Its dorsal fin is largely translucent and has a partly pale yellowish, partly blueish base, and a narrow orange edge with a light blue line below it. The entire caudal fin is coloured deep orange.

Specific traits

are the bright lines bordering the lateral band, the lyreate caudal fin, and the lack of distinctly produced fin-membranes in the dorsal fin.

Similar species

are *Apistogramma bitaeniata, A. gibbiceps, A. cacatuoides,* and *A. luelingi,* in which males however have more or less distinctly produced fin membranes in the anterior part of the dorsal fin. Except for *A. bitaeniata* all species furthermore have abdominal lines or stripes.

The

natural habitat

of *Apistogramma paucisquamis* lies in northern Brazil where this species appears to be endemic

to the central and lower catchment areas of the Rio Negro. One of the authors managed to examine the natural biotopes of this fish in three different years at different seasons. It seems that this Cichlid prefers the shallow zones with water-levels of 10 to 40 cm where cover is provided by a thick layer of leaf-litter near the banks of the relevant rainforest streams. It was found that the fish is much more rare in places where the banks are steep. All localities shared the feature of very soft and acidic black water with a total and carbonate hardness of $<1\,°dH$, a conductivity of 10 µS, and a pH of 4,3 to 4,7. The water-temperature varied between 26 and 29 °C.

Care

The maintanance of these fish requires an aquarium of moderate size with sand as substrate and ample hiding-places which are provided by a dense vegetation. Feeding is no problem since all common kinds of food are willingly accepted.

The

breeding

in captivity is not as easy. Very soft and acidic water is required whose values come close to the conditions found in the natural habitats. Only this guarantees a normal development of the embryos.

Table 15

Location:	Right bank of the Rio Negro south of Novo Airão in the area of the Anavilhanas Islands
Clarity:	clear
Colour:	dark brown, tea-coloured
pH:	4,3
Total hardness:	$<1\,°dH$
Carbonate hardn.:	$<1\,°dH$
Conductivity:	10 µS
Depth:	up to 50 cm
Current:	slight
Water-temp.:	26 °C
Date:	27.3.1986
Time:	11.00 hrs

◆ *Apistogramma personata*
KULLANDER, 1980

is another species which looks interesting, but which is unfortunately only known from preserved material. It is a moderately slender

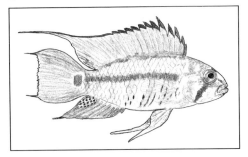

Probable appearance of *Apistogramma personata* ♀

form which was discovered by King Leopold of Belgium and the ichthyologist Dr. J. P. GOSSE in 1967. In order to draw a picture of this species' body-shape and colour-pattern, a summary of the data published by KULLANDER is given here.

The fin membranes of the dorsal fin spines increase in height from front to rear and remain at approximately at the same height from the fifth spines on. In male specimens, they are moderate long to long and pointed. In the holotype, the fin membranes three to eight are distinctly produced with the fifth being the longest. It has twice the length of the spine. The soft portion of the dorsal fin is pointed with a filamentous elongation which is formed by the second and third soft ray. Whilst it may exceed over the caudal fin in males, it usually reaches only up to the centre of the caudal fin in females. The soft part of the anal fin is also pointed and thread-like produced, but only extends up to approximately the centre of the caudal fin in male specimens. Juveniles and females have truncate caudal fins with rounded corners whilst these have filamentous streamers on the top and bottom edges in males with a total length of more than 4,5 cm giving them a bifurcate shape.

No information is available on the colouration of live specimens thus the indications

made here are limited to a description of the colours and patterns of preserved ones. The fish has a yellowish ground-colour which darkens to brownish shades towards the back. Only the first transversal bar is distinct whereas all the following ones are reduced to indications. The lateral band begins immediately behind the eye. Initially, it covers one scale in breadth widening to one and a half scales in the posterior part of the body. It is sharply defined and extends up to the last transversal bar ending slightly below the lateral line. A lateral spot is absent, but in young specimens the lateral band is more intensely coloured where it is crossed by the transversal bars. The suborbital stripe is broad whilst the frontal stripe is indistinct. A dark band crosses the head between the eyes and has the shape of an upside down triangle. Abdominal stripes are absent, but the transversal bars are clearly more intensely coloured in the belly region. Both sexes have a small black spot immediately below the lower lip, but this trait may be missing in individual specimens. The caudal spot may be quadrangular or rounded. The dorsal fin is coloured slightly smoky with the tips of the fin membranes being darker. The elongations are however colourless. The anterior membranes are fairly dark. The soft section of the anal fin carries three rows of spots and the entire anal fin is whitish at its base becoming dark towards its end. It is bordered dark with four rows of spots in female specimens. The caudal fin is colourless with seven or more or less arched rows of spots in the males which are however absent from the top half of the fin. In contrast, females have only up to five of these rows which in addition are less well pronounced. Male specimens have white ventral fins whilst the spines and the outer fin-membranes are black in females. The sexes can easily be distinguished by the shapes of their dorsal and caudal fins.

The holotype is the largest specimen known. It measures 65,3 mm in total length. The largest known female has a total length of 44,2 mm.

According to this, *Apistogramma personatus* appears to be an average sized species which is probably allied to *A. gibbiceps*.

Specific traits

are the dark band which crosses the head between the eyes with a shape of an upside down triangle and the combination of the presence of a caudal spot with the absence of a

Similar species

Apistogramma gibbiceps lacks a superorbital stripe and a caudal spot. Its lateral bands ranges up onto the caudal fin and rows of spots or speckles are absent from the soft parts of the dorsal and anal fins.

This species furthermore has obliquely arranged abdominal stripes.

Apistogramma brevis lacks a superorbital stripe. Depending on the mood, this species however often displays one or even two lateral spots and horizontal abdominal stripes. The dorsal fin has no produced fin membranes.

Apistogramma bitaeniata has a more elongate and slender body-shape, lacks a caudal spot, and the rows of speckles are confined to the central parts of the caudal fin. It furthermore differs regarding the filamentous streamers of the caudal fin.

The

natural habitat

of this species is only known from the type locality. It was originally collected in the vicinity of the Brazilian village of Assai in the region dominated by the Rio Uaupes. This area

The large rivers mean life to the continent.

▶ *Apistogramma pertensis*
(HASEMAN, 1991)

For a long time, this species was difficult to identify. Its close resemblance to the species *Apistogramma meinkeni* was part of the problem. Furthermore, this fish has been imported more frequently during past few years only so that observations could only be made very recently.

Apistogramma pertensis is a very slender species where the males have high, almost sail-like dorsal fins. The tips of the fin membranes of the first four spines are often isolated whereas all the other membranes are fused together. The tips of the rayed section of the dorsal and anal fins are not especially long and usually only reach up to the centre of the

Distribution of *Apistogramma pertensis*

Apistogramma pertensis ♂

107

caudal fin. A dark lateral band begins behind the eye and ends immediately in front of a round caudal spot. The suborbital stripe is visible in most cases. The ventral fins are long and pointed whereas the caudal fin is round and symmetrical. Seven semicircular rows of speckles are distinctly recognizable. Depending on the mood the lateral band may fade and a lateral spot may become visible. During courtship and imposing behaviour this pattern plus the caudal spot may completely disappear. Males of this species reach approximately 7 cm, females some 5 cm in total length. Distinguishing between the sexes is easy in adult specimens when the males have developed their larger dorsal fins and longer ventral fins.

Specific traits

of these fish are the slender and elongate body-shape and the sail-like dorsal fins of the males. They have a round symmetrical caudal fin, a round caudal spot, and partly enlarged ventral fins.

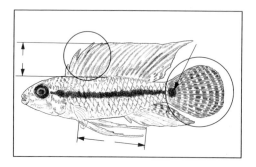

Similar species

Apistogramma meinkeni is more high-backed and less slender. In contrast the males have a less high dorsal fin, an oval, partly asymmetrical caudal fin, and an oval caudal spot.
Apistogramma iniridae lacks a caudal spot with the lateral band extending up onto the caudal fin.
Apistogramma uaupesi is more high-backed and has a different colour-pattern. The tips of its fin-membranes of the dorsal fin are not fused together.

The
natural habitat

apparently ranges over a vast area extending from Santarem through Manaus up to the western catchment areas of the Rio Negro in Brazil.

Care

The maintanance of these attractive slender fish is optimal in soft, slightly acidic water. For a positive development adequately sized, richly planted aquaria with ample hiding-places are recommendable. The water-temperature should range around 28 °C. Peaceful company fishes prevent the *Apistogramma* from becoming shy.

Pairs which once have bonded usually stay together permanently, i.e. partners are generally not exchanged. A high quality of the water should be maintained including exchanges of a third to a quarter of the water-volume every 10 to 14 days, and attention should be paid to a varying diet.

Once they have reached maturity, the fish will soon start

breeding.

For a successful reproduction, this species however requires specially conditioned water. It should be very soft and very acidic with the total and carbonate hardness ranging below 5 °dH and a pH of 5,2 to 5,5 which can be achieved by filtration over peat.

But even if provided with these water-values the development of the clutch is not always guaranteed. The spawning act and the parental care for the fry follow the ordinary scheme of all *Apistogramma*-species. The juveniles have difficulties to feed even on newly hatched nauplii of the Brine Shrimp shortly after they swim freely and should therefore be offered smaller live food. An alternative may be a "milk" made up of MikroMin powder-food and water out of the breeding tank which is carefully injected by a syringe into the school of the small fish. However, once the first 14 days have been mastered, their further rearing is easy.

▶ *Apistogramma piauiensis*
KULLANDER, 1980

is yet another species which has not been imported alive. Its description is based on specimens which were caught by the American ichthyologist ROBERTS in August 1968. The largest specimen in the series is a female of

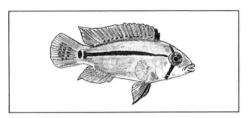

Probable appearance of *Apistogramma piauiensis* ♀

Distribution of *Apistogramma piauiensis*

30,6 mm in total length. It was designated to be the holotype of the species. Both the paratypes are juveniles and thus no information exists about how adult males may look. In addition to this one does not know anything about the colouration in life so the following data about colour and pattern refer to the preserved holotype according to KULLANDER.

Head and body of this fish are moderately elongate. The spines of the dorsal fin increase in length posteriorly, but are approximately of almost the same length from the fifth spines on. The tips of the fin membranes are short and rounded. The soft section of the dorsal fin is pointed, but lacks an elongation. It ends in the first third of the caudal fin. A similar situation is found in the anal fin which however is even shorter. The caudal fin is rounded.

The ground colour of the preserved female specimen is light grey with a dark, i. e. brownish pattern. It lacks transversal bars or these are only recognizable as indications. Only the seventh transversal bar is distinct at mid-body. It however does not extend much over the width of the lateral band. Indistinct fusing spots are found along the base of the dorsal fin. A dark lateral band is present and begins immediately behind the eye and extends up to the seventh transversal bar. It covers approximately one scale in width and runs above the lower lateral line. A lateral spot is absent, and

the suborbital stripe is moderately broad. The superorbital stripe runs up onto the nape and is very distinct. The intensely coloured caudal spot has the shape of an egg. The dorsal fin has a dark shade with the anterior two fin membranes being black. The bases of the fin membranes are spotted whilst the soft part of the fin is spotless.

The anal fin is also dark and lacks a spotted pattern whereas the caudal fin is smoky without any pattern except for some indications of speckles on the central fin membranes. The ventral fins are whitish with the spines and their membranes being black. The juvenile specimens are grey with an indistinct brownish pattern with little contrast. A cladistic relationship may exist with *A. caetei*, but similarities may also be found in *A. regani* and *A. geisleri* which can however be distinguished by their colourations and morphometric data. As far as is presently known, *Apistogramma piauiensis* is the easternmost species recorded from Brazil to date.

Natural habitat

All the known localities lie in the Estado do Piaui in Brasil in the vicinity of Buriti do Lopez. One is the Rio Longa and another one is a lake-like water-body, the Lagoa Seca, approximately one kilometre from the

Rio Parnaiba which belongs to the flooding area of this river. According to ROBERTS this water-body had a length of three hundred or four hundred metres and a width of almost one kilometre in August 1968. On the other hand, its maximum depth was only approximately one metre. The ground was partly muddy with boulders and rocks here and there. Aquatic plants were completely absent. During times of high-water it is to be supposed that there is ample of flooded emerse vegetation and this water-body is connected to swamp areas in which aquatic plants grow.

Besides of *Apistogramma piauiensis* approximately 20 to 30 other species of fishes were found including in others a small species of *Cichlasoma*.

Small water-courses and accumulations of rest-water are frequently found in the rainforests. As this one, they are habitats for a variety of Cichlids and Catfishes.

► *Apistogramma pulchra*
KULLANDER, 1980

The specimens which served for the description of this species also originated from the collections made by King Leopold of Belgium and the Belgian scientist Dr. J. P. GOSSE. Eight males and one female specimen are presently

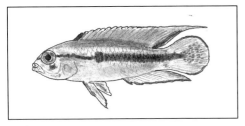

Probable appearance of *Apistogramma pulchra*

Distribution of *Apistogramma pulchra*

known. The largest male measures 43,9 mm in total length; the only female has a length of 26,8 mm. According to KULLANDER this species belongs to the *A. pertensis* species-complex.

A. pulchra has a slender elongate body-shape with a moderate elongate head. The spines of the dorsal fin increase posteriorly, but are of almost the same height from the seventh spine on. The tips of the fin membranes are moderately long and more or less truncate in shape. The soft section of the dorsal fin is pointed and elongated in the largest male with the second or third ray almost ranging up to the end of the caudal fin. The same applies to the anal fin although it is slightly shorter. The caudal fin is rounded.

The colouration of live fish is unknown. In preserved specimens the ground colouration is yellowish, slightly darkening towards the back, with a brown pattern and conspicuously dark-edged scales. This species lacks transversal bars. Its back and nape are coloured dark, and a dark lateral band extends from the eye up onto the anterior portion of the caudal fin. Its breadth is one scale up to the lateral spot and one and a half to two scales behind it. The individual scales are conspicuously bordered dark. The lateral band is almost absent in the largest male available. A suborbital stripe cannot be found, but an indistinct light spot below the

eye can be recognized. Only the smallest specimen has a frontal stripe. There is no caudal spot visible. The dorsal fin is dark with the tips of the membranes being translucent. The soft portion of the dorsal fin is either colourless or dark with light edges. The anterior fin membranes are coloured black. The anal fin is translucent to whitish and is bordered dark.

The caudal fin has a dark edge and may have no pattern or approximately five or six rows of small speckles. The ventral fins are whitish.

It is to be expected that distinguishing between the sexes is easy due to their different colourations. To date, the females are however almost unknown.

Specific traits

of this species are the absence of a caudal spot and that the unequally broad lateral band extends up onto the caudal fin; the latter being bordered dark. In comparison with similar species this form has a lower number of spines in the dorsal fin and a different colour-pattern.

Similar species

Apistogramma pertensis has a spot on the base of the caudal fin and its dorsal fin is higher.

A. meinkeni has a caudal spot, is more high-backed, and also has a higher dorsal fin.

A. iniridae is relatively similar, but may have obliquely arranged abdominal stripes in the posterior belly-region and on the tail which, depending on the mood, may also appear as almost quadrangular dark blotches. Furthermore, the appearance of the caudal fin is different by the entire fin having a vertically spotted pattern. This species also has a higher dorsal fin.

A. gephyra lacks a lateral spot, has a lanceolate caudal fin, and no unequally broad lateral band.

The natural habitat

is only known from the type-locality. This is a small side-arm of the Rio Candelas which in turn is a tributary to the Rio Madeira. The collecting site is on the Rio Petro, approximately 25 km off the village of Porto-Velho in the southwest of Brazil.

The water-level decreases by a couple of metres during times of low-water and leaves the Amazon-villages "stripped".

◆ *Apistogramma regani*
KULLANDER, 1980

The type specimen was collected by King Leopold of Belgium and J.P. GOSSE in 1967. Since then it has been found out that fully grown males may reach approximately 6 cm and old females 4 cm in total length. The sexes are distinguished by the different shapes of the dorsal and anal fins.

A. *regani* has a moderately high-backed body with the head also not being especially high. The length of the spines increases from the front to the rear end, but they are of almost equal length from the fourth to the seventh spine. The tips of the fin membranes are only moderately long, rounded in juveniles, pointed in adults, and never produced. Adult specimens have a pointed soft rayed section of the dorsal fin which may even have a thread-like streamer in large males ranging up to the end of the caudal fin. A similar situation is found in the anal fin which is however generally shorter. The caudal fin is rounded.

Distribution of *Apistogramma regani*

Since there are always problems with the proper identification of this species, the colour-pattern of the type specimens is summarized here according to KULLANDER. The

Apistogramma regani ♂

transversal bars are distinctly developed, but more faint than the lateral band. At their crossings they may however be more intense thus leading to an appearance of a spotted band. The transversal bars range down to the level of the base of the pectoral fin or even to the base of the anal fin. They are usually broader than their interspaces. A narrow lateral band begins behind the eye and extends up to the seventh transversal bar above the lower lateral line. It covers only half a scale with the maximum breadth being one scale. The lateral spot is small and round in shape. It is situated on the second transversal bar not exceeding its breadth. The cheek-band and the frontal stripe are distinct and this also applies to the four abdominal stripes which are formed by the dark edges of the relevant scales. The top stripe ranges from the upper insertion point of the pectoral fin up to approximately above the anterior edge of the anal fin. The fourth abdominal stripe, i.e. the bottom one, extends from the insertion of the ventral fin up to the area above the base of the spinous section of the anal fin. The elongate pitch black caudal spot is broad and high. The dorsal fin is translucent to dark with the first two fin membranes being black. The base of the fin is dark and the rayed section shows two to three rows of spots. In its pattern it resembles the anal fin which also has two or three rows of spots in its soft portion. The caudal fin is translucent and marked with four to nine very distinct rows of spots which run as stripes from edge to edge.

The ventral fins are dark at their bases whereas their outer edges are white.

According to KULLANDER specimens from different localities may be subject to a considerable amount of variability regarding their colourations. This refers to the ground colouration as well as to the transversal bars, the lateral band, and the caudal spot.

Specific traits

are the relatively short tips of the fin membranes of the dorsal fin, the rounded caudal fin, and the distinct transversal bars. The conspicuous, narrow, oval spot which extends over the entire height of the caudal

peduncle and the absence of a lateral spot are further characteristic features.

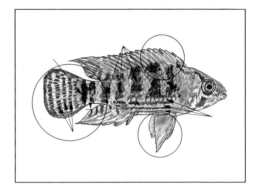

Similar species

The "Yellow-cheeked *Apistogramma*", *Apistogramma* sp., which is yet to be described scientifically, has a striking resemblance, but can nevertheless be easily distinguished by the yellow cheeks and the males having an unpatterned caudal fin.

The

natural habitat

lies in the wider vicinity of the city of Manaus in Brazil. The species has been recorded from

Table 16

Location:	Swampy lake on one of the Anavilhanas Islands on the left bank of the Rio Negro
Clarity:	clear
Colour:	dark brown, tea-coloured
pH:	4,3
Total hardness:	<1°dH
Carbonate hardness:	<1°dH
Conductivity:	12 µS
Depth:	20 to 30 cm
Current:	none
Water-temperature:	26°C
Date:	26.3.1986
Time:	11.00 hrs

black- as well as from white-water rivers. The type locality is the island group of the Anavilhanas which is situated shortly upstream off Manaus on the left bank of the Rio Negro. Another locality is a small lake, the Lago Redondo, approximately 25 km southwest of Manaus on the right bank of the Rio Solimoes (Rio Amazonas). *Apistogramma regani* has repeatedly been recorded together with *A. pertensis* and *A. gephyra*.

Care

Keeping *A. regani* is easy. No unusual require-ments are to be fulfilled regarding the quality of the water although a pH of below 7 has proven to be of advantage. The species is peaceloving and is adequate for a community tank with other small species of fishes. Small to moderately large aquaria are suitable for their captive keeping. Densely arranged groups of plants, small caves between rocks, and other hiding-facilities are a must. A fine substrate and clean water are preconditions for a long-term husbandry. The temperatures should range between 25 and 27 °C, and the keeper should pay attention to a varying diet.

Apistogramma regani ♂

◆ *Apistogramma resticulosa*
KULLANDER, 1980

This pretty species of *Apistogramma* was apparently first caught during an expedition to Brazil by Dr. Herbert AXELROD and the French ichthyologist GÉRY in August 1976. Its description is based on six specimens. The name refers to the vertical narrow dark streaks on the scales below the lateral band. Observations in captivity have shown that this is a peaceful fish whose habitual features include it in the regani-group.

This species has a moderately elongate body-shape. The spines of the dorsal fin increase in length up to the fifth spine with the following ones then being of almost equal length. The tips of the fin membranes are little pointed to rounded. They rarely exceed the spines in height. The soft section of the dorsal fin is pointed with the second and third ray forming a streamer which approximately extends up to the centre of the caudal fin. The

Distribution of *Apistogramma resticulosa*

anal fin has a similar shape, but is shorter. The caudal fin is rounded. A. resticulosa has been imported alive and even been bred in captivity.

Apistogramma resticulosa ♂

Male specimens are mainly coloured bright blue with the chest and belly regions being pearl-white to light ivory. The body-scales are bordered light blue and the cheeks are speckled with bright red and green streaks and spots. The suborbital stripe is pale. The dark transversal bars are reduced to mere indications. The second and sixth transversal bar are especially reduced to dorsal blotches.

A narrow lateral band begins immediately behind the eye and ends on the seventh transversal bar. It is thus not connected with the dark oval spot on the base of the caudal fin. The fins are transparent with a light blueish tinge. The anterior two fin membranes of the spines of the dorsal fin are darker than the following ones. The soft portion of the dorsal fin is marked with two to three rows of speckles which also appear in a similar arrangement on the anal fin.

The caudal fin is largely unpatterned except for three to four very feebly visible rows of tiny speckles in the posterior central part.

In contrast, brownish beige colours are predominant in the females turning into a light ivory shade in the belly region. The body-pattern is similarly coloured except for the anterior fin membranes of the dorsal and ventral fins which are deep black. The caudal spot and the cheek-band are also black.

Whilst males reach lengths around 5 cm, females are fully grown with just under 3 cm. The sexes can be distinguished easily by their different colourations. Depending on the mood, the lateral band may fade. During periods of parental care the females assume a yellow colouration and temporarily lose the lateral band.

Specific traits

are the bright blue body-colouration, the narrow lateral band which ends immediately in front of the caudal spot, and especially the narrow vertically arranged dark stripes on the edges of the scales.

Apistogramma resticulosa ♀

This species has small black speckles on the posterior portion of the gill-cover.

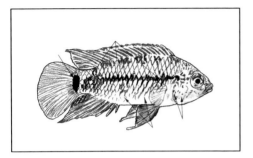

Similar species

Apistogramma caetei has a comparable colouration, but a broader lateral band which ends on a clearly visible seventh transversal bar. The caudal spot is slightly smaller. Its entire caudal fin is patterned with semicircular, almost vertically arranged rows of light speckles which could also be referred to as a reticulated pattern. In certain moods, the lateral band may transform into a partly interrupted zigzag-band. A clear point of distinction is the presence of obliquely arranged abdominal stripes in varying intensity which may also appear as an accumulation of speckles.

A superficial resemblance is furthermore found in *Apistogramma geisleri* and *Apistogramma regani*, but these species have different colourations and patterns.

The

natural habitat

is only known from the type locality. The type series was collected in the Rio Xicanga, a small stream 5 km west of the village of Humaita on the mighty Rio Madeira in central Brazil, and in a rest-water pond approximately 18 km west of this settlement.

Care

Keeping this relatively small growing species is easy. Aquaria with a minimum length of 70 cm, densely planted, with a fine grained substrate, small caves, and suitable company fishes are recommendable.

Slightly acidic water-values have been found necessary for a successful long-term keeping. This, of course, includes permanently clean water so that exchanges of a quarter to a third of the water-volume every 8 to 10 days is obligatory.

The

breeding

of this species is easy if an adequate environment is maintained and usually occurs by itself. *Apistogramma resticulosa* forms a male-mother-family structure with the male rarely collecting a harem, but rather tends to a lasting partnership with one specific female.

The latter is by far less aggressive than females of other *Apistogramma* species. Although the male is not permitted to participate in parental care for the fry, it is usually not chased away immediately if it comes close. Once the juveniles are a week or two of age the male may even occasionally stay with them.

The breeding requires soft, slightly acidic water-values. Whilst temperatures of 25 °C are suitable for this species' husbandry, 27 to 29 °C are advisable during reproductive periods.

Immediately after swimming free the young fish feed on newly hatched nauplii of the Brine Shrimp with MikroMin providing a valuable addition to their initial diet. During the first days, the juveniles form a dense school guided by the mother which viciously defends them when necessary.

It is frequently observed that a second clutch is laid only two to three weeks later. In this case it is advisable to remove the first group of juveniles from the tank since they are considered enemies of the second breed once these begin to swim and are consequently chased away or simply eaten.

▶ *Apistogramma roraimae*
KULLANDER, 1980

The description of this species was based on five specimens collected by the Belgian ichthyologist Dr. J. P. GOSSE in November 1962. The holotype is the largest known female measuring 27,8 mm in total length. The largest known male has a total length of 23,6 mm.

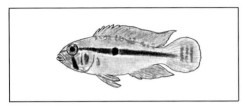

Probable appearance of *Apistogramma roraimae* ♂   Distribution of *Apistogramma roraimae*

Despite these small sizes the specimens examined by KULLANDER were already sexually mature. This could indicate that *A. roraimae* might be the smallest representative of the genus *Apistogramma* and thus the smallest of all Cichlids. On the other hand, it should be taken into consideration that very few specimens are known to date, and that reaching maturity does not necessarily have to do with maximum size in species of *Apistogramma*. KULLANDER was furthermore in doubt to which cladistic group this species might be assigned.

Unfortunately, *A. roraimae* has never been imported alive so that its colours in life are unknown. Therefore, reference is made to the original description by KULLANDER for an overview: *Apistogramma roraimae* has a moderately slender body-shape with a relatively high head. The spines of the dorsal fin increase in height from front to rear, but are of almost the same length from the fourth or fifth spine on. The tips of the fin-membranes are moderately long and pointed. The soft section of the dorsal fin is also pointed, but lacks a filamentous elongation. It extends little over the base of the caudal fin. A similar situation is found in the soft part of the anal fin. The caudal fin is rounded.

Since live specimens are unknown, nothing is known about their colouration. The ground

colour of preserved material is whitish yellow, obviously faded with time. The dark pattern is brown.

Transversal bars are absent in this species, but there is a pattern of blotches on the base of the dorsal fin which ranges onto the fin itself. A dark lateral band begins immediately behind the eye. It covers approximately one scale in width and extends up to the base of the caudal fin ending above and on the lower lateral line. The flanks are marked with a round lateral spot whose diameter does however not exceed the width of the lateral band. This spot is pitch black. The suborbital stripe is straight and moderately broad whilst the superorbital stripe is very indistinct. Abdominal stripes and a caudal spot are absent. The fins are more or less colourless and the first fin membranes of the dorsal fin are not dark. The holotype has pale transversal stripes in the centre of the caudal fin and its base is marked with a weak continuation of the lateral band. The anterior fin membranes of the ventral fins are black.

Specific traits

As this species is not known from its colours in life, the specific features indicated here refer to the preserved type material. These are however fairly general. Nevertheless the lateral band which ranges up onto the base of the caudal fin, the absence of a caudal spot, and the rounded caudal fin with its pale transversal stripes in the centre are noteworthy. It appears that the lateral spot is always very deep in colour.

Similar species

The only similar species is *Apistogramma gephyra*, which lacks a lateral spot and has a lanceolate caudal fin.

The natural habitat.

All localities known to date are in the area around the town of Boa Vista in the immediate catchment region of the Rio Branco in northern Brazil. The type specimen was collected 10 km south of the town on the road to Caracarai in the district of Roraima. Biotopes were streams and small depressions in the ground which were only temporarily filled with water. No information is available regarding the biology of this species.

The research of travelling aquarists is supported by native experts who help to catch fishes and give an indication about the diversity.

▶ *Apistogramma* sp.
(Broad-banded *Apistogramma*)

is no doubt a very attractive discovery. It was first imported in 1971. A photograph of this fish was misidentified as *Apistogramma klause-witzi* by MEINKEN which is a synonym of *Apistogramma bitaeniata*. A short while later it was however recognized that the "Broad-banded *Apistogramma*" is a species which has never been described scientifically.

The fish is moderately high-backed and elongate. Male specimens have extremely produced fin membranes in the dorsal fin with already the third membrane being as long as the body is high. Due to this the entire dorsal fin appears unusually high. It is slightly produced in its soft section with its tip exceeding over the centre of the caudal fin. The caudal fin is lyreate. The anal fin is also produced reaching just up to the centre of the caudal fin.

Depending on the mood, a broad lateral band may become visible which begins behind the eye and ends on the base of the caudal fin. Three to four abdominal stripes are present as pale indications. In the upper half of the body the colouration is dark beige to olive and light grey in the lower half. The dorsal fin is mainly wine-red with yellowish orange tips in the posterior portion. This colouration continues on the top quarter of the caudal fin. Its remaining parts are coloured as the anal fin, i. e. yellow with a light blue bordering below. The ventral fins are light in their anterior sections and otherwise transparent without colour. The gill-cover is marked with a few dark red speckles and a broad suborbital strips. This feature is also shown by the females whose chest-

Apistogramma sp. ♂ (Broad-banded *Apistogramma*)

The interspaces between the strong arched leaves of the water-hyacinths are the habitats of many species of small fishes.

slightly acidic water is probably an important precondition for an optimal environment in captivity.

Specific traits

of the males are the extraordinarily long membranes of the dorsal fin spines, the lyreate caudal fin, and the broad black cheek-band.

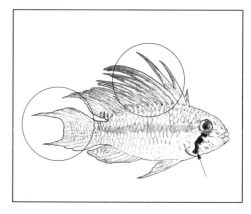

Similar species

Apistogramma bitaeniata has a less high, but more elongate body. Only the third to seventh fin membrane are produced in the dorsal fins of the males. The suborbital stripe is very indistinct, and depending on the mood, there may be a second, though more faint, band parallel to the lateral band. During periods of parental care the females display a dark longitudinal band and a different pattern.

Apistogramma cacatuoides
The great elongation of the membranes of the dorsal fin is restricted to the anterior ones in males of this species. The lateral band is always distinctly visible. The back is marked with five dark blotches which belong to the arrangement of transversal bars. The lips are thick and bulky in comparison and the ventral fins have filamentous elongations. The highly contrasting abdominal stripes are conspicuous.

The

natural habitats

lie all in the catchment of the Orinoco.

colouration is especially interesting. The ground-colour of the body is yellow whilst the back is brown. The dorsal and anal fins are bordered with black; the anterior portion of the ventral fins are pitch black. There is no lateral band on the body but a black lateral spot. Further black spots are found on the bases of the pectoral fins. The mouth-angles are bordered with black and there may be an indication of a large black blotch on the posterior part of the gill-cover.

It appears that the husbandry and breeding of this species is not free of problems. Soft,

▶ *Apistogramma* sp. (Yellow-cheeked *Apistogramma*)

This scientifically undescribed species is closely allied to *Apistogramma regani*. Both species are strikingly similar regarding morphometry and anatomy, but clear differences in their individual colour-patterns provide a basis for an easy distinction. Aquarists refer to this Dwarf Cichlid, whose males reach approximately six and females some four centimetres, as the "Yellow-cheeked *Apistogramma*".

The dark pattern of its colouration includes a large, vertically arranged caudal blotch which may extend over the entire height of the caudal base in both sexes, a lateral band which is reduced to five or six lateral spots, and broad transversal bars which however appear during certain stages of excitement. During those phases the males often also display three short abdominal stripes which begin just below the insertions of the pectoral fins and end above the anus already. During times of parental care

Distribution of *Apistogramma* sp. (Yellow-cheeked *Apistogramma*)

the females are coloured deep yellow. They initially display a lateral band which subsequently breaks up into several lateral blotches.

Male of the "Yellow-cheeked *Apistogramma*"

The colour pattern of the males largely depends on the mood and may be so variable that one did not identify specimens of different colour phases to belong to the same species if one would not know better. Dominant males in a neutral mood often display shining blueish green flanks without any black pattern. They have a yellowish zone on the head which may extend onto the gill-covers and even the belly area, but which is usually reduced to a spot on the lower part of the gill-cover.

Specific traits

of this species are the vertical caudal blotch, an unpatterned caudal fin in the males, and a yellow colour-zone on the head which led to its common name of "Yellow-cheeked Apistogramma".

Amongst the

similar species

Apistogramma regani is especially noteworthy. The males of this species however have a distinct pattern of five to seven transversal stripes on the caudal fin.

The

natural habitats

of these fish lie in the wider vicinity of the city of Manaus in northern Brazil. Localities are especially known from the catchment of the lower Rio Solimoes shortly before its fusion with the Rio Negro, for example from the water-bodies of the Lago Janauari. The "Yellow-cheeked Apistogramma" prefers ponds and streams as biotopes, but also inhabits the shallow zones of larger water-courses with no or little current if appropriate micro-biotopes are available there.

The preferred depth of water is 10 to 20 centimetres. They lead a relatively hidden life in the thick loose layer of leaf-litter which is found at the bank-zones of all rainforest water-courses.

One of the authors had the opportunity to study the natural habitats of the "Yellow-cheeked Apistogramma" at various seasons during the years 1986 to 1987. All of them were typical white-water biotopes with very murky water. Analyses of the water revealed a pH between 6,5 and 6,7. At water-temperatures of 26 to 27 °C the conductivity was measured at 20 to 100 micro-Siemens. The total as well as the carbonate hardness were always below 1 °dH.

Care

According to the observations made in the wild, the husbandry of the "Yellow-cheeked Apistogramma" requires a densely planted aquarium. The availability of a sufficient number of hiding-places is especially important due to the fact that this species obviously has a high rate of interspecific aggression which soon leads to seriously injured specimens if the husbandry conditions are inadequate.

The captive

breeding

of the "Yellow-cheeked Apistogramma" was also repeatedly successful in moderately hard water with a pH around 7,5. The juveniles can easily be reared with the larvae of the Brine Shrimp.

Table 17

Location:	Paraná do Janauari: lake southeast of Manaus (Brazil) in the catchment of the Rio Solimoes
Clarity:	very murky
Colour:	brownish yellow (white-water)
pH:	6,7
Total hardness:	<1 °dH
Carbonate hardness:	<1 °dH
Conductivity:	100 µS
Depth:	up to 40 cm
Current:	none
Water-temperature:	27 °C
Date:	19.3.1986
Time:	11.00 hrs

◗ *Apistogramma* sp. (Orange-finned *Apistogramma*)

As to how far this is a good species is yet to be investigated.

Presently, aquarists however consider these fish to be a separate species which might belong to the *bitaeniata*-complex due to their general appearance. The fish has a contrasting black pattern. The body is moderately high and slightly elongate. The pointed membranes of the spines of the dorsal fin increase in length up to the fifth membrane and subsequently remain at this level. The soft section of the dorsal fin is produced and ranges up to the centre of the caudal fin, and the same applies to the anal fin. The transparent caudal fin is lyreate and marked with five vertically arranged rows of speckles. It is feebly blue to yellowish orange coloured especially on its upper and lower edge. The dorsal fin is also coloured feebly yellowish orange and bordered with red. A bright blue colouration borders the anal fin. The short ventral fins are yellowish to orange.

A suborbital stripe is present, and a dark lateral band runs from behind the eye to the hind edge of the gill-cover and then continues up to the quadrangular caudal spot covering one scale in width. The back is coloured dark merging with the lateral band in the posterior half of the body.

Several differently broad abdominal stripes merge to an irregular dark broad band which extends up onto the caudal peduncle.

To date, only a few specimens have been imported alive and nothing is known about their husbandry, breeding, or even the natural distribution of the "Orange-finned *Apistogramma*".

Apistogramma sp. ♂ (Orange-finned *Apistogramma*)

Specific traits

These fish are easily recognized by their contrasting dark colour-pattern and the quadrangular caudal spot which is connected to the upper and lower edge of the caudal peduncle by narrow bands. This species furthermore has a lyreate caudal fin.

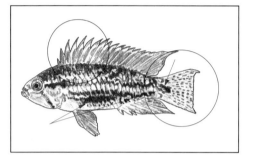

Similar species

Apistogramma bitaeniata has a different colour-pattern, no comparable abdominal stripes, and lacks a caudal spot. It apparently grows larger.

Apistogramma paucisquamis lacks produced fin membranes in the anterior dorsal fin, has no caudal spot, and also is smaller in size.

KOSLOWSKI, (1985) did not exclude the possibility that the "Orange-finned *Apistogramma*" may be a cross-breed of some sort. The specimens examined so far showed a high degree of variability of the scutellation which is a characteristic phenomenon of hybrids.

The main road of Requena on the Rio Ucayali in Peru

♦ Apistogramma sp. (Parallel-striped Apistogramma)

This is a high-backed, little elongate species which has no produced fin membranes between the spines of the dorsal fin. The predominant ground-colouration usually is greyish blue. A lateral band of one scale in breadth begins behind the gill-cover and extends up to shortly in front of the rectangular caudal spot. This lateral band may however be reduced to five quadrangular blotches in certain moods. Two to three abdominal stripes run up onto the caudal peduncle below the lateral band. These are responsible for the common name of this species. A light blue stripe is found below the eye, and the outer edge of the dorsal fin is similarly coloured. The caudal fin

Apistogramma sp. ♂ (Parallel-striped *Apistogramma*)

127

is rounded to truncate. The breeding colouration of the females is yellowish golden.

Males reach 8 cm in total length whilst females are fully grown at approximately 5,5 cm. The husbandry of this species is easy with neutral to slightly alkaline water-values being sufficient. Soft and slightly acidic water is however advantageous for a successful reproduction. Large specimens are not especially productive. The juveniles are relatively small and should be fed with the smallest available live food and MikroMin. Freshly hatched nauplii of *Artemia salina* are often still too big during the first eight days after swimming free and can only be handled without problems thereafter.

Specific traits

are the high-backed body-shape and the lateral band which is narrow right behind the eye, but covers an entire scale behind the gill-cover. It ends immediately in front of the rectangular caudal spot and may temporarily be reduced to five quadrangular blotches. The two to three abdominal stripes, which range from the insertion of the pectoral fin up onto the caudal peduncle, must furthermore be mentioned.

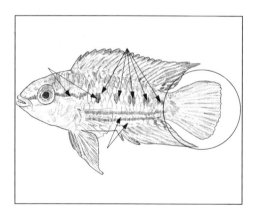

Similar species

Apistogramma cacatuoides has a different colouration, a bifurcate caudal fin, and the lateral band is never dissolved into quadrangular blotches.

Apistogramma commbrae is smaller in size and has a differently shaped caudal spot. Its lateral band is also never broken up into quadrangular blotches. No data are available on the

natural habitat

of this species. Since it is often caught in small numbers together with other fishes and imported from Iquitos, it is to be presumed that it originates from the north of Peru.

On occasion, ponds remain amidst the vast meadows of the cattle farms even during the dry season. They are utilized as "reserve water-tanks" and form biotopes suitable for a variety of small fishes.

▶ *Apistogramma* sp. "Rio Caura"

belongs to the larger representatives of the genus. Under aquarium conditions, the males reach a total length of 7,5 cm and the females just under 5,5 cm. Male specimens may become fairly high-backed and then appear quite bulky. Further morphological characteristics for the males include the conspicuously enlarged membranes of the spinous dorsal fin and a truncate caudal fin which is often asymmetrically produced in the upper half in old specimens. The posterior parts of the dorsal and anal fins are generally greatly produced and distinctly exceed the caudal fin in length.

The colouration of the males is fairly variable and is not only depending on the mood but also subject to the conditions predominant at the individual collecting localities. The greyish brown to beige ground-colouration which usually turns into a bright orange brown

Distribution of *Apistogramma* sp. "Rio Caura"

on the lower parts of the head has a blueish metallic gleam on the body. The more or less

Male of *Apistogramma* sp. "Rio Caura"

transparent caudal fin has a slightly to deep orange colouration. The base of the pectoral fin is coloured alike. The anterior part of the iris at the height of the preorbital stripe is coloured bright red and males display two obliquely arranged bright blueish green stripes below the eye.

The black body pattern so typical for this genus consists of a lateral band which is at least fairly broad in its central portion and which may be reduced to a zigzag-band or sometimes, though rarely, may disappear completely in certain moods, a preorbital, a superorbital and a suborbital stripe, and the distinctly outstanding caudal spot. The transversal bars are remarkably broad, but seldom displayed and usually only present as indications. They are generally visible as cloudy indications pattern below the dorsal fin.

Outside reproduction periods the females have a creamy to greyish yellow ground-colouration with a dark lateral band which distinctly ends before the caudal spot. The lateral spot usually is not especially obvious. The dorsal region is distinctly marked with the bases of the transversal bands which extend onto the base of the dorsal fin. The females also have the bright red blotch in the iris.

During parental care they assume a bright lemon-yellow colouration and a great contrast in formed by the membranes of the first two spines of the dorsal fin, the anterior edges of the pectoral fins, the lower bordering of the anal fin, and the suborbital stripe being coloured pitch black. The dark lateral band is reduced to six lateral blotches when the fry starts swimming free. It is especially noteworthy that caring females may display a black midventral stripe on the ventral part of the body which ranges from the base of the anal fin up to the chest region or even up to the lower lip and which widens anteriorly to a broad band. The throat thus becomes conspicuously black.

Specific traits

of the males are the more or less translucent, uniformly orange coloured caudal fin which lacks any pattern of any other colour. Furthermore, this fin is truncate or asymmetrical in shape in adult specimens, but never bifurcate.

Similar species

A great deal of resemblance exists in *A. hoignei*, but the fish of the Rio Caura lacks the dark spotted and lined patterns on the head typical for A. hoignei. Whilst the latter usually has four spines in the anal fin — a number which is rather unusual for the genus — all specimens from the Rio Caura examined to date had only three. Finally the fish of the Rio Caura grows distinctly larger.

The

natural habitat

and the distribution of this species of *Apistogramma* is confined to the southern catchment of the Rio Orinoco in central Venezuela. The fish inhabit the left as well as the right tributaries to the Rio Caura. One particular locality on the Rio Tiquire is a vast flooding area which is meandered by several streams and bordered with forests.

The Dwarf Cichlids resided there in the extremely shallow areas of the water-courses with no current. The ground was covered with a thick layer of leaf-litter thus providing ample cover. Aquatic vegetation was absent from these very shady water-bodies, but the flooded emerse vegetation provided additional hiding-places. The majority of specimens were caught in zones of 20 to 40 cm in depth.

There, their shared the biotope with the Tetra *Pristella maxillaris*, the Killi *Rachovia maculipinnis*, and juveniles of the predatory Characin *Hoplias malabaricus*.

The brownish coloured, relatively clear water had a temperature of 25,5 °C whilst the air measured 29 °C. Its pH was 5,8, the conductivity was measured at 35 micro-Siemens/cm. The total as well as the carbonate hardness were below the detectability level of 1 °dH.

Another collecting site in the catchment of the Rio Sipao lies in a swampy area which is drained by a larger, rapidly flowing stream and largely lies open in the sun with only a few palm-trees and bushes providing shade. In this biotope the Dwarf Cichlids resided in the little or not flowing zones with water-depths of between 10 and 30 centimetres. Cover was provided by emerse vegetation hanging into

Table 18

Location:	Swamp in the catchment of the Rio Sipao west of Maripa on the road to Caicara
Clarity:	moderately murky
Colour:	none
pH:	5,8
Total hardness:	<1 °dH
Carbonate hardness:	<1 °dH
Conductivity:	30 μS
Depth:	10 to 30 cm
Current:	slightly flowing
Water-temperature:	27 °C
Air-temperature:	25 °C
Date:	14.8.1989
Time:	11.00 hrs

the water or aquatic and swamp-plants such as *Hydrilla verticillata*, *Bacopa* sp., and *Eichhornia diversiflora*.

Care

Caring for this species is not difficult. The fish should have an at least partly densely vegetated aquarium which is additionally decorated with pieces of bog-oak. Fine gravel is recommendable as substrate. If kept in pairs, a tank measuring half a metre in length may be sufficient.

Breeding

The fish form a male-mother-family structure during periods dedicated to reproduction. The female preferably spawns at the ceiling of a cave-like hiding-place and solely cares for the embryos and subsequent larvae. In larger aquaria and in the presence of several females, the males collect a harem in their territories. Breeding was repeatedly successful in moderately hard water with pH-values in the neutral to slightly alkaline zones.

Female of *Apistogramma* sp. "Rio Caura" in breeding colours

◆ Apistogramma sp. (Red-wedged Apistogramma)

This scientifically undescribed species has not only been referred to as "Red-wedged *Apistogramma*" but also as "Sail-finned *Apistogramma*". Both names however refer to the same species although the red colouration may be absent from the caudal fin in specimens offered as "Sail-finned *Apistogramma*". Experiments have shown that changed conditions for breeding and husbandry, for example changed water-values, may result in very different colourations in the offspring even from the same parental specimens. In the following, this species is therefore named the "Red-wedged *Apistogramma*".

Males reach a total-length of 10 cm and females are fully grown at 5 cm. The specimens of this species have a slender elongate body-shape with the males growing a very high dorsal fin. The fin membranes are fused from the first spine on and are of equal height

Distribution of *Apistogramma* sp. (Red-wedged *Apistogramma*)

throughout the entire fin. A broad lateral band begins immediately behind the eye and extends up onto the caudal fin where it usually is espe-

Apistogramma sp. ♂ (Red-wedged *Apistogramma*)

cially contrasting and never appears as a caudal spot. Below and above this pattern the otherwise colourless and transparent caudal fin is coloured red to reddish brown. This pattern looks like a wedge tapering and fading towards the end of the fin and is the basis for its common name. Below the lateral band there are usually three abdominal stripes which may range up to the caudal peduncle.

Large males have a large lyreate caudal fin and ventral fins which extend up to the caudal fin if pressed against the body.

As to whether or not the "Blue-throated *Apistogramma*" represents the same species is still to be investigated.

The females have a more rounded to truncate caudal fin and a moderately high dorsal fin. During reproduction periods the lateral band is reduced to a lateral spot and the body assumes a yellowish orange colouration. The sexes can be distinguished at very young age by their differently shaped caudal fins. Adult males display a dark anal spot.

Specific traits

are the extremely high sail-like dorsal fins whose membranes are fused from the first spine on and the large lyreate caudal fin in the males. Further points of distinction are the lateral band with the pseudo-caudal-spot, the very long ventral fins, the abdominal stripes, and finally the red to reddish brown wedge-like pattern above and below the end of the lateral band which may however be absent in individual specimens. A faint pattern of speckles in the central part of the caudal fin may already be displayed by young males.

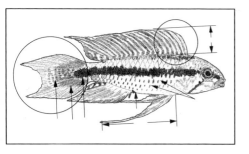

Similar species

Both sexes of *Apistogramma iniridae* have a rounded caudal fin.

Apistogramma pertensis has a distinct caudal spot and a rounded caudal fin. Furthermore, its anterior membranes of the dorsal fin stand free.

Apistogramma meinkeni has a less high dorsal fin and the first membranes of the dorsal fin stand free. The shape of the caudal fin is rounded and asymmetrical. The caudal spot is distinctly recognizable.

Very little is known about the

natural habitat

but it is to be presumed that the "Red-wedged *Apistogramma*" inhabits the area of the southern Orinoco and northern Rio Negro in the boundary region between Brazil and Columbia.

Care

Keeping this beautiful slender species of *Apistogramma* is not always hassle-free. For a healthy growth soft and slightly acidic water is important and the splendid fin-growth is also dependent from a soft water-quality.

Large males are often highly aggressive against each other and this causes the need for large aquaria. The species is sensitive towards a decreasing cleanliness of the water. However, if attention is paid to an environment suitable for Dwarf Cichlids, the husbandry of the "Red-wedged *Apistogramma*" is easy.

The

breeding

is nonetheless another story. It is important to take into consideration the fact that these fish originate from a biotope which is characterized by extremely soft and acidic water. As is the case with *Apistogramma iniridae* and *Dicrossus filamentosus*, amongst which the "Red-wedged *Apistogramma*" is sometimes found as side-catch, breeding is exclusively successful in this extreme water-milieu. Own experiments confirm this presumption. Successful reproduction was observed at water-values of approximately 170 micro-Siemens, a hydrogen-ion concentration of 5,4, and a water-temperature of 27 °C on average. Small caves on the ground are the preferred spawning sites for the females.

The observation made indicate parallels with the West African species of the genus *Pelvicachromis* since the female partially closes the entrance of the cave with substrate, e. g. sand or fine gravel, so that only a narrow opening remains. If only breeding caves are available which do not permit being shut, it is observed that the larvae are frequently moved by the mother.

During reproduction the females assume a yellowish orange body colouration and display a quadrangular lateral spot. At temperatures of 27 °C on average the development of the offspring is completed after 192 hours. The juveniles measure 4,7 mm in total length at this stage and are capable of feeding on newly hatched nauplii of *Artemia salina*.

Already during the development of the fry the female is a devoted mother. During their first few days of swimming free the juveniles form a dense school guided and guarded by the mother whilst the male simultaneously defends the breeding territory and is not permitted near the young fish. The further development of the juveniles was 80 % successful after 8 days at a temperature of 27 °C, a conductivity of 165 micro-Siemens, and a pH of 5,3.

In a personal communication, Karl-Heinz LÖHNDORF (Kiel, Germany) reported that breeding was still possible at a pH of 5,7, but at a much worse ratio. The hydrogen-ion concentration does however do only have an impact on the success-ratio, but also influences the sex-ratio. At a pH of 5,3 98 % of the juveniles were males. This problem is common with some other *Apistogramma* species, and is also noted with West African Dwarf Cichlids. Thus it appears there is still a lot of research to be done.

Apistogramma sp. ♀ (Red-wedged *Apistogramma*) in breeding colouration

► Apistogramma sp.
(Red-spotted Apistogramma
or
Black-edged Apistogramma)

This scientifically undescribed species belongs to the high-backed, less slender bodied representatives of the genus. Males reach just under 8 cm in total length and females grow up to approximately 4 cm.

The sexes can easily be distinguished. Not only that the males become distinctly larger, they additionally have produced ventral fins and long tapering soft rays in the dorsal and anal fins. The dorsal fin extends up to the central area of the caudal fin and up to behind the first third of the caudal fin in case of the anal fin respectively. Adult males furthermore develop a slightly bulkier head and thicker lips. The membranes of the dorsal fin increase in length up to the fourth spine and then maintain an equal length up to the rayed section. The caudal fin is rounded, and the ventral fins range up to the anterior insertion of the anal fin when pressed against the body. Laterally, a band ranges up to a dark, almost triangular spot on the base of caudal fin. It is formed by the dark anterior edges of scales arranged in two parallel rows. Another row below these

has scales with red centres and thus forms a row of red spots below the lateral band. This particularity accounts for the fish's common name. Females rarely display a lateral band, but more often a pale superorbital stripe and a contrasting, though short, suborbital stripe. Their dorsal fins are marked with a black edge which ranges from the first spine over the entire spinous section. The rounded ventral fins with their black borderings are especially noteworthy. Furthermore, there is a black spot on the lower base of the pectoral fins. The soft rayed portions of the dorsal and anal fins are rounded posteriorly.

The species is peaceful and adequate for a community aquarium with other peaceloving fishes. It is obviously identic with the specimens referred to as "Black-edged Apistogramma".

Specific traits

of male specimens are the bulky body-shape, the thick lips, the slightly high dorsal fin, and the row of red spots below the lateral band which may extend up onto the gill-cover. Females in contrast have black-edged dorsal and anal fins and rounded ventral fins which are bordered dark. The caudal fins are rounded in both sexes.

Apistogramma sp. ♂ (Red-spotted *Apistogramma*)

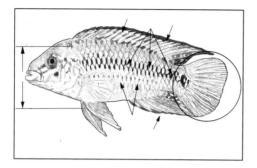

Similar species

Apistogramma cacatuoides males also have thick lips and have a bulky body-shape. The anterior membranes of the dorsal fin are however greatly produced and the caudal fin is bifurcate.

The

natural habitat

lies in the catchment of the upper Orinoco.

Care

Keeping this species is easy. According to experiences made so far, this species does not require specially conditioned water and does well in moderately hard, slightly alkaline water. On the other hand it is crucial to keep this fish in an adequately large, well structured aquarium with a rich growth of aquatic plants. Since the males tend to accumulate harems, i. e. one male facilitates several females in his territory, the ground space need be large enough. It seems to be important that the water is kept very clean at all times and a varying diet is offered. Maturity can already be reached at a length of approximately 4 cm.

Accordingly, it will soon come to

breeding

and the species is fairly productive. Due to this, a sufficient space of ground must be available as breeding territory. If one intends to rear large numbers of juveniles, this environmental factor is necessarily to be taken into consideration since the females otherwise engage in permanent quarrels.

The male successively mates with all females and subsequently protects the entire breeding area as the breeding territory. It is recommendable that each female has a ground space of 40×40 cm available. The juveniles are devotedly cared for. The nauplii of the Brine Shrimp are a suitable first food.

Apistogramma sp. ♀ (Red-spotted *Apistogramma*)

◆ *Apistogramma* sp. Turucui-*Apistogramma*

In the very recent past, European aquarists obtained some Dwarf Cichlids which have been unknown to science. Amongst these new species was a form of *Apistogramma* which is especially noteworthy for its unusual appearance. The colouration contains a striped pattern which is not known in this manner from any other representative of this genus.

The males of the new species have a yellowish to beige ground-colour with a pattern of up to nine very narrow dark lateral stripes on the flanks which are composed of individual small spots. They resemble the abdominal stripes found in several species of the *Apistogramma cacatuoides* species-complex. In

Distribution of *Apistogramma* sp. "Tucurui"

Male of *Apistogramma* sp. "Tucurui"

female specimens this peculiar pattern is confined to the lower half of the body. In the male, the entire head is also speckled with numerous small black spots. The caudal fin is more or less colourless. The distant area of the dorsal fin, whose anterior membranes are coloured black, and the anal fin are light blue. The breeding colouration of the females includes a noteworthy longitudinal row of six black lateral blotches and a same number of dorsal spots.

The new species was first imported from Brazil by Arthur WERNER in 1988.

Amongst the

specific traits

which enable an easy identification of this new species, the pattern of narrow dark longitudinal stripes on the flanks is certainly the most remarkable one.

Similar species

The colour-pattern of this Dwarf Cichlid is so unique that a confusion with any other species is hardly possible. The only other known species of Apistogramma in which males also have a pattern of small black spots laterally is *Apistogramma guttata* from Venezuela.

In this species, the membranes of the anterior part of the dorsal fin are clearly produced.

The

natural habitat

of the "Tucurui-*Apistogramma*" lie in the catchment of the Rio Tocantins in the northeast of Brazil. The specimens found to date all originate from an area between Jacunda Nova and the Tucurui Dam in the State of Pará.

Care

According to experiences made so far, keeping these fish has turned out to be fairly easy. It was however observed that this attractive Dwarf Cichlid may show an unusual amount of aggression towards other species of *Apistogramma*. Even if provided with a generously spacious aquarium it is hardly possible to keep several males together.

The

breeding

of this interesting form has repeatedly been successful in soft, slightly acidic water.

Female of *Apistogramma* sp. "Tucurui"

◗ *Apistogramma staecki*
KOSLOWSKI, 1985

Distribution of *Apistogramma staecki*

This colourful and interesting species was first collected and imported alive by the authors in 1983. It is a small growing fish with an attractive colouration whose males reach total lengths around 5 cm and females approximately 3 cm. Male specimens are moderately high-backed and less elongate. The dorsal fin is moderately high with the membranes of the anterior spines being slightly produced. The rayed section of this fin is only slightly produced and does not exceed the first third of the caudal fin in length. The same applies to the anal fin. The caudal fin is lyreate, but this shape is only recognizable clearly in adult males. The ventral fins are moderate in length with prolonged spines which range up to the anterior caudal peduncle. Depending on the mood a dark lateral band may appear. It begins immediately behind the eye and extends at a small triangular spot on the base of the caudal fin. The transversal bars are reduced to five dark blotches on the back. A black suborbital stripe ends at a small transversal band on the

Apistogramma staecki ♂

lower edge of the gill-cover. In certain moods, this band may be displayed solely in the form of a black spot.

The caudal fin is transparent with six vertical rows of pale light speckles. The same pattern, but more distinct, is also found in the soft posterior section of the anal fin and as a faint indication in the same section of the dorsal fin. The body-colours are dominated by a pale zinc-yellow whilst the gill-covers stand out in a bright cadmium-yellow. During courtship or while imposing the lateral band fades or completely disappears and a dark lateral spot becomes visible instead. The caudal fin, and also the caudal peduncle and posterior parts of the dorsal fin then assume a tomato-red colouration. The caudal fin is marked with up to seven transversal bands — a pattern which is otherwise exclusive to *Apistogramma hippolytae*. Besides the other features, this links the species with the *steindachneri*-group.

Female specimens of this form not only remain smaller in size, they also have a round caudal fin and black membranes in the anterior portion of the ventral fins. Both are important factors to consider for the distinction between the sexes.

Specific traits

of adult males are the lyreate shape of the caudal fin, the black edge of the dorsal fin, and a lateral band which ends on a small triangular caudal spot. Another small transversal spot on the lower gill-cover is also worth to be mentioned as it represents a rudiment of the suborbital stripe. The species is fairly small growing.

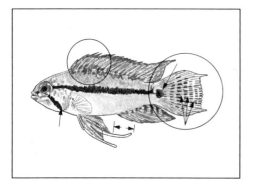

Similar species

Apistogramma steindachneri has a different colouration and the first two membranes of the dorsal fin are coloured black. The presence of a lateral blotch above the lateral band at the height of the third transversal bar is another important point of distinction. These fish grow larger and are slightly more high-backed.

Apistogramma hippolytae has a lateral band which ends in front of a large rectangular caudal spot. It furthermore has a rounded to truncate caudal fin and a lateral spot at the height of the third transversal bar above the lateral band.

Apistogramma gibbiceps lacks a caudal spot and the lateral band ends on the caudal fin. These fish display abdominal stripes which may sometimes appear as blotches.

Apistogramma cacatuoides has abdominal stripes and a different colour-pattern.

The

natural habitat

as known so far lies in the vicinity of the town of Trinidad in the north of Bolivia. This is an area of cattle farming thus the landscape is predominated by flat meadows. The collecting localities during the expedition in 1983 were situated along the road to El Colegio and Loreto south of Trinidad. Since the meadows of the cattle farms are often flooded during the rainy seasons, it was tried to elevate the connective roads. Soil was moved from either side of the planned road to achieve a level above the water-level. The resulting depressions on both sides of the road were soon filled with water and thus formed biotopes for a variety of interesting species of animals.

The artificial ponds are connected to smaller water-courses or larger rivers during the rainy seasons only although they may be kilometres in length. The surface of these lakes is usually covered with a dense carpet of water-hyacinths which obviously subdue all submerse plants.

There are only a few places which are vegetated by large specimens of a species of *Echinodorus* which stick out high above the water-surface. The depth of the water in these lagoons is mainly 50 to 60 cm and the dense layer of water-hyacinths with their strong large leaves extends down to a depth of 20 to 30 cm. Below, there is free space without any vegetation as it is isolated from most of the light by the dense carpet on the surface. The ground is usually muddy with a layer of rotting plant remains. Small fishes were exclusively found amongst the labyrinths of the floating plants. In between the strong, large, and arched leaves of the water-hyacinths small and even tiny cavities exist which are used by a variety of small fishes as places to reside or as territories and spawning caves as is the case in *Apistogramma staecki*. This plant-zone provides an efficient cover from the predatory fishes which live in the space clear of vegetation below the "hyacinth-carpet". There, the small fishes would have only a slight chance to survive.

In 1983, the authors could record this species of *Apistogramma* in a surprisingly dense population. The water-analyses were also extremely interesting and we found that with the hydrogen-ion concentration decreasing the density of the *A. staecki* populations were increasing.

If the water was less acidic, the species shared its habitat with another new species which was recently described as *Apistogramma linkei*. Whenever the pH value ranged in the neutral or even slightly alkaline zones, only the "Yellow-chested *Apistogramma*" could be recorded. This indicates that the acidic level determines the distribution of these species.

Care

Keeping this species is easy when the observations made in the natural biotopes are taken into consideration and the fishes are provided with a dense vegetation near the ground as zones for retreat. The decoration should also contain small caves between stones or bog-oak.

It was surprising to observe that the fish does not require specially conditioned water. However, although husbandry and even breeding is possible in moderately hard, slightly alkaline water, a soft, slightly acidic environment is nevertheless of advantage. The cleanliness of the water and a varying diet are important. The fish is a very peaceloving one and does well in a community tank together with species with a comparable behaviour.

The

breeding

occurs almost by itself according to observations made so far. For a healthy development the fish need tranquillity and adequate aquaria as described in the chapter on husbandry. The females spawn on the ceiling of small cavities. The species forms a male-mother-family structure. A tendency of the males to accumulate harems was observed only on rare occasions. The female cares for the clutch and the male defends the territory.

The eggs and larvae develop better in soft, slightly acidic water. The eggs are slightly reddish in colour. They hang down from the ceiling of the cave on short stems where they are firmly attached. After 3,5 hours a rapid cell-splitting can be observed already. Approximately 48 hours later the almost completely developed embryo can be seen through the egg-shell. The yolk-sac shows small dark spots. The eye-sockets and the embryonic stem are clearly recognizable and strong

Table 19

Location:	Appr. 10 km south of the town of Trinidad towards El Colegio and Loreto (Bolivia)
Clarity:	slightly murky
Colour:	brown
pH:	5,7
Total hardness:	<1 °dH
Carbonate hardness:	<1 °dH
Conductivity:	94 µS at 29 °C
Nitrite:	not measured
Depth:	up to 80 cm
Current:	almost none
Water-temperature:	29 °C
Date:	12.7.1983
Time:	16.00 hrs

Apistogramma staecki ♀

Apistogramma staecki ♂ in imposing colouration

movements of the body or the embryonic stem are sometimes observed. These are the first attempts to break through the egg-shell.

Approximately 55 hours after spawning the embryos emerge from the eggs. Then they lay on the ground in small groups or hang on the walls of the cave. A few hours later the small bodies have assumed first indications of a pattern in the form of small dark speckles. The larvae have a length of 3,6 mm at this stage. After 96 hours their development has advanced. The eyes have received a dark grey pigmentation, the mouth is recognizable, and the heart-beat can clearly be observed.

Another 24 hours later the development of the larvae appears to be almost completed. The iris of the eye has become golden, and mouth, lips, and the frontal bulge are well formed. A dark spotted pattern has become visible on the tail and caudal peduncle. The adhesive organ of the head is still functional. After approximately 160 hours the larval development is eventually completed. A tiny air-bubble is visible inside the body which indicates that the swim-bladder is filled. Light silvery spots have appeared on the caudal fin and peduncle. The adhesive organ and the "adhesive thread" have disappeared. A few hours later the juveniles begin to swim and are henceforth guided and protected by their mother. The observations described above were made at a water-temperature of 28 °C and the process lasted approximately 164 hours.

Freshly hatched nauplii of the Brine Shrimp are an adequate first food also in this case. It may be supplemented by a "food-milk" made up of MikroMin powder-food and water from the aquarium. The rearing does not cause specific problems although the juveniles grow slowly despite given food several times a day and a good water-quality. The species is not very productive.

Blooming water-hyacinths in the north of Bolivia

◆ *Apistogramma steindachneri*
(REGAN, 1908)

Distribution of *Apistogramma steindachneri*

is a species whose males may reach up to 9 cm in total length.

Originally described as *Heterogramma steindachneri*, the fish was subsequently given a variety of other names — such as *Apistogramma ortmanni rupununi*, *Apistogramma ornatipinnis*, and *Apistogramma wickleri*. All these are however considered to be synonyms today.

This is most colourful and largest species of the so-called *steindachneri*-group. Males have a caudal fin of lyreate shape. The posterior part of the body, the central section of the caudal fin, and the anal fin are light blue in colour. Depending on the disposition, a dark lateral band may appear beginning behind the eye and extending up to a small triangular caudal spot. The edges of the scales on the body above the lateral band are more or less deep black posteriorly. The suborbital stripe widens on its way down and stands out distinctly whereas the superorbital and preorbital-stripe are weakly developed or may be completely absent. A triangular spot at the height of the third trans-

versal bar may be visible temporarily. It lies directly on the lateral band. Adult males have pointed ventral fins which are however not especially long and extend to the second spines of the anal fin only if pressed against the body. The anterior two membranes of the dorsal fin are black.

Apistogramma steindachneri ♂

Females of this species reach total lengths of up to 6 cm. The soft sections of their dorsal and anal fins are also pointed, but otherwise little produced.

Specific traits

of this species are the almost triangular spot on the base of the caudal fin and another triangular spot on the flank above the lateral band. Furthermore, the lateral band extends up to the caudal spot.

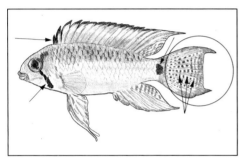

When reaching approximately 5 cm in length the males develop a lyreate caudal fin whilst females retain the rounded shape of theirs.

Similar species

Apistogramma hippolytae grows smaller, has an oval caudal spot, and a wide dark blotch above the lateral band. The latter ends on the seventh transversal bar in front of the caudal spot. Depending on the mood up to seven stripes may appear on the caudal fin which is slightly rounded to truncate in shape.

Apistogramma rupununi is very similar to *A. hippolytae* and both species may thus be easily confused. *A. rupununi* however has a narrower lateral spot which only extends to the upper lateral line.

As to how far a relationship may exist with *Apistogramma ortmanni* is still be thoroughly investigated. According to the data published in the original description specimens of this species have a rounded caudal fin and two to four abdominal stripes. Furthermore, the lateral band is said to range up onto the caudal fin.

The

natural habitat

lies in the Guayanas and in the east of Venezuela. Localities are especially known from areas of the Essequibo River and the Demerara River in British Guyana which flows into the Atlantic Ocean near the capital Georgetown.

Care

According to experiences made so far, keeping this species has turned out to be fairly easy. Well structured aquaria with a rich growth of plants, a fine substrate, and numerous small caves as hiding-places are suitable to adequately house this fish. Regarding the water-quality A. steindachneri is fairly adaptable and happy with moderately hard, slightly alkaline water. Notwithstanding this, its longevity is higher in soft, slightly acidic water and the specimens display brighter colours.

Adult males tend to collect "harems" and it is therefore recommendable to keep several females with a male.

The

breeding

of this species requires appropriately sized breeding territories for each female. The species is very productive and 250 young fish per clutch are no exception. A minimum ground-space of 40×40 cm is adequate as such territory. Since the males often spawn with several females in succession, suitably sized breeding aquaria are necessary in order to prevent losses amongst the territorial females. If these are not available, the number of females must be reduced.

The rearing of the juveniles is easy. Newly hatched nauplii of the Brine Shrimp and MikroMin in the form of a "food-milk" injected directly into the school of fish by means of a syringe helps to satisfy the apparently never ending hunger of the young fish during the first days. Provided regular water-exchanges, i.e. depending on the size of the aquarium and the number of juveniles a third of the volume every two to five days, the young fish grow rapidly and may measure some 3 cm after 12 weeks already.

◗ Apistogramma taeniata
(GÜNTHER, 1862)

A single specimen collected by H.W. BATES in 1852 served GÜNTHER as holotype for the description of this fish as *Mesops taeniatus* ten years later. This name is however regarded as a synonym of *Apistogramma taeniata* today. The type specimen is a male of 42,1 mm in length. However, all subsequent authors who described fishes under the name of *A. taeniata* erred with regard to the specific features.

Apistogramma taeniata is the type species of the entire genus *Apistogramma*, but is systematically fairly isolated since it does not share many traits with other members of the genus. The holotype of this species is a very old specimen in an extremely bad state of preservation. It has lost all its colours and most of its scales and the fins are so badly damaged that their shapes cannot be identified any more.

In order to draw a picture of how this fish might look as good as possible, some remarks of Sven KULLANDER may be quoted here: According to GÜNTHER the preserved fish was brownish, had a rounded caudal fin, no produced membranes in the dorsal fin, and displayed a black lateral band which ranged up into the caudal spot.

Furthermore, the presence of a suborbital stripe and a caudal stripe were mentioned. REGAN, who described the appearance of this fish in 1906, additionally indicated that the anterior three membranes of the dorsal fin

Distribution of *Apistogramma taeniata*

were black and that all vertical fins would be more or less distinctly spotted. He furthermore described a pale vertically expanded caudal spot, a narrow pre-, a broad suborbital stripe, and two rows of spots in the posterior parts of the dorsal and anal fin respectively.

Specific traits

of *Apistogramma taeniata* are the shape of the muzzle and especially the unusually long last spine in the dorsal fin.

Similar species

Leaving the pattern aside and with some fantasy one could compare the appearance of the body with species like *Apistogramma caetei* and *Apistogramma resticulosa*. These however lack the height of the head, the unusual shape of the mouth, and the long last spine of the dorsal fin.

The

natural habitat

The locality of the type specimen is the Rio Cupari, a tributary to the Rio Tapajos, approximately 200 km south of the town of Santarem in the Brazilian state of Pará.

The lengendary dangerous Pinranha shows its "real" face.

▶ *Apistogramma trifasciata*
(EIGENMANN & KENNEDY, 1903)

Distribtuion of *Apistogramma trifasciata*

is a relatively small Cichlid which is very frequently offered by pet-shops in different varieties. Whether or not these may be considered different morphs is questionable since they often result from different breeding conditions. For example, it was established that male specimens which have been reared in moderately hard, slightly alkaline water only develop moderately long membranes in the dorsal fin. In contrast, specimens from an environment of soft, slightly acidic water have much brighter colours and partially unusually long membranes of the dorsal fin.

As is the case in many other *Apistogramma*-species the husbandry in soft acidic water favours not only a much better state of health but also influences the growth of the fins to a surprising extent. Two subspecies of *Apistogramma trifasciata* have been described: *Apistogramma trifasciata haraldschultzi* and

An *Apistogramma trifasciata* ♂ which has been reared in very soft water

Apistogramma trifasciata maciliensis, but both names have subsequently been dumped and are nothing but synonyms today.

Apistogramma trifasciata is a very peaceful species. Males reach total lengths of approximately 6 cm whilst the female are fully grown at a mere 3,5 cm.

A distinction between the sexes is possible at an early stage already when the males begin to grow produced anterior membranes in the dorsal fin. In addition the posterior soft rays of the dorsal and anal fins become longer and pointed, and the filamentous appendices of the ventral fins begin to grow which are features not found in females.

Specific traits

of subadult males are that the second to fourth membrane of the dorsal fin are produced to a different extent. A lateral band ranges from behind the eye up to the base of the rounded caudal fin. A lateral spot, a caudal spot, and abdominal stripes are absent.

The most characteristic feature of this species however is a black line which runs from the upper insertion point of the pectoral fin over the belly down to the first spine of the anal fin. It is one of the stripes to which the scientific name refers — *trifasciata* means "with three stripes".

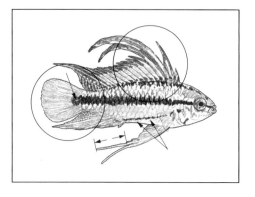

Similar species

Adult males of *Apistogramma cacatuoides,* A. *luelingi,* A. *bitaeniata,* and the scientifically

undescribed "Broad-banded *Apistogramma*" also have greatly enlarged membranes in the anterior part of the dorsal fin. All aforementioned species however grow much larger and have a lyreate caudal fin. In *Apistogramma norberti,* which has a rounded caudal fin, the dorsal fin has a comparable shape. This species however differs by the possession of distinct abdominal lines.

The

natural habitats

of *Apistogramma trifasciata* are spread over the countries of Brazil, Bolivia, Paraguay, and Argentina. The distribution ranges from the Rio Guaporé in the northwest throughout the entire Rio Paraguay up to the Paraná where the city of Santa Fé is indicated to be the southernmost locality. Due to this vast distribution it is not really surprising that specimens from distant localities show a certain amount of variability. This obviously was the reason for the description of the abovementioned subspecies which are however invalid today.

One of the authors had repeatedly the opportunity to examine the natural habitats of *Apistogramma trifasciata* in the Rio Guaporé and in different sections of the Rio Paraguay in

Table 20

Location:	Lago de Mandioré in the catchment of the Rio Paraguay north of Corumbá
Clarity:	fairly clear
Colour:	brownish
pH:	7,6
Total hardness:	1 °dH
Carbonate hardness:	4 °dH
Conductivity:	60 µS
Depth:	up to 50 cm
Current:	none
Water-temperature:	25 °C
Date:	10.8.1991
Time:	14.00 hrs

Bolivia. These were partly rivers of the clear-water type, but others carried white-water and were very murky accordingly. Despite these differences the biotopes of these fish were comparable in so far that the specimens were exclusively found amongst the cover provided by a dense vegetation which either consisted of aquatic or swamp-plants or a dense carpet of floating plants. They were very frequently found living syntopically with *Apistogramma borelli* and *Apistogramma commbrae.*

Otherwise the syntopic ichthyofauna at the collecting sites included the Tetra *Hyphesso-brycon callistus* and the Killis *Pterolebias lon-gipinnis* and *Pterolebias phasianus.*

Analyses of the water made at different collecting localities of *Apistogramma trifasciata* in the months of July and August in 1987 and 1991 revealed values of a total hardness of <1 to $2\,°dH$, a carbonate hardness of <1 to $4\,°dH$, and a pH of between 6,9 and 7,6. At water-temperatures of 24 to 27 °C the conductivity was measured at 15 to 100 µS/cm.

Care

Keeping this fish is easy. Richly vegetated aquaria with a number of caves are as important in this case as with all other species of *Apistogramma*. The species does not have special

The short-finned form of *Apistogramma trifasciata* ♂

requirements regarding the quality of the water, but it should not be ignored that soft, slightly acidic water is of advantage in any respect. The cleanliness of the water and a varying diet are however points important enough to pay special attention to. A male cares for several females. If the breeding aquarium is thus spacious enough two or three females may be kept together with one male. The species is sensitive to intestine parasites.

The

breeding

is easy and occurs by itself if the environment is properly maintained. The female spawns on the ceiling of a small cave. If the cave is too small for the male, the fertilization occurs by sperm being released into the water and shovelled into the cave. To achieve this the male positions himself in front of the cave entrance and fans the water against the eggs with the caudal fin. The parental care is the exclusive task of the female.

This species is not especially productive and to obtain 40 to 60 juveniles from a fully grown pair is a good average result. The rearing of the juveniles is easy. The first food should consist of the nauplii of the Brine Shrimp and MikroMin made up as "food-milk".

Apistogramma trifasciata ♀

▶ *Apistogramma uaupesi*
KULLANDER, 1980

is, no doubt, a very pretty slender species of *Apistogramma* which has apparently never been imported alive. This fish was also collected by King Leopold of Belgium and Dr. GOSSE during an expedition through the northwest of Brazil in 1967.

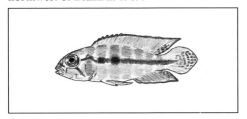

Probable appearance of *Apistogramma uaupesi* ♂

Distribution of *Apistogramma uaupesi*

The largest known male measures 37 mm in total length, the largest female 34 mm. For its identification there are only the data available published by its original describer. According to KULLANDER *Apistogramma uaupesi* has a slender elongate body with a moderately elongate head. The spines of the dorsal fin become increasingly longer from front to rear with the tips of the membranes being moderately long and pointed, but not produced. The soft section of the dorsal fin is also pointed and not produced. It extends up to the central caudal fin. A similar situation is found in the case of the soft portion of the anal fin. The caudal fin is roundish to lanceolate in males and rounded in females and juveniles. The appearance of live specimens is unknown. Preserved specimens have a yellowish ground-colouration with the markings appearing brown. There is a pattern of transversal bars which is however never distinct and often reduced to indications. It is more distinct in females and juveniles than in adult males. The transversal bars are broader than their interspaces. Their intensity is highest on the back where they appear as blotches which however never extend onto the dorsal fin.

A moderately broad lateral band begins behind the eye which is clearly set off in the holotype, but speckled in smaller specimens.

It covers approximately one and a half scales in width and ranges up to the base of the caudal fin where it ends below the lateral line.

The lateral spot is roundish, small, and not as broad as the lateral band. A spot is frequently observed where the second transversal bar crosses the lateral band. The superorbital stripe is only found in juveniles. The suborbital stripe is narrow and confined to the cheek-areas. Abdominal stripes and a caudal spot are absent. The dorsal fin is dark at the ends of the fin membranes, but transparent otherwise. Its soft section holds two to three rows of spots. The anal fin is tinted dark or colourless. It is bordered dark in the type specimen and has two to three rows of speckles. The caudal fin is dark and marked with distinct vertical rows of spots in its posterior section. The lateral band faintly continues on its scaly anterior part. The ventral fins are white.

There is apparently no distinct difference between males and females.

Apistogramma uaupesi was assigned to the *pertensis* species-group by its describer.

Specific traits

The vertical rows of light spots in the posterior part of the caudal fin are regarded as being especially characteristic.

Similar species

Apistogramma meinkeni is to be mentioned in the first instance here although this species has a spot on the base of the caudal fin.

Although *Apistogramma iniridae* has a resembling body-shape it distinctly differs in its colouration. The tips of the fin membranes of the dorsal fin are fused in *A. iniridae*.

Apistogramma gephyra is similar, but lacks a lateral spot.

The

natural habitat

of *A. uaupesi* is so far only known from the locality of the type specimens. This is a stream near the village of Trovao on the right bank of the Rio Uaupes. *Apistogramma elizabethae*, *A. brevis*, and *A. meinkeni* were recorded from the same area. Further data on the collecting site are not available.

The "cultivation" of the vast South American rainforest-areas proceeds rapidly.

▶ *Apistogramma viejita*
KULLANDER, 1979

For the description of this species three specimens were available which had been collected by the Swede HONGSLO in Columbia. This series consisted of a male specimen of 40 mm in total length and a female of 26 mm. The third specimen was damaged and measured only 15 mm. The sex could not be determined due to its state. On occasion a few specimens of this species have been imported alive and were thus accessible to the aquarists. During a collecting trip through Columbia one of the authors had opportunity to in others examine the type locality of this species and its wider vicinity. It was most interesting to observe that there are at least three different colour-

Distribution of *Apistogramma viejita*

Apistogramma viejita ♂ Colour-morph I

153

varieties of *Apistogramma viejita* which are to date considered one species despite their dissimilar colour-patterns. They are referred to here as

Apistogramma viejita I
Apistogramma viejita II
Apistogramma viejita III.

Colour-morph I was found in a small water-course between Puerto Lopez and Puerto Gaitan and on a site near Puerto Gaitan. It was however also recorded from the type-locality of *Apistogramma macmasteri,* from water-courses which cross the road from Villavicencio to Restrepo.

Colour-morph II was collected in the lagoon of the headwaters area of the Rio Manacacias whose water flows east towards the Orinoco.

This variety is especially stunning with its red spots on the gill-covers.

Colour-morph III also originates from a small lagoon whose water however flows into the Rio Manacacias in the west.

The varieties II and III are separated by the highland watershed although their collecting sites are not even 30 km far from one another. The distance to the localities where morph I was found is approximately 50 km.

The females of *Apistogramma viejita* are uniquely coloured. Their breeding colouration is basically yellowish golden with a pattern of rectangular black blotches which are the remains of the lateral band.

Further black elements of the pattern are a caudal spot, a suborbital stripe, and six dorsal blotches to which the transversal bars are reduced. The throat is also black, and there are a midventral stripe and a black anal spot. These female features are characteristic for the species although it could not yet be determined whether the females of all three colour-morphs display these traits. It is fact that the females of colour-morph III are furnished with these features.

Apistogramma viejita is closely allied with *Apistogramma macmasteri* and *Apistogramma hongsloi* and often especially difficult to distinguish from the first mentioned. In this connection the shape and size of the spot on the base of the caudal fin is important.

Unfortunately, this spot is displayed in varying intensity depending on the specimen's actual mood. Therefore, a detailed description of the habitus and colour-pattern may help with identification problems.

Apistogramma viejita has a moderately elongate body. The length of the dorsal spines increases from the first to the fifth spine and then continues at the same height. The third to sixth membrane of the dorsal fin are produced in the type specimen; they do however not exceed the respective spines in length. The fourth fin-membrane is the longest. In females, the membranes are short, but pointed. In the males, the soft section of the dorsal fin is produced reaching the centre of the caudal fin in length. The same applies to the anal fin which is slightly shorter. The caudal fin is rounded.

The description of the colour-pattern according to KULLANDER may also be useful for identification purposes. The transversal bars are developed, but do not stand out very distinctly and the anterior two are only visible in small specimens. The third and fourth bar hardly exceed the lateral band whilst bars nos. five to seven range up to the edge of the body, their length being equal to the height of the caudal fin. The pigmentation of the transversal bars is most dense on the base of the dorsal fin and even extends onto the base of it. The lateral band begins immediately behind the eye, but only ranges up to the fifth transversal bar. Thereafter it is continued as a row of connected rectangular blotches. A distinct lateral spot is absent. The suborbital stripe is moderately broad and the superorbital stripe extends up to the nape. There are three abdominal stripes, the first of which running from the top of the base of the pectoral fin to the caudal peduncle whilst the second connects the lower edge of the pectoral fin with the caudal peduncle. The third stripe is arranged below the second and ends at the base of the anal fin. These stripes are composed of elongate spots. The caudal spot is oval to semicircular in shape. The fins are usually colourless or dark in small males with the first two spines and membranes of the dorsal fin being black. The soft portion of the dorsal fin has no pattern of spots or speckles. Males have four rows of spots in the

Apistogramma viejita ♂ Colour-morph II

Apistogramma viejita ♂ Colour-morph III

posterior part of the anal fin. The caudal fin lacks any pattern of spots or speckles.

Specific traits

of the males are the high dorsal fin and the produced membranes in this fin. The lateral band which is reduced to a row of blotches between the second transversal bar and the caudal peduncle should also be taken into consideration. The oval to rectangular caudal spot is a useful identification feature.

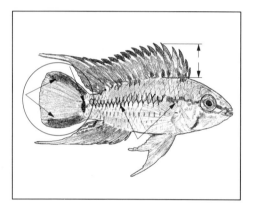

Similar species

Apistogramma macmasteri often displays greatly contrasting transversal bars or an intensely coloured lateral band which is reduced to a row of rectangular blotches. Furthermore, it has a high and wide caudal spot. Its dorsal fin is lower and has less produced membranes if compared directly. This species grows larger and its males have a rounded to truncate, according to SCHMETTKAMP even a lyreate caudal fin. The red top and bottom borderings of the caudal fin are atypical and rather a trait of *Apistogramma viejita*.

Apistogramma hongsloi has a different colour-pattern, a differently shaped caudal spot with a usually more faint intensity, and a broad, often dull lateral band. Its colouration is dissimilar. The dark scales forming the lateral band have light centres so that the band appears in a more reticulated pattern.

The

natural habitat

extends from the green borderzones of the eastern Cordillera near Villavicencio up to the steppes east of Puerto Gaitan which are dominated by the vast dry cattle farms of the so-called Llanos in the Departemento del Meta. Suitable biotopes are found in the approximately 250 km long catchment area south of the Rio Meta in central Columbia.

The Colour-morph I of *Apistogramma viejita* was originally caught in a stream 10,5 km from the town-limits of Villavicencio in direction of Restrepo. This appears to be a watercourse which heads for the Rio Guatiquia. The water is usually clear with some current. The region between Villavicencio and Restrepo is cattle-land with green meadows. The depth of the water-course did usually not exceed 40 cm.

The colour of the water was slightly brownish and clear with the ground consisting of sand and fine gravel. Submerse plants were

Table 21

Location:	Lagoon on the road to Puerto Gaitan, 2,5 km off the village of Canó los Brincos; a tributary to the Rio Manacacias (Columbia)
Clarity:	clear
Colour:	brownish
pH:	5,3
Total hardness:	below 1 °dH
Carbonate hardness:	below 1 °dH
Conductivity:	3 µS at 28,5 °C
Nitrite:	below 0,1 mg/l
Depth:	usually between 5 and 20 cm
Current:	slight
Water-temperature:	28,5 °C
Date:	12.3.1982
Time:	14.00 hrs

rare and the vegetation mainly consisted of emerse bank-plants and grass which grew especially in the shallow, often just five to ten centimetres deep zones of these water-bodies. The small numbers of *Apistogramma viejita* were only found here living together with *Aequidens metae* and a species of *Pyrrhulina*.

The described area is also the collecting locality of the type specimen of *Apistogramma macmasteri* and accordingly both species should occur here sympatrically. The second site of the Colour-morph I lies approximately 150 km to the east, i.e. exactly 56 km off the village of Puerto Gaitan. It is a rest-water in a depression which is connected to an up to 6 metres broad water-course. It forms the centre of a green island of approximately 100 metres in diameter which is surrounded by a dry steppe. The river flows to the south mouthing into the Rio Yucao which in its further course flows into the Rio Meta north of Puerto Gaitan. This small oasis is cut by the road from Puerto Lopez to Puerto Gaitan. Here, the

species is also not common and found exclusively in the few vegetated zones. As is the case in the biotope described above, the water is extremely soft and very acidic. Side-catches contained species like *Mesonauta festivum*, *Geophagus daemon*, *Aequidens metae*, and several species of Tetra. Another collecting site of the Colour-morph I lies two and a half kilometres before Puerto Gaitan. It is another small oasis formed by numerous palmtrees and situated directly on the road. A small stream of usually only one metre in breadth with a water-depth of partly only 5 cm is responsible for the change in the landscape.

The centre of the oasis is formed by a lagoon with crystal clear brownish water in a depression of approximately ten metres in diameter and a depth of one to one and a half metre. Whilst the deep zones of the lagoon are inhabited mainly by Tetras and large *Aequidens metae*, the shallow bank-areas and the also very shallow stream are the right biotopes for *Apistogramma viejita*. The more dense

Apistogramma viejita ♀

the vegetation is, the more numerous is this fish. At this place it was possible to collect 20 medium-sized *Apistogramma* in an area of just a few square metres. The banking zones and the plant-free areas especially contain rich sediments of iron. Examination of the water revealed that this is another case of very soft, acidic water. The water-temperature was established to be 28,5 °C whilst the air-temperature was measured at 29,5 °C around 14.00 hrs. There was a slight breeze under an almost cloudless sky. The locals refer to this stream as the Canó los Brincos; it appears to be a tributary to the grand Rio Manacacias which flows into the Rio Meta approximately 15 km farther north.

Approximately 80 km east of Puerto Gaitan, between the headwaters areas of the Rio Muco and the Rio Guarrojo, there lies a collecting site of *Apistogramma viejita* Colour-morph II. It is also a lagoon and a small water-body which is embanked by dense brush and solitary trees cutting through the land as a narrow shallow stream. The lagoon measures approximately 30 by 12 metres and is free of submerse vegetation. Shallow bank-zones are absent. Its depth was not measured, but may be estimated to be one metre. The ground was

dark to black and muddy. The entire ground of the immediately vicinity was like a tossing carpet of grass which made walking difficult. It was thus not without danger to proceed into the partly swampy and marshy areas or to try to catch fishes in the stream itself as one often sunk up to 50 cm deep and was unable to free oneself without helping hands. Although the biotope was examined on a day with an overcast sky, the air-temperature was 35 °C at 11.30 hrs. Besides the Colour-morph II of *Apistogramma viejita* with its beautiful red spots on the gill-covers and the broadly bordered caudal fin, especially pretty Tetras were caught. This included the Red-mouthed Tetra *Hemigrammus rhodostomus,* the Lemon-tetra *Hyphessobrycon pulchripinnis,* a species of Hatchetfish, and the Red Phantom-tetra *Megalamphodus sweglesi* — to mention just a few. This site was situated east of the plateau towards the Orinoco lowlands. The collecting site of the Colour-morph III in contrast laid west of the plateau.

Table 22

Location:	Palmtree oasis appr. 50 km southeast of Puerto Gaitan in the vicinity of the Rio Manacacias in eastern Columbia
Clarity:	clear
Colour:	greyish brown
pH:	5,1
Total hardness:	below 1 °dH
Carbonate hardness:	below 1 °dH
Conductivity:	15 μS at 28,5 °C
Nitrite:	below 0,1 mg/l
Depth:	up to 60 cm
Current:	very slight
Water-temperature:	28,5 °C
Date:	14.3.1982
Time:	15.00 hrs

Apistogramma viejita ♀ with its characteristic black colouration on throat and belly

Colour-morph III was found to inhabit an idyllic small oasis, whose lagoon and water-course were set up relatively deep and whose slightly ascending banks were vegetated with a slender grass-like plant similar to the swamp-plants of the genus *Eleocharis*. The small, partly shallow water-body housed a variety of fishes, but *Apistogramma viejita* could only be found in the very shallow, up to 5 cm deep zones of the banks amongst dense grass. This variety is rather drab if compared with both the other morphs and its assignment to the species *A. viejita* may not be a final conclusion.

Here, females were caught in the breeding colours characteristic for this species. The water was very soft and acidic also at this site. Its temperature was measured at 28,5 °C at 15.00 hrs. whilst the air-temperature was 37,5 °C in the shade at the same time. This oasis was embanked by palmtrees which provided shade to the water all day round. It was situated only a few kilometres east of the Rio Manacacias.

Care

Keeping *Apistogramma viejita* in an aquarium is not difficult. An adequate environment is created by a dense vegetation and ample caves amongst rock constructions. The natural shyness of this species can only be helped if numerous hiding-facilities and some peaceful company fishes are provided. Since most of the specimens offered are wild-caught fish, attention need most definitely be paid on the water-values of their original biotopes and soft, acidic water should exclusively be used.

The species is sensitive towards intestine parasites and preventive treatment is therefore advisable. Care should especially be taken when *Tubifex* or Red Mosquito-larvae are fed. This kind of live food should be conditioned before use. *Apistogramma viejita* is an interesting aquarium-fish.

Provided with a varying diet and regular exchanges of water every fortnight, the specimens will soon start

breeding.

This species also forms a male-mother-family structure in which the male defends a claimed territory and the female cares for the fry.

The success of breeding however depends on the use of soft, acidic water. *Apistogramma viejita* is not very productive although breeds of 60 to 80 juveniles from large parental specimens are not especially rare. As is the case in all species of *Apistogramma*, this species is a cave brooder. The eggs, larvae, and subsequent juveniles are cared for by the female only and the male is not allowed to come close to or even participate in the parental care for the offspring before their second or third week of life. The young fish are capable of feeding on newly hatched nauplii of *Artemia salina* without problems. They are cared for by the parents for approximately four to six weeks when another spawning may take place.

The most important preconditions for a healthy development and growth are feeding them several times per day and very clean water which may induce the necessity of frequent partial water-exchanges.

The Genus Apistogrammoides
MEINKEN, 1965

The genus *Apistogrammoides* is monotypical which means that it holds only a single species. As the generic name already indicates there is a very close relationship with the species of *Apistogramma* which is not only restricted to a large amount of superficial resemblance but also includes the general behavioural pattern.

The most important point of distinction between these two genera is the number of spines present in the anal fin. Whilst six to nine of those spines are found in *Apistogrammoides*, the species of *Apistogramma* usually have only three. The exceptions are however *Apistogramma luelingi*, *A. hoignei*, and *A. commbrae* which frequently or even regularly have four spines. The presence of five or six anal fin spines in *Apistogramma*-species was only found in extremely rare and exceptional cases.

The distribution of the genus ranges over the central and lower Rio Ucayali and the upper Amazon region. Its one and only representative is one of the smallest Cichlids known.

▶ *Apistogrammoides pucallpaensis*

MEINKEN, 1965

Distribution of *Apistogrammoides pucallpaensis*

The only species of the genus is a real dwarf with the males reaching total lengths of around 4 cm and the females just over 3 cm. The body is relatively high and strongly compressed laterally. The caudal fin is rounded lacking pointed tips. The anterior membranes of the dorsal fin are not enlarged. The top half of the body of the males is greyish brown to dark grey whilst the bottom half is whitish. The flanks have a pretty metallic glimmer. The scales are distinctly set off from each other by being bordered dark. Beginning at the upper lip, a black lateral band extends up to the base of the caudal fin.

The nape and the back are marked with some indistinct cloudy black blotches. An arched black band runs from the nape through the eye down to the lower angle of the gill-cover. The base of the tail is marked with three black spots in a vertical row which are framed by a narrow bright golden corona. The lower half of the head, and the area of the gill-cover especially, shine green whilst the lips have a metallic blueish green glimmer. The caudal fin

Apistogrammoides pucallpaensis ♂

160

is wine-red with a pattern of tiny light blue dots. The dorsal fin is bordered with black and gleams yellowish green whereas the anal fin is blueish green and also has a broad black bordering. The pectoral fins are colourless and translucent, the ventral fins show some light shades of blue with the anterior spines being coloured black.

The much less colourful females are basically brownish, but may display a metallic greenish gleam on the flanks. Some bright green speckles may mark the gill-covers. A dark lateral band which extends from the upper lip to the base of the tail may be overlaid with five to six transversal bars in a state of excitement. The pectoral and ventral fins are more or less colourless, the dorsal fin is green, and the anal fin coloured yellow. The determination of the sexes on the basis of colouration is therefore fairly easy.

Specific traits

are the spots on the base of the tail which are arranged in a vertical row and the transversal band on the caudal peduncle in front of them.

In comparison with the species of *Apistogramma,* the presence of up to nine spines in the anal fin is the most important and obvious point of distinction.

The
natural habitats

of *Apistogrammoides pucallpaensis* lie in northern Peru and the extreme south of Columbia in the catchment areas of the Rio Ucayali and the upper Amazon River. During the years 1984 and 1985 we had opportunity to examine several localities of this species more closely (STAECK 1987). Water-temperatures of 23,1 to 26 °C were established, and the conductivity ranged between 127 and 510 µS/cm.

The total hardness varied from 4 to 17 °dH, the carbonate hardness from 5 to 16 °dH. The pH was constantly 7,1. According to our observation this cichlid prefers to reside immediately below the water-surface where cover is provided by a carpet of floating plants as is so commonly the case on the edge of white-water biotopes.

Apistogrammoides pucallpaensis ♀

Care

For the husbandry of these small fish, separate aquaria should be utilized.

If there is no other option than to keep them in large community tanks, special protective means must be taken for these "dwarfs". Of course, no large, aggressive, or too nervous fishes should be kept with them. Furthermore, extensive zones of dense vegetation should cover a dark substrate of fine grain. Several rock constructions and small caves are also important. In the case of wild-caught specimens only live food will be accepted and the nauplii of the Brine Shrimp are an adequately sized prey. The water should be of soft to moderately hard quality with a pH of around 7. The temperature may range around 28 °C. A high standard of cleanliness should be obligatory.

Provided a not too large number of company fishes and a healthy plant-growth, this type of husbandry should not be too difficult. The fish preferably reside near the ground amongst the plants and if sufficient cover is available between plants, rocks, and pieces of bog-oak, their initial shyness will soon vanish.

Their interesting behaviour is especially noteworthy during

breeding

periods. The parental care is little different from that of the species of *Apistogramma* except for a few details. In *Apistogrammoides pucallpaensis* an intermediate stage between a male-mother- and a father-mother-family structure can be observed. The parental specimens spawn between rocks or branches of wood. The female takes over the task to care for the eggs and the larvae. Once the juveniles begin to swim it can be observed that the male also temporarily guides the offspring. Initially it is usually the female, but sometimes also the male which stay in the dense school of the juveniles, or the male even guides a small group independently and separately from the female. Despite their small size the young fish are capable of feeding on newly hatched nauplii of the Brine Shrimp immediately once they have begun to swim free. They grow surprisingly rapid during the first days. After approxi-

mately three weeks the school departs and the young fish become independent. Taking the small size into consideration this species is fairly productive and a single clutch of an adult pair may result in up to 80 juveniles.

The Genus Biotoecus
EIGENMANN & KENNEDY, 1903

With only two species — one of which was only described in 1989 — the genus *Biotoecus* belongs to the smallest genera of Cichlids. It has been given little attention by the aquaristic enthusiasts, one reason for which may be the fact that there were almost no imports.

Both species of *Biotoecus* have a fairly unusual body-shape which makes their identification easy. One of the features characteristic for the genus is a slender body with a pointed head and an unusually elongate caudal peduncle. Another trait which is very unusual amongst South American Cichlids is the ratio of spines and rays in the dorsal fin. With the exceptions of the genera *Symphysodon* and *Pterophyllum* all South American Cichlids have more spines than rays, but both species of *Biotoecus* have more rays in the dorsal fin.

Originally it was generally presumed that the genus *Biotoecus* would belong to the cladistic group of the Geophagines. KULLANDER (1989) could however demonstrate that the resemblance of the species-group is of superficial nature only so that it is now unclear who the closest allies of both the *Biotoecus*-species are.

The distribution range of the genus *Biotoecus* is relatively small being restricted to the northern parts of South America. Localities are known from the Orinoco region in Venezuela and from the catchments of the Rio Negro and the Amazon River in Brazil. Although the fishes inhabit fairly easily accessible areas they have surprisingly infrequently been caught. It is therefore to be presumed that they do not have high population densities in the areas inhabited. It is however also possible that they have simply been overlooked due to their small sizes.

▶ *Biotoecus opercularis*
(STEINDACHNER, 1875)

Although this Dwarf Cichlid ranks amongst those longest known to science, it has remained almost unnoticed by the aquarists up to date. It was described as *Saraca opercularis* by the zoologist STEINDACHNER of the Vienna museum more than hundred years ago. Since the generic name was however preoccupied, EIGENMANN & KENNEDY replaced it with their name *Biotoecus* in 1906.

Reaching a maximum total length of just under 5 cm *Biotoecus opercularis* is one of the smallest Cichlids known. It has a pointed head and a fairly slender body which ends in an unusually elongate caudal peduncle. The colouration of this fish is far from being spectacular or even conspicuous. Except for the whitish belly region it is mainly greyish green. In certain situation of light the gill-covers and flanks however assume a delicate light green gleam. Five dark dorsal blotches mark the area between the base of the dorsal fin and the

Distribution of *Biotoecus opercularis*

caudal peduncle. In addition to the distinct caudal spot there are another six of those spots at mid-body of which the anterior three may fuse with the dorsal ones to form mood-

Male of *Biotoecus opercularis*

163

dependent transversal bars. All fins are more or less transparent. Breeding females have orange to slightly brownish red coloured ventral fins.

The distinction of the sexes does not cause problems as there is a distinct sexual dimorphism present. Adult males have clearly enlarged ventral fins and old specimens have filamentous prolongations of the top and bottom edges of the caudal fin.

Specific traits

of *Biotoecus opercularis* are the body-shape, the unusually elongate caudal peduncle, and the presence of three spines in the anal fin.

Similar species

A similar species is of course the second representative of the genus, *Biotoecus dicentrarchus*. This species however has the membranes of the first two spines of the dorsal fin enlarged. Another specific feature is that there are only two spines in the anal fin.

The

natural habitats

of *Biotoecus opercularis* lie in the north of Brazil where the fish preferably inhabits black-water rivers and accordingly has a fairly wide distribution. The localities recorded to date concentrate in the catchment of the left tributaries of the Amazon River between the Rio Negro and the Rio Trombetas. In the region dominated by the Rio Negro, the species has in others been caught in the vicinity of the town of Barcelos, in the area of the Anavilhanas Islands, in the Rio Urubaxi, and in the Rio Branco.

Care

For the maintanance of *Biotoecus opercularis* a small aquarium with a length of half a metre may be adequate. Its bottom should be covered with a few centimetres thick layer of fine sand. In order to feel at ease, the shy fish require much cover and many hiding-facilities. Accordingly, the tank should be decorated with a dense ground-vegetation. Using bog-

oak roots cavities and caves can be created which are required by the fish as breeding-sites.

The small mouth indicates that these fish feed on very small prey, preferably invertebrates. Their diet should therefore consist of e. g. mosquito-larvae or tiny species of shrimp.

The

breeding

in captivity has repeatedly been successful. As is the case in many other species of Dwarf Cichlids, *Biotoecus opercularis* is an adapted cave brooder which spawns on the ceiling of a breeding-cave. Digging at the subsequent spawning site is obviously part of the courtship behaviour. During periods of parental care, the partners form a father-mother-family with a strictly organized work-sharing between male and female. After spawning the female exclusively cares for the eggs and larvae inside the breeding-cave whilst the male protects the breeding-territory. As soon as the fry has however completed the larval stage both parents jointly guide and guard the school of juveniles.

The rearing of the offspring is difficult in so far that the young fish are too small to feed even on newly hatched nauplii of the Brine Shrimp. During their first days they are therefore to be fed with an alternative type of food, e. g. a "milk" of fine-powdered dry-food.

For a successful breeding it is absolutely necessary to emulate the conditions of the natural biotopes which means that only clean and acidic water guarantees a healthy development of the embryos. KILIAN (1989) reported on a successful breeding at a water-temperature of 28 Celsius, a conductivity of 20 to 38 micro-Siemens/cm, and pH values between 6,6 and 6,8.

The Genus Crenicara
STEINDACHNER, 1875

also holds only two species and is thus another of the very small Cichlid genera. It was however temporarily a fairly large genus in the past when one followed the opinion of the English ichthyologist REGAN (1905) and assigned to it all species which aquarists generally had referred to as the "Chequered Cichlids". In 1990, KULLANDER came back to the arrangement already suggested by STEINDACHNER and re-transferred the smaller "Chequered Cichlids" to the genus *Dicrossus*.

The two high-backed, much larger species were the only ones left in the genus *Crenicara*. The maximum total length of the males of these species makes it difficult to still regard them as "Dwarf Cichlids".

Together with the single representative of the genus *Mazarunia* and the species of the closely allied genus *Dicrossus*, they form the group of the Crenicarines. Typical features of the species of *Crenicara* are the high-backed body-shape, the chequered spotted pattern on the flanks of the body, the small, low-set mouth, and the orange-red coloured ventral fins of the female fish.

The genus *Crenicara* inhabits a wide area in Guyana and the Amazon basin. In the south, records from the central Rio Ucayali, the upper course of the Rio Madeira, and the upper Rio Guaporé mar the limits of their range. The two species have an allopatric distribution which means that they do not occur together.

Although the *Crenicara*-species can actually be warmly recommended for a husbandry in an aquarium, they have been receiving much less appreciation than the small "Chequered Cichlids" of the genus *Dicrossus*. A reason for this may certainly be the fact that they are less frequently imported since their population density in their natural habitats is sparse and catching them takes a lot of effort.

Shallow zones near the banks are the preferred biotopes of species of *Apistogramma* and *Crenicichla*.

◗ *Crenicara latruncularium*
KULLANDER & STAECK, 1990

The name of this only very recently described Cichlid (lat. *tabula latruncularia* = chess-board) refers to the chequered pattern of dark blotches which marks the flanks of these fish. Live specimens do however not often display this pattern since it is highly dependent on the mood and state of excitement. The "chess-board" pattern appears most distinctly in situations of distress. It is reduced to a longitudinal row of three to four blotches in the central parts of the anterior body in specimens in a neutral disposition. The rows of dark blotches fuse to form two lateral stripes in breeding females.

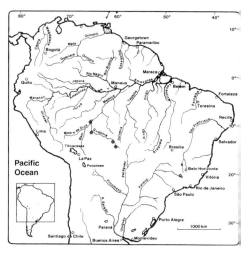

Distribution of *Crenicara latruncularium*

Specific traits

of live specimens are the colour-patterns of the lower head-region.

Crenicara latruncularium displays a pattern of three to four obliquely arranged gleamy green lines on the reddish brown ground-colour of the cheeks. The gill-covers have a very similar colour-pattern, but here it is much more irregular. This feature is much more distinct in adult males than in females.

Male of *Crenicara latruncularium*

Similar species

Crenicara punctulatum
An important feature for distinguishing between the two species of *Crenicara* is the number of spines in the dorsal fin. Whilst *Crenicara punctulatum* has 16 to 17 of which, *Crenicara latruncularium* usually has only 15. The first mentioned species never has 15, the latter never has 17.

The Chequered Cichlids of the genus *Dicrossus* are distinctly smaller in size.

The

natural habitat

as known from the localities to date is confined to the border region between Brazil and Bolivia and covers the catchments of the Rivers Guaporé and Mamoré. The fish was collected amongst others in the vicinity of the towns of Pontes e Lacerda and Vila Bela in Mato Grosso. All sites were characterized by a rich growth of the aquatic plants *Echinodorus* sp., *Ottelia brasiliensis*, *Eichhornia azurea*, *E. diversifolia*, and *Cabomba piauhyensis* amongst which the fish resided.

In most the cases the water-bodies were more or less static. One locality, i.e. a sand-bank in the Guaporé, however had a remarkably strong current. Other species of fishes recorded by us from the same biotopes were several species of *Corydoras*, numerous Tetras, and the Cichlids *Apistogramma trifasciata*, *A. inconspicua*, *Aequidens plagiozonatus*, *Mesonauta festivus*, and *Satanoperca pappaterra*.

One of the authors performed water-analyses at three different localities and recorded water-temperatures of between 20 and 24 °C, pH-values of 6,0 to 7,1, and a conductivity of 20 to 70 micro-Siemens/cm. The total as well as the carbonate hardness of the always crystal-clear, almost colourless water was below the detectable level of 1 °dH.

Care

According to experiences made so far, this is a rather easy, but fairly skittish species. It should therefore be kept in a large community aquarium together with other South American fishes of a more vivid temperament. All on its own in a separate species-tank, this Cichlid tends to exclusively reside hidden amongst plants.

It is furthermore crucial not to disturb these sensible fish unnecessarily since they react with week-long fear to any greater change in their environment or to catching. An adequate decoration includes a substrate of fine sand and a dense vegetation from which *Echinodorus* species should not be omitted.

Breeding

Crenicara latruncularium belongs to the polygamous substratum brooders.

Observation in a large community aquarium showed that the males maintain a territory with several spawning sites which may serve a number of females as territories. As is the case in other open breeders, the fish spawn on a horizontal substratum which, in my specimens, always was a large leaf of a Sword-plant *(Echinodorus)*.

After spawning the females drives her partner away from the clutch. As soon as the larvae are hatched they are transferred to a shallow depression in the sand which has been prepared before. All direct actions of parental care are exclusively performed by the female fish.

Table 23

Location:	Sand-bank in the Rio Guaporé 20 km downstream from Vila Bela da Santissima Trinidade
Clarity:	crystal clear
Colour:	none
pH:	6,3
Total hardness:	<1 °dH
Carbonate hardness:	<1 °dH
Conductivity:	20 µS
Depth:	up to 1 m
Current:	strong
Water-temperature:	20 °C
Date:	8.8.1987
Time:	11.00 hrs

◗ *Crenicara punctulatum*
(GÜNTHER, 1863)

This species rarely shows the characteristic "chess-board" pattern and when present, it is of a more faint intensity. A very dark lateral band however is usually present. The males display a yellowish grey to bright yellow colouration of the body whereas females are rather whitish grey. The ventral and anal fins of the females are fire-red.

Both sexes may occasionally show other colourations and patterns.

Male specimens grow up to approximately 12 cm whilst females are fully grown at just under 8 cm. The species is peaceful and ideal for a community aquarium.

Distribution of *Crenicara punctulatum*

Specific traits

are the presence of more than 15 spines in the dorsal fin and the yellow colouration of the chest and belly in the male specimens.

Similar species

Crenicara latruncularium has only 15 dorsal spines and displays obliquely arranged, greenish shining streaks on its reddish brown cheeks. All the species of *Dicrossus* are more slender and much smaller.

Crenicara punctulatum ♀

168

The
natural habitat.

A few individual catches of *Crenicara punctulatum* were made in the region between Pucallpa and Iquitos in Peru. Specimens from here slightly differ regarding their colouration from those of other localities by the Peruvian specimens having more orange shaded bellies and lower caudal regions. Other records were made south of Manaus, in the catchment of the Rio Madeira in Brazil, and in the vicinity of Gluck Island in the area of the Essequibo River in Guyana.

Care

According to experiences made so far, care of this interesting Cichlid is not always easy. Medium size aquaria with moderately hard to soft water are adequate if richly planted. As this species is very shy by its nature, one should not forego for some company fishes, such as Characines, Live-bearing Toothcarps, or small South American Cichlids in order to create an environment where interesting obser-

vations are possible. For a long-term husbandry a varying diet is as obligatory as a "healthy" water poor in nitrate and of slightly acidic quality. Care must be taken if diseases are treated since the species reacts very sensitively to chemicals.

The
breeding

of *Crenicara punctulatum* is not difficult and has repeatedly been successful. Female and male jointly choose a spawning site whereby the female plays the more active part. By intense "cleaning", i.e. plucking from a leaf-surface, she defines the chosen site where eventually up to 150 eggs are being laid in varying intervals during a period of approximately half an hour. In between, these are fertilized by the male. Thereafter, the male is driven away from the spawning locality and the female solely cares for the clutch. Once the larvae have hatched the intensity slightly decreases and approximately seven days later the juveniles begin to swim. Freshly hatched nauplii of *Artemia salina* should be offered as first food.

Crenicara punctulatum ♂

The female guides the offspring for approximately three weeks. On reaching 2 cm in size, the young fish already develop the typical red ventral and anal fins.

The number of juveniles is relatively small in comparison with the large number of eggs laid and it would be interesting to find out as to how far the result can be enhanced in very soft, acidic water. Prof. Dr. Dietrich OHM of the Institute for Psychology of the Technical University of Berlin (Germany) made some highly interesting observations on *C. punctulatum*. Due to the conditions in its natural habitats a change of the sex, i.e. from female to male, is possible.

The results were obtained in numerous experiments with the following particulars: In a school of 10 juveniles, one specimen always grew larger and turned out to be a male, easily recognizable by the originally intensely red coloured ventral and anal fins loosing their colour and becoming the two to three times longer fins with their characteristic blueish shining colouration. The body-colouration also changed accordingly. During the phase of change, the different behavioural patterns of both sexes become visible. This male henceforth mates with the remaining females. If it is removed, the next largest and strongest female begins to change into a male. The development, or change of the sex respectively, continues until the complete transformation of all females. It is apparently the first case of sex change recorded in Cichlids.

Aquarium-fish collectors of Puerto Gaitan in the Llanos of eastern Columbia sort their catch into plastic-bag lined boxes of different colours before transporting them to Bogota.

The Genus Crenicichla
HECKEL, 1840

Containing approximately 50 described species and more than 30 scientifically unrevised forms, *Crenicichla* presently is the largest genus of South American Cichlids (KULLANDER 1990). Since its representatives are moderately large to large Cichlids with an almost exclusively predatory ecology, they play no important role in the hobby. By reaching lengths of 20 to 30 cm in many cases, they are rather appreciated for the pot in the countries of their distribution.

However, seven species have been described which can be considered true Dwarf Cichlids due to their small body-sizes and which are recommendable fishes for the aquarium. Other Dwarf-*Crenicichla* are known from the collections of zoological museums (KULLANDER 1990).

Generic features of these Cichlids, which are also referred to as Pike Cichlids on account of their predatory ecology, are a very elongate, slender body and a large, deeply bisected mouth with a usually slightly protruding lower jaw. Some of the smaller *Crenicichla* however feed on small prey and have a differently shaped mouth.

Some of the smaller *Crenicichla* species have a very limited distribution which is the result of a strictly rheophile ecology.

They have adapted to extremely torrential waters and are thus preferably found in the immediate vicinity of rapids. Rheophile *Crenicichla* have been described from the rapids of the Rio Tocantins, the Rio Trombetas, and the Rio Tapajós. Due to their limited distribution and the small size, they have been discovered only recently, and their descriptions were published only at the end of the eighties and in the early nineties.

A biotope of *Crenicichla notophthalmus* at the Rio Negro

◗ *Crenicichla compressiceps*
PLOEG, 1986

This attractively coloured Dwarf Cichlid is one of the species which have become known to science as well as to the aquarists only relatively late. For example, it was imported to Germany in 1990 for the very first time.

The maximum total length of male specimens does supposedly not exceed nine centimetres with females staying approximately two centimetres smaller. Compared with other dwarf forms of the genus *Crenicichla,* this species has a fairly high, compressed body-shape. Another characteristic feature is the laterally compressed head to which its scientific name refers. The fish has a mainly greyish green to dark grey ground-colouration with the lower head and belly regions being always distinctly lighter. The flanks are marked with six or seven narrow transversal bars of light yellow colour, the first two of which extend to the lateral band only which itself is exclusively visible in the anterior portion of the body. The

Distribution of *Crenicichla compressiceps*

upper parts of these two transversal bars are often much darker so that one might refer to them as a shoulder-blotch. All unpairy fins are coloured yellow.

Male of *Crenicichla compressiceps* from the Rio Araguaia

The caudal fin as well as the posterior sections of the dorsal and anal fins are patterned with very narrow dark transversal lines.

Depending on the collecting site these three fins either show a narrow black or a bright red edge. Since a sexual dimorphism is almost non-existent, the determination of the sexes is extremely difficult in sub-adult specimens. An indication may be given by the vertical striped pattern of the unpairy fins which is more distinct in the males.

The

specific traits

of *Crenicichla compressiceps* include its small size, the relatively high body, the pattern of light stripes on a dark ground-colour, and the pattern of vertical lines on the caudal fin.

Amongst the

Similar species

there are *Crenicichla regani* and *C. notophthalmus* to be mentioned due to their small sizes. Both species however have entirely different colourations; for example female specimens have a conspicuous black pattern in the dorsal fins.

The

natural habitats

of *Crenicichla compressiceps* lie in the north of Brazil where this Cichlid apparently endemically inhabits the catchment areas of the Rio Tocatins and the Rio Araguaia. Most the localities are rapids or torrential water-courses with mainly rocky grounds. Since however records have also been made in other types of biotopes, this fish does not appear to belong to the extremely rheophile species.

Detailed information on the ecology of *Crenicichla compressiceps* was published by STAWIKOWSKI & WARZEL (1991). They observed these Cichlids in the vicinity of rapids near the banks where heaps of rocks were scattered on a sandy ground. Cavities amongst rocks or caves which had been created by the fish themselves underneath rocks formed spawning-sites and the centres of breeding territories in these bio-

topes. They were jointly defended by a bonded pair. It appears to be noteworthy that the specimens were obviously extremely bound to their chosen locality and upon being disturbed and driven away, always returned to their territory.

Measurements taken revealed a clarity of up to two metres, water-temperatures between 25 and 28 °C, and a pH between 6,0 and 6,5. The total as well as the carbonate hardness were below 1 °dH (STAWIKOWSKI 1991).

Care

Crenicichla compressiceps requires an aquarium which provides enough space and hiding-facilities since it is a highly territorial fish which viciously defends its domain against conspecifics. Due to an ecology near the ground, the available ground-space is obviously more important than the height of the aquarium. In order to create an environment similar to nature, sand and rocks are required.

Planting the tank is of course possible if it does not confine the swimming space too much. Due to its small mouth this Dwarf Cichlid feeds on small items and should therefore be offered appropriately sized prey.

During times of

breeding

Crenicichla compressiceps forms a father-mother-family structure with a clearly defined "work-sharing" between the parents. Being cave brooders, they prefer a spawning site under a rock from where they have removed the sand. Initially, only the female cares for the clutch whilst the male guards the territory. Once the juveniles swim both parents jointly guide and protect the school.

The breeding is not very difficult and was also successful in relatively hard water of 17 °dH total hardness and a pH of 6,8 (STAWIKOWSKI 1991).

▶ *Crenicichla notophthalmus*
REGAN, 1913

Distribution of *Crenicichla notophthalmus*

was described as early as 1913 by the English ichthyologist REGAN when he was busy with a revision of a group of Cichlids allocated to this genus and is thus one of the species long known. The original description was based on two specimens with total lengths of 60 and 65 millimetres respectively which both originated from the vicinity of the city of Manaus. Since then it was found out that the maximum length of the males may be approximately 13 centimetres. Females grow distinctly smaller. Since this species has a clearly defined sexual dimorphism it is easy to distinguish between males and females. The females are prettier with the back being greyish green and the lower region of the body light blue. A fairly conspicuous trait of mature specimens is the orange coloured belly. The pattern of the anteriorly blueish violet to deep red coloured dorsal fin is especially splendid in females. There are one or more roundish black blotches which are encompassed by a partly signal-red, partly white aura. The upper edge of the caudal fin is marked with a white

Female of *Crenicichla notophthalmus*

or light blue band which is bordered dark on the top. The posterior part of the iris and its lower edge are bright red. Depending on the mood, eleven dark transversal bars may be present on the upper half of the body.

Male specimens are greyish green above the fairly narrow lateral band and beige below. The posterior portion of the gill-cover has a tinge of greenish yellow. The unpairy fins may be pale wine-red and have a narrow black edge and a whitish blue submarginal line.

The most important of the

specific traits

by which this Cichlid may be recognized is the dorsal fin of adult males. The membranes between the first five dorsal spines of Crenicichla notophthalmus are distinctly produced and fused only at the base.

Similar species

A subject of possible confusion is *Crenicichla regani* which has about a same size. In addition the females have a similarly patterned dorsal fin. Males of this species however lack produced membranes in the dorsal fin.

All the other species with black blotches in the dorsal fin, e.g. *Crenicichla proteus,* additionally differ in size which usually exceeds 15 centimetres.

According to the present state of investigation, the

natural habitats

of *Crenicichla notophthalmus* are confined to the catchment of the Rio Negro. One of the authors was able to catch this fish on the left bank of the river near the Anavilhanas Island-group where juveniles of four to six centimetres lived together with *Apistogramma gephyra* and *Taeniacara candidi* concealed amongst a thick layer of submerged leaf-litter which covered the ground of the bank of the watercourse.

Care

Since this fish has a fairly well pronounced intraspecific aggression which may even be directed towards the partner outside seasons dedicated to reproduction, it is recommendable to utilize aquaria as large as possible. In addition to an at least partly dense vegetation, a couple of cave-like hiding-places amongst roots and rocks are necessary. The bottom of the tank should be covered with a layer of coarse sand. Being a predatory fish, this Cichlid requires a diet of appropriately sized live food including other fishes and shrimps.

Breeding

will only be successful if the water-values in the aquarium match those of the natural habitat. Otherwise the embryos will develop abnormally and are eventually eaten by the mother. This means that the fish must be kept in fairly soft water with a distinctly acidic reaction. Spawning takes place in a cave-like hiding-place, and it is the female which directly cares for the offspring whilst the male is in charge of the protection of the territory.

Table 24

Location:	Lago Arará on the left bank of the lower Rio Negro
Clarity:	clear
Colour:	brown, tea-coloured
pH:	4,3
Total hardness:	<1°dH
Carbonate hardness:	<1°dH
Conductivity:	10 µS
Depth:	up to 50 cm
Current:	none
Water-temperature:	28°C
Air-temperature:	26°C
Date:	21.3.1987
Time:	9.00 hrs

◗ *Crenicichla regani*
PLOEG, 1989

This Cichlid has been known to aquarists for many years, but was referred to under a variety of names until it was formally described scientifically recently. The maximum length of this fish should be somewhere around 13 centimetres with females being considerably smaller. Due to the fact that the colour-pattern is subject to great variation throughout the wide distribution range, a description can only be relative.

Male specimens often have a dull grey body-colouration. Depending on the mood, a pattern consisting of a relatively broad lateral band and ten to eleven dark transversal bars in the region of the back may become visible. The cheeks and the gill-covers are usually yellow.

The posterior section of the dorsal fin may be light or deep wine-red in colour depending

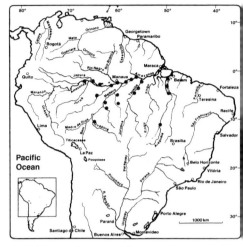

Distribution of *Crenicichla regani*

on the origin of a particular specimen. The upper edge of the caudal fin is black with a

Female of *Crenicichla regani*

whitish blue and a brownish red stripe below. The hind half and the lower edge of the iris are bright red.

The by far more colourful females can easily be identified by their reddish bellies. Furthermore, they have one or more irregularly shaped pitch black blotches in the dorsal fin which are often framed by a white aura. In rare cases these blotches may be fused to form a banded pattern.

The

specific traits

of this Cichlid include its small body-size, the relatively broad lateral band, the more or less distinct lanceolate shape of the caudal fin, and the conspicuous pattern of the dorsal fin in the females.

Most of the

similar species

in which the females have comparably patterned dorsal fins grow much larger. An exception may be *Crenicichla notophthalmus,* a species which can however easily distinguished by means of the differently shaped dorsal fin. The membranes between the anterior spines are distinctly produced. This species furthermore differs by having a clearly narrower lateral band.

The

natural habitats

of *Crenicichla regani* are spread over Brazil. Here, the species inhabits a remarkably vast area of central South America covering a considerable part of the Amazon region. Larger tributaries to the Amazon River from which this species has been recorded include amongst others the Rio Madeira, Rio Tefé, Rio Tapajos, Rio Tocantins, and the Rio Trombetas.

Due to the vast distribution range it is not surprising that the fish has adapted to a variety of biotopes. Specimens were caught in very torrential water-courses as well as in more or less stagnant waters.

Furthermore, it is remarkable that the range extends very far to the south, i.e. into

regions where the water-temperatures may drop to only 20 °C during the winter. Despite all the mentioned differences a feature shared by all the water-courses inhabited by *Crenicichla regani* appears to be the presence of fairly soft, distinctly acidic water.

Care

of this Cichlid requires an awareness of the fact that it has a pronounced territorial nature and may behave fairly unsocial towards conspecifics. This extreme amount of aggression may even be directed towards the breeding partner outside the reproduction season. Despite their comparatively small size the fish therefore should be kept in aquaria as large as possible which are furnished with many hiding-facilities in thickets of aquatic plants and caves below rocks or pieces of bog-oak. Coarse sand is a recommendable substrate.

Since this Cichlid has a mainly predatory ecology, it requires powerful food accordingly. An adequate diet therefore should include mosquito larvae and shredded meat of fish and shrimps.

Breeding

Crenicichla regani is a cave brooder which rears its offspring in a father-mother-family. Whilst the direct care for the clutch is performed by the female, it is the male's task to keep potential predators of the eggs and juveniles out of the breeding territory.

The fish preferably spawn on the ceiling of a cavity which they create themselves below a rock or a root by removing substrate. It has unfortunately turned out that the reproduction of these fish in captivity is only successful when the water-values in the aquarium come close to the conditions found in the natural habitats.

Proper development of the eggs is possible only in very soft, distinctly acidic water.

The Genus Dicrossus
STEINDACHNER, 1875

was described more than hundred years ago by the scientist STEINDACHNER of the Vienna museum on occasion of the description of *Dicrossus maculatus* and thus ranks amongst the longest known genera of Cichlid fishes. Subsequently, it was dumped by the English Ichthyologist REGAN in 1905 when its one and only representative was transferred to the genus *Crenicara*. Most of the succeeding authors followed this opinion and allocated to this genus all "Chequered Cichlids" known at their times. It was not before 1990 that the organization of REGAN was reversed again by KULLANDER. Since then the large, high-backed species are considered to belong to the genus *Crenicara* whereas the small slender "Chequered Cichlids" are again referred to as *Dicrossus*. Together with the sole representative of the genus Mazarunia and the two species of *Crenicara,* the Cichlids of the genus *Dicrossus* form the group of the Crenicarines.

The genus *Dicrossus presently* holds only two defined species. This is added by another two forms which have not yet been described. One of which is completely unknown to the aquarists and the other one has only been imported sporadically in a few single specimens. The distribution of the genus is restricted to the northeast of South America and definite records were made in the upper Orinoco, the Rio Negro, the Rio Tapajós, and the lower Amazon River exclusively (KULLANDER 1990).

Important features of the Cichlids of this genus are the slender and elongate body-shape, the small low-set mouth, and the "chess-board" pattern of spots on the flanks to which the common name "Chequered Cichlid" refers. All species are attractive fishes for the aquarium whose husbandry can however be recommended to those aquarists only who are experienced with the keeping of more complicated species.

Most of the species of *Dicrossus* feel really well in very soft, acidic water.

Dicrossus filamentosus inhabits the black-waters of the Rio Negro.

◗ Dicrossus filamentosus
(LADIGES, 1958)

Due to two different publications by its describer Prof. Dr. Werner LADIGES in two different years, there is some uncertainty about the date of the original description of this species. However, the paper titled "Bemerkungen zu einigen Neuimporten" published in the aquaristic journal "DATZ" in 1958 has clearly priority above the paper *"Crenicara filamentosa* spec. nov., ein neuer seltener Cichlide aus Südamerika" in the "Internationale Revue der gesamten Hydrobiologie" which was actually meant to be the original description, but which did not appear before 1959. The name *Dicrossus* sp. FERNANDEZ-Y'EPEZ 1969 is nothing but a synonym of this species.

This fish is the prettiest and unfortunately the only species of its genus offered more frequently by the pet-shops. Males reach a total length of around 8 or 9 cm, while their standard length, i.e. without the length of the caudal fin, is about 5 cm. In contrast, females grow

Distribution of *Dicrossus filamentosus*

up to just under 6 cm in total length. The difference in size is however based on the enormously produced streamers of the caudal fins of the males — otherwise both sexes

Dicrossus filamentosus ♂

179

have an almost equal body-length. These prolongations are characteristic for this species, and the scientific name refers to them. It is an unfailing feature to distinguish between the sexes and is developed already at a size of approximately 4 cm total length. To date, two differently patterned forms are known. Males

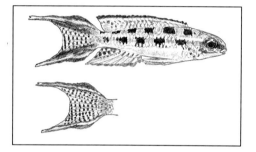

of the one form have a small speckled wedge marking the central part of the caudal fin and their respective females develop fire-red ventral fins and a partially equally coloured anal fin after the first spawning.

This colour-variety originates from the area of the Rio Negro in Brazil. Males of the second variety have a large spotted zone between the top and bottom borderings of the caudal fin and their females exclusively have transparent fins after the first spawning. They are found in the Columbian Orinoco region. Whether or not those females with a truncate, almost "bifurcate" − instead of a rounded − colourful bordered caudal fin may belong to a certain local variety is still to be investigated.

Specific traits

are the chequered lateral pattern which may be transformed into a lateral band during imposing or courtship behaviour and the extremely produced filaments of the top and bottom sections of the caudal fin of male specimens.

Similar species

Males of *Dicrossus maculatus* have a higher dorsal fin, long ventral fins, and no bifurcate, but a lanceolate, pointed caudal fin.

Table 25

Location:	Rio Guarrojo between La Calata and Abariba in eastern Columbia
Clarity:	clear
Colour:	brownish
pH:	5,3
Total hardness:	below 1 °dH
Carbonate hardness:	below 1 °dH
Conductivity:	1 to 3 µS at 30 °C
Nitrite:	below 0,1 mg/l
Depth:	up to 1 m
Current:	moderate
Water-temperature:	30 °C
Date:	13.3.1982
Time:	13.00 hrs

The
natural habitat

was described by Prof. Dr. Werner LADIGES as "probably on the upper Amazon River". On account of side-catches to the Red Neon-tetra (*Paracheirodon axelrodi*) we learnt about its occurrence in the Rio Negro region in northwestern Brazil. Collections made by the Swede T. HONGSLO recorded the fish from a second locality in the western Orinoco area. Whether or not these populations are connected is however still unknown. HONGSLO caught his specimens in the steppes along the Rio Guarrojo near where it flows into the Rio Vichada. The latter eventually mouthes into the Rio Orinoco near Puerto Narino where there is another collecting site. The region around Puerto Inirida, some 80 km more south, also holds biotopes inhabited by *Dicrossus filamentosus*. These are however forested regions where the species lives in small shallow water-courses.

The data captured at the collecting sites are highly interesting.

Whilst the air-temperature measured 29,5 °C between 9.00 and 13.00 hrs, that of the water was established at 31 °C. The pH was recorded to be 5,5. The water had a dark teacolour in the forest and was beige in the lagoon in the savannah area. The results of our own water-analyses in the upper course of the Rio Guarrojo are illustrated in Table 25.

The water-values of the individual savannah-lagoons may deviate from those indicated for the river, but in general they agree with regard to very soft and strongly acidic water in which the pH may considerably drop below 5. These extreme compositions should be taken into consideration when it comes to keeping or even breeding.

Care

Discrossus filamentosus actually requires small aquaria only since this is a small fish.

Moderately sized tanks however offer some advantages and those of 70 to 130 cm in length and a width of 40 or 50 cm are ideal for their successful keeping. Although the height of the aquarium is of secondary importance it should not fall short of 25 cm. An appropriate envi-ronment should include a substrate of fine gravel with a grain-size of one to two millimetres, a very dense plant-growth of preferably fine plants such as the Java-moss *Vesicularia dubyana* and the Java-fern *Microsorum pteropus*, but also of a few specimens of *Echinodorus*, and also some pieces of bog-oak and a few calcium-free stones.

For a successful long-term keeping, the quality of the water is obviously of utmost importance. Soft, acidic water with a total and carbonate hardness below 5 °dH, a pH below 6, and temperatures between 26 and 29 °C are essential. If these values are exceeded, the husbandry will fail on the long run.

An efficient filtration is furthermore crucial for the necessary aeration of the water. Regular exchanges of approximately a quarter of the water every week are very advisable. The species is sensitive to intestine parasites so that preventive treatment should be obligatory in certain intervals. The pet-shop industry will offer advice.

Dicrossus filamentosus ♀

Dicrossus filamentosus are extremely peace-loving and ideal for a community aquarium with other small fishes. Some more active species like Characines should definitely be present, but one should especially forego larger Cichlids in small tanks. Caves are not essentially necessary.

The

breeding

of this species is often very difficult and hardly ever successful if left to its natural course. Most breeders therefore prefer an artificial rearing which means they remove the fertilized eggs from the female and hatch them in a separate tank. It is however to be considered the last possibility since this kind of reproduction cheats the mother fish of important behavioural processes and may eventually lead to its entire suppression. Only the natural procedure of reproduction is recommendable although it may be written easier than done and artificial hatching may sometimes be the only way to reproduce a certain species. Experiments have shown that the natural reproduction is possible under certain conditions. What's the problem though? For the breeding of *Dicrossus filamentosus* one should use the aquarium described in the chapter on husbandry. The vegetation should be very dense so that fish have sufficient places to hide and thus zones providing security. The water must be very acidic, soft, and poor in nitrates. Values of 1 to 2 °dH in total and carbonate hardness lead to a conductivity below 60 micro-Siemens, and a pH around, or even better below 5 should be made available. The temperature may range between 28 and 29 °C. The filtration through peat has been proved to be of advantage. The pH need to be monitored constantly since such an extremely soft water is very instable. The breeding group, a male and one to three females, should be kept together with three or four not too large dither fish. These company fish in the breeding aquarium reduce the natural shyness of the "Chequered Cichlids" and thus allow more detailed studies. Nevertheless, this species requires a calm environment in and in front of the tank and situations which may cause distress have to be carefully avoided.

Despite adhering to all these recommendations, the breeder might still face a tough test of his patience. It is however nothing but patient waiting which may eventually lead to the ultimate goal.

First signs of an intention to spawn are an increasing frequency of courtship posings by both sexes and a more frequent plucking on a usually horizontal leaf whose vicinity of 10 to 15 cm is defended as a territory. Both partners replace their "chess-board pattern" by a dark lateral band of more contrast with increasing frequency. During this time the specimens are especially colourful. The spawning eventually only lasts approximately 30 minutes. The females lays on average 120 to 150 light ivory coloured eggs on the leaf she has so carefully "cleaned" before with the male fertilizing them between her individual laying-phases. Once the spawning is completed the male is chased away and the female cares for the eggs alone. The male may follow the motivation of another female already a short while later and father a second clutch. Once spawning is finalized there is no trace of bonding any more.

During these early stages the female is a very attentive mother. She resides above the clutch and fans fresh water over the eggs with strong movements of the pectoral fins almost without interruption.

The littering of particles of dirt and microscopic organisms on the eggs is thus prevented. Eggs which do not develop are carefully and attentively plucked out of the clutch. The above mentioned red colouration of the ventral fins appears at this stage. The following hours show whether all criterions for a successful development and rearing of the fry described above have been met. If this is not the case, the female would eat all the eggs and the hope for juveniles is — once more — destroyed. Approximately 48 hours later the larvae hatch and are subsequently relocated by the female several times a day. The site is changed at least once a day. Six to seven days after spawning on average their development is completed, and a "proud mother" guides a school of often more than 100 young fish through the aquarium. The juveniles immediately begin to feed on newly hatched nauplii of the Brine Shrimp. The devoted care of the mother unfortunately subsides subsequently and a part of the juveniles get lost in the large aquarium or become victims of the company fishes. They are however not the only ones which reduce the number of the young fish — the mother also appears to incidently swallow some when she collects them. This is now the second critical phase of the development. Experiences breeders say that if the female is unable to rear her juveniles without losses one should rather suck them up with a pipe and house them in a separate tank filled with the same water.

Despite all efforts to keep the water very clean — frequent partial exchanges of the water are necessary — and a varying diet, the growth-rate is not overwhelmingly large. At an age of approximately four month the young fish have grown to a mere 4 cm in total length.

At this stage one can already distinguish between the sexes.

Dicrossus filamentosus ♀ with juveniles

▶ *Dicrossus maculatus*
STEINDACHNER, 1875

Distribution of *Dicrossus maculatus*

After almost forty years a legend became reality when Arthur WERNER, Wolfgang FRIEDERICH, and Erich FRECH managed to import the mythical "Chequered Cichlid" *Dicrossus maculatus* again in 1988. Although the literature indicates that the fish would occur along the mighty Amazon River, the Brazilian Solimoes, and in numerous tributaries and lakes, it had been impossible to find this beautiful and interesting species before. It was A. WERNER who eventually caught a larger number of this fish in an area south of Santarem.

Dicrossus maculatus resembles the widely known *Dicrossus filamentosus* very much and only larger males exhibit distinct feature which distinguish them. Whilst male *Dicrossus filamentosus* develop a clearly lyreate, i.e. forked, caudal fin, the males of *Dicrossus maculatus* grow an oval to slightly lanceolate tail-fin and additionally much longer ventral fins with almost filamentous streamers.

Dicrossus maculatus ♂

Furthermore, the males of the latter species are slightly larger and may reach up to 9 cm in total length. In contrast, females do not grow much larger than 5 cm. *Dicrossus maculatus* was scientifically described by STEINDACHNER as early as in 1875. In 1936, Ernst AHL described his *Crenicara praetoriusi* which is considered a synonym according to today's knowledge. Werner LADIGES published about *D. maculatus* in 1951 for the last time. Thereafter it appears that only a minor number of specimens have been imported so that the species did not experience a wide distribution in the aquaria of the enthusiasts. The specimens caught in 1988 eventually made studies possible again. Interesting results disclosed a surprisingly close resemblance of *Dicrossus filamentosus*. Whilst however the black-water *D. filamentosus* turned out to be very instable if permanently kept in moderately hard, slightly alkaline water, observations made so far indicate that the clear-water *D. maculatus* is much more tolerant towards the same type of aquarium-water. Regardless of this fact, both species definitly require very clean water.

The description of the

breeding

of this fish by LADIGES in 1951 was largely confirmed by more recent observations, and there are many parallels with *D. filamentosus* also in this respect. This fish is a substratum brooder as well which spawns on a solid surface such as strong leaves or stones. Open caves like lying flower-pots are equally acceptable sites. As the eggs are transparent to slightly yellowish and relatively small, they are often overlooked. The female cares for the fry alone. The male dedicates himself to the protection of the territory on a large scale, but is not permitted near the clutch. *Dicrossus maculatus* tends to polygamy which means that one male tolerates several females in his territory and successively spawns with all of them. Due to this it is possible to simultaneously observe several females with their schools strolling through a large aquarium. The mothers attentively care for their offspring. In contrast to the red ventral fins of females of *D. filamentosus*, *D. maculatus*-females have yellow ones which are

bordered black after spawning. The anal fin is however coloured red. With the aid of the female the embryos break through the egg-shells after approximately three days at a

The Rio Chinipo, a typical clear-water river, during a period of low-water in the vicinity of the village of Chicosa on the Rio Ucayali in the south of Peru. The river is mainly inhabited by Cichlids and Catfishes.

temperature of circa 29 °C. They are immediately transported to small depressions in the substratum or hidden in nooks between plants or roots by the mother. These hiding-places may be changed several times a day. The female almost constantly stands above the developing fry and fans fresh water to them through movements of the body and the fins.

Another three to four days later the larvae are able to swim and roam through the breeding territory in a dense school below the mother fish. Individual run-aways are caught with the mouth by the mother and brought back to the school. "Antagonistic fishes" which come close to the school are viciously attacked and chased away. This protective and caring instinct as well as the dense school behaviour lasts some time.

Although these fish originate from moderately soft, almost neutral water according to present knowledge, soft, acidic water has proved to be of advantage for their captive breeding. Due to the fact that the swimming larvae are very small and have a tiny mouth it is necessary to provide them with adequately small food. Even freshly hatched nauplii of *Artemia salina* are usually too large as first food. The juveniles of one clutch may number 70 to 100. It is unfortunately no exception that only 5 % of the young fish are males so that there is a very unbalanced sex-ratio. This result is apparently favoured by low pH-values which seemingly generally favour the development of female offspring.

Dicrossus maculatus ♀

▶ *Dicrossus* sp.
(Red-finned *Dicrossus*)

This species was first introduced by the Dutch-man W.A. TOMEY in 1981 and has not yet been given a scientific name. The males of this new species reach a maximum size of 9 cm whilst female are fully grown at a total length of approximately 7 cm. These fish are usually very shy.

The species has a slender and elongate body-shape. The membranes of the dorsal fin are not produced and the colouration of this fin is mainly reddish violet. On its top it is bordered bordeaux-violet with a narrow light blue submarginal line. This colour-pattern is also recognizable in the spinous section of the dorsal fin near its base whereas the lower part of the rayed portion is transparent and uncoloured. The anal fin is almost completely reddish violet whilst this colouration is confined to the lower half of the caudal fin. Its upper

Distribution of *Dicrossus* sp. (Red-finned *Dicrossus*)

half is transparent and uncoloured except for a narrow bordeaux-violet hind edge with a

Dicrossus sp. (Red-finned *Dicrossus*)

187

narrow light blue submarginal line which run halfway down resembling the pattern of the dorsal fin. The ventral fins are light ivory in colour. The ground-colour is light grey in the upper and light ivory coloured in the lower portion of the body. The caudal stripe is well developed whilst a superorbital and a suborbital stripe are absent. A dark blotch marks the hind edge of the gill-cover. A row of four rectangular spots runs from the nape up to the base of the rayed section of the dorsal fin. Another three parallely arranged rows of rectangular or closely spaced dots, more precisely referred to as double-dots, extend from behind the head up onto the caudal peduncle. The central and lower row end parallely and close to each other immediately in front of the base of tail-fin.

Depending on the mood, the fish may display indications of pale transversal stripes between these two rows of dots over almost their entire length. Dorsal and anal fins are not produced. The shape of the caudal fin is oval, more rounded in female specimens. According to information received from Mr. TOMEY, the colouration is largely dependant on the individual's disposition. Illumination, decoration, and the presence of company fishes have a great influence.

Similar species

Dicrossus filamentosus males have a long filamentous lyreate caudal fin. This species furthermore has a "chess-board pattern" of two rows of alternating quadrangular blotches.

Dicrossus maculatus closely resembles this species regarding its habitus, but specimens of this species display a double-row of five alternating, fairly large, dark, almost quadrangular blotches on their flanks. This pattern could also be referred to as a "chess-board pattern".

The

natural habitat

of this fish lies in the catchment of the upper Rio Negro in Brazil.

So far, only individual specimens were sporadically imported into Europe which were mainly side-catches of the Red Neon-tetra

and *Dicrossus filamentosus.* The collection of the museum of Sao Paulo holds specimens which were caught in the Rio Marani (KULLANDER 1990).

W. A. TOMEY allegedly collected his specimens west of the city of Iquitos in northern Peru in a small unnamed stream in the dense rainforests between the Rio Mazan and the Rio Nanay which is exclusively accessible by means of a canoe. These water-courses are between 20 and 110 cm deep depending on the season. They have clear brownish water whose colour usually resembles "coke". After rainfalls this water becomes murky and light brown. No aquatic plants were recorded and it is only branchwork which has fallen or grown into the water, leaves, and sunken leaf-litter which provide cover for the fishes. This species is a ground-dweller which is, according to the present state of knowledge, not common in the described biotope.

Specific traits

are the three, respective four parallel rows of double-dots or rectangular spots on the flanks.

Care

The aquarists keeping this species should take sufficiently large aquaria with adequate hiding-facilities into consideration. A generous vegetation with a number of hiding-places amongst rock constructions, pieces of bog-oak, and bamboo-tubes are important. Placid company fishes which are not shy should be kept with them. One should definitely forego the aggressive fishes like certain Barbs or larger Cichlids. A fine substrate of very dark colour is recommendable. Slightly soft water and average temperatures of 27 °C appear to be necessary for a successful long-term husbandry.

The

breeding

of this species has not been successful despite intense attempts at various places under very different conditions.

The Genus Laetacara
KULLANDER, 1986

is a genus which has been described only very recently for a couple of Dwarf Cichlids. It is intended to hold those small Cichlids which were previously clustered in the genus *Aequidens*, i.e. in the *Aequidens dorsiger* species-group. Four scientifically described *Laetacara* species are presently recognized. There are however at least another two species known which undoubtedly also belong to this genus, but which still lack a formal scientific description. These two forms have already been kept in captivity. According to recent research there are hints that the species of Laetacara are not so closely related to the genus *Aequidens*, but more so with the species of *Cichlasoma*.

Regarding the colour-pattern the general generic features of *Laetacara* include a distinctly developed lateral spot and another, fairly conspicuous dark blotch in the centre of the dorsal fin. Both are often connected with each other by a broad dark band. Another trait shared by these Cichlids is a relatively high-backed and stout body which is little compressed laterally and which thus gives the fishes a fairly round appearance. There is no distinct sexual dimorphism.

The genus *Laetacara* is widely distributed in South America. The northern border of its range is formed by the catchment of the upper Orinoco in Venezuela, whilst in the south it is limited by the Paraguayan Paraná.

The small species of *Laetacara* are especially recommendable for a husbandry in the aquarium without reservations. Their pros include comparatively low space-requirements, their easy-to-meet environmental needs, their quite colourful patterns, and the fact that they not damage even very fragile plants. In contrast to the majority of other Dwarf Cichlids they are substratum brooders which rear their juveniles in a parental family structure.

Habitat of *Laetacara dorsigera* in Bolivia (Rio Paraguay)

The best known small species of this genus is

▶ *Laetacara curviceps*
(AHL, 1924)

in which the males reach approximately 8 cm and the females some 6 cm in total length. These small fish are very hardy in captivity.

They have become known relatively early and rank amongst the standard assortment of the aquaristic hobby ever since. The species is very colourful. Its sexual dimorphism is not always distinct and only recognizable with some certainty in adult specimens. Females are not only smaller in size, but also have shorter ventral fins and often a larger blotch at the base of the central portion of the dorsal fin which may, in direct comparison, be twice the size of that of the male. Juveniles are hard to distinguish from those of other small species.

Various colour-varieties are occasionally offered. For example, one morph is charac-terized by an additional fire-red band closely above and parallel to the front part of the lateral band. Deviations of the pattern on other parts of the body are also known.

Specific traits

Laetacara curviceps displays a dark lateral band which usually extends over the lateral spot up to the caudal fin. In comparison with related species its body-shape is slightly lower and more elongate. Furthermore, the turquoise-blue ground-colour is specific.

Similar species

Laetacara dorsigera has a different colouration, its lateral band does not exceed over the lateral spot, the body-shape is slightly higher, and the specimens appear to be shorter in length. Depending on the mood, the species may display a broad dark superorbital stripe and transversal bars on the tail.

Laetacaraq curviceps ♂

Laetacara sp., the "Orange-finned *Laetacara*" grows slightly larger, has a lateral band which does not extend over the lateral blotch, usually has a light green body-colouration, and a yellowish golden to yellowish orange coloured lower part of the caudal fin and anal fin. This species also displays a superorbital stripe and a barred pattern of the caudal fin.

Laetacara sp., the "Bulge-headed *Laetacara*" shows a deviating colouration and depending on the mood, three to four abdominal stripes which is otherwise not known from any other *Laetacara*-species. This species additionally has a broad, dark, obliquely arranged stripe on the edge of the gill-cover and a dark blotch behind the eye above the lateral band. According to the presently available information, the

natural habitat

of *Laetacara curviceps* lies on either side of the Amazon River. As to how far this may include similar, but other species is unknown. Ecological data on this species are not available.

Care

Keeping these small sturdy fish is easy. One should use small or moderately sized aquaria which are richly planted for their keeping.

The species does not need a particular water-quality. Since they are however fairly shy by nature, not only a dense vegetation but peaceful company fishes should also be present. Decoration items should include pieces of bog-oak and some flat stones with a smooth surface; the latter may later be used as spawning sites. Cave-constructions are not essential.

The species is sensitive to intestine parasites and the pathogen of Hexamitosis. Regular exchange of the water should be obligatory.

Problems regarding their diet have never been reported.

The

breeding

of this species is by no means difficult and may often be observed under ordinary husbandry conditions. The species belongs to the substratum brooders and cares for its young in a so-called parental family. The pair usually spawns on a solid obliquely arranged object. The spawning site is preferably chosen behind some plants or other type of cover, thereby also hiding the act away from the observer outside the tank. The clutch is generally arranged in a circle of approximately 4 cm in diameter. At a temperature of 25 °C the larvae hatch after some 48 hours. Both parental specimens are very attentive, but sometimes the female appears to be more active. After the larvae have hatched the female carries them in her mouth to a small depression in the ground. The male occasionally participates in this activity. During the course of the subsequent 8 days, both parents often transfer the embryos to other depressions. The territory with the breeding site and the depression as its centre is very small during this period of development and may extend to only 15 or 20 cm in diameter. The juveniles begin to swim after 10 days and initially stay together in a tight school. They do not necessarily limit their range to levels near the ground, but also explore the medium levels of the aquarium. One parent usually resides in the school whilst the other defends the territory, the tasks constantly alternating. Both parents are attentive and courageous defenders of their offspring. The female assumes a darker colouration during this period and the territory is expanded to some 35 to 40 cm in diameter. The school loosens increasingly and the juveniles may form a congregation of already 8 to 10 cm in diameter on their second day of swimming free. Young fish which wander too far from the crowd are picked up with the mouth by the parents and brought back to the centre of the school.

Approximately 100 to 150 juveniles may be expected from a young pair of only 5 to 6 cm in length and, provided with soft water, up to 98 % of the descendants may successfully develop. Just after swimming free, the young fish measure approximately 4 mm in length and immediately feed on freshly hatched nauplii of the Brine Shrimp. They grow with moderate rapidness, initially show a spotted pattern, and may measure 8 to 9 mm after approximately two weeks. The parents care for their young for two to three weeks. Once bonded, a pair usually stays together for a whole fish-life.

▶ *Laetacara dorsigera*
(HECKEL, 1840)

is a fish with a reputation for its splendid ruby-to purple-red body-colouration. Unfortunately these colours are displayed only when a specimen feel very well — but then in all its brightness. The common name of "Red Laetacara" is however suitable. If the red colour fades, the remaining ground-colouration is a mere light greyish brown. A sexual dimorphism is not always clearly recognizable.

Although the males grow approximately 2 cm larger than the females and thus reach total lengths of around 8 cm, this feature, the longer ventral fins, and a conspicuous blotch in the dorsal fin are useful for the determination of sex in the case of adult specimens.

The following synonyms have been established for this species: *Aequidens dorsiger, Aequidens frenifera, Aequidens flavilabris* and *Aquidens thayeri.*

The "Red Laetacara" are extremely peaceful and should exclusively be kept together with other calm and peaceful fishes.

Distribution of *Laetacara dorsigera*

Specific traits

are, in addition to the red body-colouration, a mood-dependent broad dark superorbital stripe and a lateral band which only extends to the lateral spot. Subadult *Laetacara dorsigera*

Laetacara dorsigera ♂

differ from *L. curviceps* of the same age by having a dark lateral spot with a surrounding light aureole and up to five vertical transversal bars of different breadth on the tail. Furthermore, their body-shape appears to be distinctly shorter and thus more high-backed.

Similar species

Laetacara curviceps is more elongate and less high than this species, has a turquoise body-colouration, and a lateral band which extends up onto the tail.

Laetacara sp., the "Orange-finned *Laetacara*" grows considerably larger than this species and usually displays a light green body-colouration with the lower part of the caudal fin and the anal fin being yellowish golden to yellowish orange.

The

natural habitats

known to date are swamp-areas around Corumba on the Rio Paraguay and farther to the northeast in the area of the Rio Guaporé and the Rio Alegre in the Brazilian frontier region to Bolivia. The majority of waters there are of soft, slightly acidic quality.

It is interesting that this species appears to have a much wider distribution than assumed so far. For example, the authors recorded L. dorsigera during an expedition in the summer of 1983 from approximately 850 km farther west, i.e. from the region of the town of Trinidad in northern Bolivia. There, the fish share their biotopes with *Eigenmannia* sp. aff. *virescens,* a species of *Hypostomus,* another one of *Rhineloricaria,* two species of *Apistogramma* which had not been scientifically described at that time, various species of Characins, *Crenicichla lepidota, Cichlasoma boliviense,* and *Aequidens vittatus.*

The collecting site is situated approximately 10 km east of the town of Trinidad towards Peroto. It is a group of small rest-water accumulations and lagoon-like water-bodies on either side of the road which were rarely deeper than 30 cm. They were connected to a small river. The ground was partially slightly muddy, but mainly consisted of loamy sand with no aquatic vegetation at almost all places. Dead branchwork and emerse vegetation which ranges up into the water at some rare places formed a few hiding-facilities for the fishes living here. The water was murky and of ochre-brownish colour with a very poor visibility. Measurements taken during sunlight hours showed an intensity of 50000 Lux at the water-surface, 20000 Lux at a depth of 10 cm, and only 5000 Lux at 20 cm. The water was very soft, acidic, and had almost no current. The values established are indicated in Table 26. The examination took place at a time of low-water.

Table 26

Location:	Rest-water accumulation some 10 km east of the town of Trinidad (Bolivia), on either side of the road to Peroto
Clarity:	murky
Colour:	brownish
pH-Value:	6,0
Total hardness:	below 1 °dH
Carbonate hardness:	below 1 °dH
Conductivity:	23 µS at 29,5 °C
Nitrite:	below 0,1 mg/l
Depth:	not measured
Current:	almost none
Water-temperature:	29,5 °C
Date:	12.7.1983
Time:	11.00 hrs

Care

One should make aquaria of 80 cm, or better 100 cm in length, 40 cm in depth, and more than 25 cm in height available to these fish. Dark sand with a grain-size of one to three millimetres is ideal as substrate. Smooth, flat, and calcium-free stones which may be arranged in small heaps should be added to a decoration with pieces of bog-oak. *Laetacara dorsigera* can easily be kept in moderately hard to hard water although water with a total hardness of up to 8, a carbonate hardness up to 4 °dH, and a pH below 6,5 is more advantageous and favours a successful breeding. Water-temperatures of approximately 25 °C are recommendable for the husbandry. A partially, or even entirely dense vegetation provides a feeling of safety to these otherwise very shy fish and thus enhances the possibilities for detailed studies. *Laetacara dorsigera* is a species which leaves aquatic plants untouched. Other fishes, such as Tetras or Live-bearing Toothcarps, should not be omitted from the aquarium. Small Cichlids, e.g. a species of *Apistogramma*, may be included. Those company fishes should however be small in numbers and actually serve only as substitutes of "antagonists" during a possible breeding. They furthermore serve the purpose that the often shy, grey, and drab *Laetacara dorsigera* turn into interesting, colourful fish. One usually acquires semi-adult specimens which are reared with a varying diet of live and flake-food and grow to mature fish at an age of 6 to 8 months. There is no point mentioning that a very clean water plays an important role and that regular water-exchanges are therefore obligatory. If *Laetacara dorsigera* is kept in a large community aquarium, attention must be paid to a rich vegetation, zones of safety with sufficient hiding-places, and adequate space for the specimens to claim suitable territories. Active or aggressive fishes should not be kept in the same tank. Although adult males may measure approximately 8 cm and females are not much smaller, they often are physically inferior to same-sized or even smaller representatives of other species. Therefore, a successful husbandry of the "Red Laetacara" during which the fish displays itself in all its potential beauty is possible only in an environment which meets all the species' requirements.

A successful

breeding

is however also to be expected then. For this purpose the temperature should be raised to 28 °C. Already two to three days before the spawning the partners indicate their intention by slight shaking of their heads and bodies. It is usually a large flat stone with a smooth surface which is chosen to serve as spawning site. *Laetacara dorsigera* is an substratum brooder. The eggs are laid on a solid object at a usually covered location between plants. Whilst the male excitedly guards the spawning territory, the female swims directly over the spawning site. At this point of time the actually peaceful company fishes which represent the "antagonistic factor" come into the game since they stimulate the attention of the parental specimens. Immediately after a spawning sequence of the female is completed, the male proceeds to the clutch in order to fertilize the laid eggs. During this time the female protects the territory.

This procedure can be observed in constant alternation. A clutch from adult specimens contains approximately 300 eggs. It is arranged in a circle of approximately five centimetres in diameter and the individual eggs have a faint reddish brown colour. One parental specimen always undertakes to reside directly above the clutch and fans fresh water over the clutch by strong movements with the pectoral fins. This avoids that particles of dirt settle on the eggs and thus spoil their proper development. At a temperature of 28 °C the embryos emerge from the eggs after 40 to 44 hours. The parents, but mainly the female, assist by taking the developing larvae into the mouth. During this, the embryos are usually sucked out of their egg-shells already and subsequently transferred to a depression in the substratum which has been created before and may measure some 4 or 5 cm in diameter and about 1 cm in depth. The metamorphosis of all juveniles from the embryonal to the larval stage may take several hours which indicates that there is some tolerance in the development time.

At this point of time, the larvae measure 3,4 mm in total length.

During the following days the depressions are changed frequently and the larvae transferred. Both parents are very active and one of them resides above the depression and arranges for fresh water in it by strong movements of the pectoral fins. However, decay and rotting plant material are occasionally also brought into the pit; probably in order to enhance the camouflage of the larvae. Approximately 4 days later, i.e. almost 144 hours after the fertilization of the eggs, the first juveniles can be observed swimming. Since the development time is apparently very variable, one can recognize that the parents try to suppress the swimming of those juveniles which have already completed their individual development. Approximately 15 hours later one may eventually observe that the fry leave the depression. At this stage the juveniles measure 4,5 mm on average and it is an exciting picture when the deep red coloured *Laetacara dorsigera* are surrounded by a school of several hundred young.

Unfortunately they are not capable to defend all their juveniles even against so-called harmless antagonistic company fishes. Therefore their number should be reduced to two specimens at maximum already before the fry starts swimming. This should of course be done as inconspicuously as possible. Another danger exists due to the fact that the small fish become fairly active already a few days after swimming free and thus generate a large loose school which is extremely difficult to protect. The parents permanently undertake to keep the school together by catching run-aways with the mouth and bringing them back. Despite all efforts one has the impression that this goal is simply impossible for the *Laetacara* to achieve.

Due to the small size of the juveniles when they begin to swim one should feed them rotaries, nauplii of *Cyclops,* and Bosmids. This should be supplemented by a "food-milk" made up of the powder-food MikroMin which is injected into the school of juveniles. Even freshly hatched nauplii of *Artemia salina* appear to be too big for them as has been shown when smaller food was not available and losses were experienced on a large scale during the first days. The small mouth of this species most likely is the major reason for this problem.

However, even if adequately sized food is available, the rearing of the juveniles is not always hassle-free. One should especially forego for drastic changes of the water-quality. Once the first 10 to 14 days have been survived the most difficult period has been managed.

The parents may now be separated from the fry and be used for breeding again. Even if this is not the intention they and "antagonistic company fishes" should be removed from the aquarium.

On the other hand, a removal of the juveniles at this point of time instead may be the cause for extremely high losses.

A healthy rearing of the juveniles requires a varying diet and the maintenance of a high water-quality. They do not grow very rapidly.

In rainforest-areas, water-courses are often the only routes.

◗ *Laetacara flavilabris*
(COPE, 1870)

This Cichlid was described under the name *Acara flavilabris* already more than a century ago and it is therefore one of the South American Cichlids longest known. Another name frequently used for this fish is the synonym *Acara freniferus*. Until the genus *Laetacara* was described it was referred to as a species of *Aequidens*.

Laetacara flavilabris seems to be the largest species of this genus.

Although specimens of more than nine centimetres in length are rarely caught in the natural habitats, this Cichlid may have grown distinctly larger than ten centimetres after several years under optimal aquarium-conditions. It has a relatively high-backed body-shape which may have either a light or a dark grey ground-colouration depending on the prevailing mood. The centre of the body is marked with a large dark lateral spot which however only becomes distinct during certain stages of

Distribution of *Laetacara flavilabris*

excitement. The spot is often connected by a broad band of same colour with a dark spot on the base of the dorsal fin. A broad lateral stripe is generally present in the anterior half of the

Female of *Laetacara flavilabris* from the Rio Coca in Ecuador

body extending from the hind edge of the eye up to the lateral spot. The cheeks are marked with a contrasting colour-pattern which is created by the front portion of the pregill-cover and the gill-cover being golden or greenish golden whereas the hind parts are black up to the respective edges. The iris has a brownish red colouration. The grey fins may display a light blueish gleam. Whilst the upper lip is always dark grey, the lower lip is always whitish. This is remarkable in so far that this feature was referred to in the scientific species-name. The term *flavilabris* means "light" or "yellow-lipped".

According to our observations *Laetacara flavilabris* occurs in various geographical colour-varieties. Specimens which we caught in the catchment region of the Rio Coca in Ecuador were, for example, uniformly grey whilst males which we observed in the vicinity of the town of Jenaro Herrero in Peru had a yellowish caudal fin with a splendid blueish green gleam on the lower parts of the head and the body.

Males can be hardly distinguished from female when they are still not fully grown since a clear sexual dimorphism is absent in this species. On the other hand, the sex of adult specimens can be determined with some certainty as the males then have developed considerably larger fins. At this stage, the ventral fins extend up to the central part of the anal fin when pressed against the body and the much enlarged anal and caudal fins may exceed the caudal fin in length.

Specific traits

of *Laetacara flavilabris* are the inconspicuous colouration with shades of grey being predominant all over the body and the conspicuously yellow coloured lower lip.

Amongst the

similar species

which might be confused with this form, Laetacara thayeri must be mentioned due to this species' size and shape. It is however readily distinguished by having a wine-red colouration and large black blotch in the dorsal fin.

The

natural habitats

of this Cichlid lie in the north of Peru, in Ecuador, and in northwestern Brazil. We caught specimens at various localities in Ecuador and Peru which were in most cases shaded rainforest streams where banking vegetation ranged up into the water and many sunken twigs and branches provided cover and hiding places. At all sites, the water was soft (total hardness <1°dH, carbonate hardness <1 to 3°dH) and acidic (pH 5,4 to 6,5).

Care

The fish turned out to be a robust and easily adapting omnivore which is not afraid to also feed on fragile plants every now and then.

Nevertheless, it should be kept in a richly planted aquarium with many hiding facilities.

Breeding

Laetacara flavilabris is a monogamous substratum brooder which rears its offspring in a parental family structure. Soft, slightly acidic water is recommendable for breeding attempts.

Table 27

Location:	Stream near the road to Lago Agrio, apr. 20 km north of the town of Coca in Ecuador (catchment of the lower Rio Coca)
Clarity:	fairly murky
Colour:	brownish
pH:	6,5
Total hardness:	<1°dH
Carbonate hardness:	3°dH
Conductivity:	95 µS
Depth:	up to 60 cm
Current:	slow
Water-temperature:	26°C
Air-temperature:	29°C
Date:	7.2.1990
Time:	13.00 hrs

♦ *Laetacara* sp.
(Bulge-headed *Laetacara*)

This small species is referred to by the enthusiasts as the "Bulge-headed *Laetacara*" although this term is not always adequate. Not all males develop a bulged forehead respectively nape at old age. This fish is very colourful and usually has an interesting pattern which partially is characteristic for the species.

A dark lateral band ranges from the hind edge of the gill-cover up to the very dark lateral spot and then continues in a more faint intensity up to in front of the caudal peduncle. Pale indications of transversal bars are visible on the caudal fin. The presence of three to four abdominal stripes is especially interesting since no other small *Laetacara*-species has this feature. The species appears to be very peaceful and may be kept under the same conditions as described for the other small *Laetacaras*. These fishes apparently also require soft, slightly acidic, and clean water for a successful reproduction.

The males of this scientifically undescribed species reaches a total length of approximately 8 cm, whilst females grow slightly smaller.

There is just an indication of a sexual dimorphism of which the enlarged spines of the dorsal and anal fins in the males are to be mentioned. Old males may develop a bulged forehead or nape.

Collecting localities are known from the rivers Tapajós, Xingú, and Tocantins.

Specific traits

are the two to four abdominal stripes. Old males may have a bulged forehead or nape, sometimes referred to as "bulged head". This feature may however also appear a less pronounced form in males of related species.

The lateral band often disintegrates into a row of almost quadrangular blotches behind the lateral spot. The most reliable trait distinguishing this form from all other small species of *Laetacara* is however the presence of a relatively broad dark, obliquely arranged stripe on the gill-cover behind the eye and above the lateral band.

Laetacara sp. (Bulge-headed *Laetacara*) ♂

◆ Laetacara sp. (Orange-finned Laetacara)

This is another new and exceptionally colourful species of *Laetacara*.

Representatives display an intense light green colouration on the anterior portion of the body which lessens towards the caudal peduncle. During courtship and imposing a slight transversal barred pattern becomes visible on the caudal fin. A dark lateral band also appears in such mood ending at the even darker lateral spot. A characteristic feature of this species is the presence of a broad dark superorbital stripe. The dorsal fin is pale to deep violet in colour and so, but less intense, is the upper part of the caudal fin. Its lower portion and most of the anal fin are deep yellowish golden to yellowish orange.

Distinguishing between the sexes of adult specimens is easy. Besides of the different adult sizes — the males reach just under 9 cm, the female a little more than 6 cm — males have

Distribution of *Laetacara* sp. (Orange-finned *Laetacara*)

produced dorsal fins which exceed the caudal fin in length and pointed anal fins which extend up to the centre of the caudal fin. These fins are also pointed in female specimens, but

Laetacara sp. (Orange-finned *Laetacara*)

199

distinctly shorter if directly compared with those of the males. This species has a relatively high-backed body-shape and a close relationship with *Laetacara dorsigera* is to be supposed.

Specific traits

This scientifically undescribed species has actually no specific features at young age. Subadult specimens resemble young *Laetacara curviceps* except for that they are more high-backed. Once they however mature, they can be readily allocated to a species by the unique colouration alone.

Similar species

Laetacara dorsigera has an entirely different colouration and is smaller.

Laetacara curviceps juveniles are fairly similar. This species however has a more elongate body-shape.

The

natural habitat

lies in the area of Puerto Inirida on the Rio Inirida and thus in the catchment of the Orinoco and the Rio Negro in the border-triangle of Columbia, Brazil, and Venezuela. During a collecting trip in 1983, Mr. SCHMITT-KNATZ recorded this species from shallow bank-zones and swampy areas. All sites had in common that the water was very clear, of brown colour, and very soft, very acidic with a pH around 5,5. The water-temperatures were established to vary between 29 and 30 °C. *Dicrossus filamentosus* and *Apistogramma iniridae* were found inhabiting the same areas.

Care

Keeping these intensely coloured, though very shy fish is easy. A moderately large aquarium of 100 cm in length, a depth of 40 cm, and a height not under 25 cm may be appropriate. A dense vegetation, some low rock constructions, other hiding places, and clean water rich in oxygen and free of nitrite are very important.

A few similarly peaceful company fishes are recommendable. Provided with a potent, but varying diet, the specimens will grow to splendid fish which will start

breeding

without problems. There is however also a fair chance that the patience of the keeper is excessively stressed. The partners spawn on a solid object near the ground. Their breeding and husbandry behaviour is comparable with *Laetacara dorsigera*. A positive development obviously requires soft, very acidic water and at a temperature of 25 °C on average, a conductivity of 139 S, and a pH of 5,5. The authors noted the following development data: The embryos emerged from their egg-shells after 69 hours on average.

Another 6 days later their development was finalized and the young fish began to swim. The species is fairly productive, and schools of 200 to 250 descendants are an average result. They are small and require very small prey-items. Freshly hatched nauplii of the Brine Shrimp are usually still too large initially and they may only be used as supplement. Microscopic live food, MikroMin powder-food made up as "food-milk", and small amounts of a liquid plant-food which are usually utilized for rearing *Artemia salina* are more adequate. The juveniles grow slowly and a high quality of the water is absolutely necessary for their progress.

A clear-water river at time of low-water

▶ *Laetacara thayeri*
(STEINDACHNER, 1875)

As this Cichlid was described as *Acara thayeri* by the zoologist STEINDACHNER of the Vienna museum more than a century ago, it is one of the longest known South American fishes. Up to the point of time when the genus *Laetacara* was defined the species was allocated to the collective genus *Aequidens*. Although it is one of the most commonly encountered Cichlids around the city of Iquitos in Peru, it is a fish rarely seen in the aquaria of the hobbyists. Wild-caught specimens may rarely exceed eight centimetres in length, but under favourable captivity conditions they may easily grow to over ten centimetres.

Fully grown representatives of this species have a stout and very roundish body-shape which makes them appear fairly plump. Whilst the region of the back is usually dominated by greyish brown to dark grey colours, the rest of the body has a beige ground-colouration with

Distribution of *Laetacara thayeri*

the lower parts having a pretty wine-red tinge. The always ochre colouration of the forehead which greatly contrasts with a pitch black

Male of *Laetacara thayeri* from the Rio Momon

preorbital and a broad superorbital stripe is especially noteworthy.

A red band bordered with shining light green lines ranges from the lower edge of the eye to the angle of the mouth. The mood-dependent black pattern of this species includes an ill-defined blotch immediately in front of the dorsal fin on the nape and a large lateral spot with a yellowish aura which usually goes over into a broad dark dorsal band. This band may extend obliquely backwards and reach up onto the dorsal fin. The lateral spot and the hind edge of the eye are connected by another black horizontal band. Four indistinctly indicated transversal bars may occasionally become visible in the posterior half of the body. The caudal fin is marked with a pattern of tiny wine-red speckles which are arranged in vertical rows. The ventral fins, the anal fin, and the posterior section of the dorsal fin are coloured light wine-red and light blue.

The hind portion of the dorsal fin is additionally bordered on its top edge with a broad orange stripe. Except for the produced fins of the males there is no distinctive sexual dimorphism or chromatism.

Specific traits

of *Laetacara thayeri* are the dark nuchal blotch, the obliquely backwards arranged band-like extension of the lateral spot, and the striped pattern between the eye and the upper lip.

Amongst the
similar species

Laetacara dorsigera need to be mentioned especially due to its similar red colouration. This species however lacks a black band which connects the lateral spot with the blotch in the dorsal fin.

The
natural habitats

of *Laetacara thayeri* are found in northern Peru and the bordering Brazil. Localities are known from the catchment of the upper and central Amazon River between the lower Rio Ucayali

and the vicinity of the city of Manaus. During several excursions the authors established that this Cichlid is very common in small water-bodies in the rainforests near the city of Iquitos.

According to our observation the fish seems to prefer those streams in the forests where the vegetation of the banks ranges into the water and where submerged twigs and branches provide ample cover and numerous hiding-places. At all collecting sites the water was very soft and acidic.

Here, the species lived syntopically with *Apistogramma bitaeniata* and *A. agassizii*.

Care

Keeping this fairly shy and edgy Cichlid requires a densely planted aquarium where the fish may always find the hiding-facilities which are necessary to make them feel well. Keeping it together with more active and outgoing species is another adequate method to overcome its natural shyness.

An important precondition for the
breeding

is a soft and acidic quality of the water which emulates the values found in the natural habitats. *Laetacara thayeri* is a monogamous substratum brooder which forms a parental family structure during times of reproduction.

Table 28

Location:	Lower Rio Ucayali: Quebrada de Baga-san
Clarity:	very murky
Colour:	yellowish ochre
pH:	6,5
Total hardness:	$<1\,°dH$
Carbonate hardness:	$3\,°dH$
Conductivity:	$85\,\mu S$
Depth:	up to 50 cm
Current:	none
Water-temperature:	$27\,°C$
Date:	1.8.1990

The Genus Nannacara
REGAN, 1905

is one of the genera of Cichlid fishes longest known to the aquarists. As early as in 1911 a species of *Nannacara* was reportedly kept in an aquarium in Germany (ARNOLD, 1912). Presently, this fairly small genus holds five species only, but there is at least another one which still awaits to be scientifically investigated.

The distribution of the genus is restricted to the northeast of South America. Localities have been recorded from the three Guyanas and their immediate vicinity, which means more to the north from the mouth of the Ori- noco and from the mouth of the Amazon River in the south. Although the species of *Nannacara* show many parallels with the genus *Apistogramma* regarding appearance and behaviour, they are not closely related to the Geophagines but belong to the Cichlasomines instead. The generic features include a reduced number of rays in the caudal fin, the presence of a membrane which connects the caudal peduncle with the last rays of the dorsal and anal fins (KULLANDER & NIJSSEN 1989), and the highly contrasting colouration of breeding females which consists of dark longitudinal and transversal bands on a light ground-colour and thus forms a plaid pattern.

Sunken wood and branchwork are favourite residing places for small species of Cichlids and Catfishes. This includes representatives of the genera *Ancistrus* and *Rhineloricara* especially.

▶ *Nannacara anomala*
REGAN, 1905

Distribution of *Nannacara anomala*

This very pretty and colourful species was probably temporarily imported for the first time in 1911. It was however only 20 years later that specimens became available again, which subsequently were successfully bred. Since that time this fish with its interesting behaviour has become a standard aquarium fish which is permanently hold in stock by the pet-shop trade.

Nannacara anomala shows many parallels to *Nannacara taenia*, a species which has long been considered to be a synonym of *N. anomala*.

Nannacara taenia is however easily identified by its temporarily appearing longitudinal banded pattern.

Whilst the just under 5 cm long females of *Nannacara anomala* have a mainly beige to yellowish body-colouration, the up to 8 cm long males display almost iridescent emerald-green colours which are in great contrast with the smoky to black coloured fins. The sexes are therefore easily distinguished. Not only that the males are larger, the anterior soft rays of the dorsal and anal fins are less produced in the females. Large males lack the lateral band characteristic for female specimens.

Nannacara anomala ♂

This species is very peaceloving and it is only during period of parental care that the female may become very aggressive and thus requires sufficient space. At such times it displays a highly contrasting pattern of dark longitudinal and transversal bands.

Specific traits

are the body-shape and the unique colour-pattern.

Similar species

Nannacara aureocephalus This species is coloured completely different.

The

natural habitat

lies in the Guyana-countries in the northeastern part of South America with records especially concentrating in the regions of the Essequibo River and the swamps south of the capital of Georgetown.

The fish preferably inhabits the very shallow zones between plants, leaf-litter, and the branchwork of the banking vegetation. In most of the cases small streams and rest-water zones of large rivers and swamps offer suitable biotopes. As far as is known, these water-bodies have very different water-qualities.

Care

The following conclusions should be drawn from the aforesaid. The aquarium should be generously planted and offer many hiding places.

The community fishes must be adequately tempered and one should forego large or aggressive species. The fish does tolerate a variety of water-qualities, but water with a slightly acidic reaction, i.e. with a pH under 7 has been proved to be recommendable. Small to moderately sized aquaria with a fine-grained substrate and a number of rock constructions which provide caves and shelters create an appropriate environment. Coconut-shells with an opening of 2 to 3 cm or bam-

boo-tubes are useful further decoration items.

A regular partial exchange of the water, i.e. a quarter to a third every week or fortnight, should be obligatory and attention must be spend on a varying diet of live and flake-food. The species is susceptible to the pathogen *Hexamita* which causes Hexamitosis. Means of preventive maintenance are therefore recommendable. Under these husbandry conditions the specimens will grow rapidly and start

breeding

without further effort. The male entices his partner very attentively and if the female has set up spawn, she will not try to escape. No signs of male aggression towards the female can be observed. The species preferably spawns inside a cave and the partnership ends immediately after the spawning act. The female alone undertakes to care for the fry and to defend the breeding territory whilst the male remains completely passive. Bonding which is known from many other species does not take place. The beige to yellowish colouration of the female now changes into a plaid pattern of black bands on a greyish brown ground-colour.

At a water-temperature of 25 °C, the development of the fry is completed after approximately 12 days. Subsequently, the female can be observed in company of 100 to 150 juveniles which stay together in a dense crowd. They immediately respond to signs given by their mother which may signal danger by jerks of the body and the fins and turning the head slightly sideways and order the young fish to stay motionless. One may observe the juveniles staying close to the ground or above stones or plants without any recognizable movements when the mother attacks a supposed enemy. This kind of behaviour lasts a couple of days.

At the time of starting to swim freely, the juveniles measure approximately 5 mm and have a camouflage pattern of small dark spots on their bodies. With regularly timed periods of illumination it may be observed that the mother will guide her school back into the breeding cave already a few minutes before the lights are switched off. The nauplii of *Artemia salina* and MikroMin are suitable first food.

▶ Nannacara aureocephalus
ALLGAYER, 1983

This very recently described species closely resembles *Nannacara anomala* regarding its habitus, but has a completely different colouration and pattern and is thus easily identified. Its original description is based on five specimens which were collected by G. OELKER in 1982 and P. ISSEMANN in 1983. The holotype is a male of 65 mm in standard length.

Nannacara aureocephalus has a relatively high body-shape and a comparatively short head. In life, males have a colour-pattern of a blueish gleaming forehead and lips. The eye is surrounded by yellow with wine-red worm-like speckles below. The cheeks and gill-covers are coloured vividly yellow and may have a number of red spots. A shade of beige is predominant on the body with a blueish glow all over. Each scale is bordered metallic blue. The dorsal fin is marked with reddish spots and an orange edge with is accompanied by a blueish submarginal line. The anal fin is patterned with longitudinal rows of blue and red dots and the same arrangement of markings is found on the rounded caudal fin.

Distribution of *Nannacara aureocephalus*

Nannacara aureocephalus ♂

This species has a distinct sexual dimorphism regarding the different sizes of the sexes. In addition to the fact that male and female are differently coloured, the male may reach a total-length of 10 to 11 cm whilst the females are already fully grown at just under 6 cm.

Specific traits

are the high-backed body and the comparatively short head, the yellow colouration in the head region, and the beige body with the metallic blue bordered scales. Males of this species also usually show a lateral band and dark blotches on the back to which one may refer to as remainders of a transversal barred pattern if one applies the standards of *Apistogramma*-species. The forehead and the lips have a blueish gleam, and there are wine-red worm-like streaks below the eye.

Similar species

Nannacara anomala-males have a colouration predominated by dark green shades and smoky grey bordered fins. They are slightly more slender and have a more elongate head in direct comparison. The head and adjacent parts lack yellow colours.

The

natural habitat

is only known from the type locality in French Guyana. It is a tributary to the Rio Mana, approximately 11 km off the village of Saut Sabbat, near the National Road No. 1. A second locality has been recorded from a tributary to the Rio Comté in the vicinity of the village Cacao in the proximity of the road leading to this village.

According to a personal communication received from ALLGAYER, the species inhabits small streams and rivers as well as stagnant water-bodies inside the rainforest. The depths of these waters were measured to be between 20 centimetres and 2 metres. The water was slightly brownish and clear and had the following values:

Total hardness: 0 to 1 °dH
Carbonate hardness 0 °dH
pH: 5,8 to 6,0
Conductivity: 30 µS

The aquatic vegetation consisted of species of *Nymphaea*.

Care

Keeping this species is easy and comparable with that of *Nannacara anomala*. It is a cave brooder as well. Males are fairly aggressive towards each other, but this fish is absolutely peaceful towards other fishes. Well structured aquaria of moderate size are sufficient for their husbandry. The natural water-values should be emulated.

Even on short excursions into the rainforest one should not forego the company of local people familiar with the terrain.

◗ *Nannacara taenia*
REGAN, 1912

Until recently, this name was considered to be nothing but a synonym of the widely known species *Nannacara anomala*. However, after imports made by Arthur WERNER in 1987 and KILIAN, SCHLIEWEN, and STAWIKOWSKI in 1988 and their subsequent observation, one may conclude that *Nannacara taenia* is in fact a good species. According to MEINKEN, the "Banded Dwarf Cichlid" was first imported in 1911, but had vanished from the captive aquaria already a few years later.

Nannacara taenia is the smallest representative of the genus with adult males reaching approximately 4 cm in total length. A specific feature is the uninterrupted striped pattern on the upper and lower half of the body as well as on the caudal peduncle. Compared with the females the males have dorsal and anal fins which end in a point and a faintly gleaming scalation.

Data on this form's distribution were doubtful until WERNER, KILIAN, SCHLIEWEN,

Distribution of *Nannacara taenia*

and STAWIKOWSKI recorded the fish from water-courses in the region of the town of Belém and "a tributary to the Guamá near the village of Boavista" in northeastern Brazil. The species was successfully bred in the meantime.

Nannacara taenia ♂

The Genus Papiliochromis
KULLANDER, 1977

was suggested by the Swedish ichthyologist KULLANDER in 1977 to accommodate the "Orinoco Butterfly Cichlid" *Papiliochromis ramirezi* which until then had erroneously been allocated to the genus *Apistogramma*. The usage of this name is however not unquestioned and some ichthyologists (in others GÉRY 1983) are of the opinion that due to formal reasons the name *Microgeophagus* would have priority since it was already used by FREY in 1959. Although the latter author did by no means intend to establish a new genus and used this name only hypothetically, he had unpurposedly provided a definition for a name which would therefore be available for use (GÉRY 1991).

The genus accommodates two species only, which have a disjunct distribution in northern (Columbia and Venezuela) and central (Bolivia and Brazil) South America respectively. Their generic features include the enlarged and black coloured anterior spines and membranes of the dorsal fin and a large black lateral blotch. Their sexual dimorphism is weakly developed. In contrast to other Dwarf Cichlids, the species of *Papiliochromis* are no cave brooders, but substratum brooders which rear their offspring in a parental family structure. It is especially noteworthy that the "Bolivian Butterfly Cichlid" shows the behaviour of a mouth-breeder whilst the descendants go through their larval development (STAECK 1987). Both parents take the larvae into the mouth in cases of supposed danger and carry them around for a longer period of time.

On the headwaters of the Rio Guarrojo in eastern Columbia

◗ *Papiliochromis altispinosa*
(HASEMANN, 1991)

Distribution of Papiliochromis altispinosa

The "Bolivian Butterfly Cichlid" made its first appearance in the aquaristic literature in the late sixties (MEINKEN 1966, LÜLING 1969). LÜLING had managed to catch a single specimen near Todos Santos in eastern Bolivia for the first time. The preserved fish was later misidentified as *"Apistogramma ramirezi"* by MEINKEN. Both authors subsequently caused a lot of confusion since they reported about this particular specimen several times and questioned the correctness of the distribution data of *P. ramirezi* due to their misidentification. The identity of this Dwarf Cichlid from Todos Santos was eventually clarified by the Swedish Ichthyologist KULLANDER in 1981. He re-examined the specimen in question and compared it with preserved material of several other museum collections. The result was that with no doubt this fish belonged to the species described as *Crenicara altispinosa* by HASEMANN in 1911.

Papiliochromis altispinosa ♂

The fact that there was not any information available on the colouration of live specimen, was reason enough for us to travel to Bolivia in order to search for this particular Cichlid. Since the region of Todos Santos has however turned into a centre of Coca-farming and drug-trade, this plan met with unforeseen problems. It eventually took a second journey in 1985 to catch a few specimens and bring them back to Germany alive.

Specific traits

A dark band runs from the nape through the hind edge of the eye onto the cheek and to the edge of the gill-cover. The species has six transversal bars marking the body with the third of which including a dark spot at its centre or slightly above the hypothetic lateral band. The base of the caudal fin shows a conspicuous blotch which extends up to the lower edge of that fin. Representatives of *P. altispinosa* have 15 spines in the dorsal fin and 14 in the pectoral fins respectively on average. The species grows slightly larger than *P. ramirezi*.

Similar species

Papiliochromis ramirezi is the only comparable species with some sort of resemblance. On the other hand, it has only indications of six transversal bars. Furthermore, there is a distinct lateral spot recognizable on the second transversal bar at the height of the lateral band. The spines of the dorsal fin number 13 to 14 and those of the pectoral fins 11 to 12. This species has a smaller adult size. All data refer to wild-caught specimens.

The

natural habitat

centres in the Rio Mamoré Basin in eastern Bolivia. The fish has been recorded from a large lake approximately 1,6 km west of San Joaquin, from the Rio Quizer 14 km outside San Ramón in direction of Limón, from the mouth of the Igarapé Palheta near Guajará-Mirim, from a small depression approximately 4 km south of Todos Santos, and from near a sandbank in the Rio Mamoré below the mouth of the Rio Guaporé.

Unfortunately, the entire area covering these localities has been subjected to urbanisation for the purpose of cattle-farming and thus the ecological circumstances have drastically changed. The specimens imported by the authors for the first time alive were caught in the vicinity of the town of Trinidad in the north of Bolivia. The collecting site was a rest-water accumulation fully exposed to the sun which was so murky that the visibility was clearly below 5 cm.

An analysis of the water at site revealed a pH of 7,6 and the total and carbonate hardness was established to be 4°dH each. The water-temperature measured 27°C and the electrical conductivity 123 micro-Siemens.

Care

Due to the water-values established in the natural habitat it was presumed that the requirements for the husbandry of the "Bolivian Butterfly Cichlid" would be easy to fulfil.

According to experiences made to date, this presumption turned out to be hundred percent correct. *Papiliochromis altispinosa* can be described to be an unlimited recommendable species for the large community tank as well as for the small species aquarium. This Cichlid only pays attention to other fishes during periods of breeding. However, amongst its own kind, the "Butterfly Cichlids" are territorial. On the other hand, according to our observations their claimed territories are usually small and their antagonistic combats are so much ritualized that injuries are avoided.

The fish readily accept all types of food. During the course of 15 months of husbandry the wild-caught specimens grew from originally 30 to 45 mm to approximately 7 cm and this is probably the maximum length reached by the species. It is noteworthy that we had to keep the fish for more than a year before first sexual activities could be observed. Although the specimens were kept in separate aquaria, several pairs bonded almost simultaneously.

Since males and females hardly differ from each other in their appearance and thus make a determination of sex a matter of guessing, we were fairly uncertain about the sex-ratio of our specimens. Some sort of hints are given by the shape of the unpairy fins only, which become slightly more filamentous in old males.

Apart from reproduction periods, the "Bolivian Butterfly Cichlid" appears to be living in solitude.

According to our observations, a

breeding

cycle begins with a pair bonding approximately one week before spawning. It was initiated by the male which suddenly began to court.

In order to attract the female the courtship behaviour included displaying the flanks, tail-lashing, head-jerking, body-shaking, digging, and cleaning the supposed breeding substratum. Female specimens engage in the same manner of courtship behaviour, but clearly less often and during a shorter period of time. In our aquaria it was observed two days before spawning.

During the courtship period the male creates four or five small depressions in the ground, which, in our case, consisted of sand emulating the situation of the natural habitat. Each of the pits was approximately 4 cm in diameter. We therefore presumed that the "Bolivian Butterfly Cichlids" would subsequently lay their eggs in such depression as is the case in *P. ramirezi*. Surprisingly enough, they however eventually always spawned on a stone in the manner of substratum brooders.

During the spawning act, both fish alternatingly slided over the stone with their genital papillae visibly everted. As soon as the female had attached a few eggs to the surface, she gave way and the male moved over the clutch in three to four circular courses. The eggs were subsequently cared for and exclusively guarded by the female almost. With the body slightly bent, it usually stayed approximately one centimetre above the clutch and fanned fresh water over the eggs with the pectoral fins. The male meanwhile mainly patrolled the borders of the breeding territory and only came occasionally close to the clutch. On those rare occasions, short reliefs could be observed, i.e. the

female left her place in order to let the male temporarily care for the clutch. However, the female usually returned after some 20 seconds already in order to proceed with her duty.

It appears to be noteworthy that the female spat some sand over the eggs. The biological meaning of this action is presumably that the sand particles enhance the invisibility of the already well camouflaged brownish coloured eggs for potential predators and thus provides an additional chance for their survival.

At a water-temperature of 27 °C the larvae hatched after 60 hours.

They were transported by both parents to small depressions which had partially been dug by the male during the courtship already. These "nests" were frequently situated on the base of plants so that the roots provided additional cover for the fry. During the course of a day, the larvae were usually twice re-located to another pit. This does however not mean that new depressions were created all the time.

Local fisherman skillfully handle their small canoes when out to catch Piranhas.

It was merely that there were four to six of such "nests" in the breeding territory which were successively used again and again. As soon as the larvae had hatched, the male became more active in the participation of parental care so that there was hardly any noticeable difference in the behaviour of both parental specimens from then on. Seven days after the spawning the juveniles had completed their larval stage and were observed swimming in a school through the aquarium guided by both their parents. From this point of time on, the parental fish began to defend their breeding territory with an increased viciousness. An ideal food for the juveniles are newly hatched larvae of the Brine Shrimp. The breeding of *P. altispinosa* was successful in ordinary tap-water. Its values in the aquarium were 7,5 pH, a total hardness of 14 °dH, and a carbonate hardness of 13 °dH.

Due to its splendid colouration, *Papiliochromis altispinosa* certainly is an important addition to the assortment of Dwarf Cichlids available to the aquarists. Since this Cichlid is much easier to breed than the "Orinoco Butterfly Cichlid" *P. ramirezi,* it might be expected that it may in future become a competitor for this species which must be taken seriously.

Papiliochromis altispinosa ♀ above a clutch

▶ *Papiliochromis ramirezi*
(HARRY & MYERS, 1948)

To introduce The Ramirezi would mean to describe a fish which has been one of the most popular aquarium fishes for many years. It has been ranking on top places of the "hit-lists" of the aquarists for decades and the wild-caught specimens imported from South America have long since been surpassed by even more colourful breeds from Asia. Unfortunately, these products of busy Asian breeders do not have much in common with the original fish any more. Accordingly, numerous artificial colour-morphs exist, which are, in case of the "Gold-ramirezi" for example, not necessarily very viable.

Distribution of *Papiliochromis ramirezi*

The basis for looking at this species however is the wild fish living in South America. The sexes of adult specimens are readily distinguished. Female grow slightly smaller in comparison, have less produced fin-membranes and spines in the anterior portion of the dorsal fin, and shorter ventral fins. Wild-caught specimens have a more intense colouration of the body containing more red in the belly-region. The habitus of this species largely resembles that of *P. altispinosa*. Wild *Papi-*

Wild-caught male specimen of *Papiliochromis ramirezi*

liochromis ramirezi reach adult sizes of around 50 mm. The names *Apistogramma ramirezi* and *Microgeophagus ramirezi* are to be considered synonyms.

Specific traits

of *P. ramirezi* are the presence of indications of seven transversal bars whose intensity varies with the prevailing mood. A dark spot of varying intensity is found on the second of these bands at the height of a rarely visible lateral band. The spines of the dorsal fin number 13 to 14 and 11 to 12 in case of the pectoral fins respectively. This species grows considerably smaller than *P. altispinosa*.

Similar species

Papiliochromis altispinosa is very similar in all respects, but there are considerable difference regarding both the species' colour-patterns and a slight deviation in the number of spines in the fins.

Preserved material shows only six instead of seven transversal bars. There are 13 to 14 pectoral fin spines and 15 spines on average in the dorsal fin. This species furthermore differs with regard to its colouration and pattern and the anterior spines of the dorsal fin are not as much enlarged.

The

natural habitat

lies in the catchment area of the central Orinoco in Venezuela and Columbia. Members of the FITOBE in others examined the biotopes of *P. ramirezi* during a study-trip through Columbia in 1982. One of the results was the final elimination of the legend of the "junglefish which inhabits the most romantic watercourses". *Papiliochromis ramirezi* profanely inhabits waters of the savannas. At the end of March, not much different from the rest of the year, the Llanos is a very dry steppe with temperatures ranging around 40 °C in the shade and a very low humidity. It is simply a dusty badlands.

The imagination that this area should be the home of splendid aquarium-fishes appears

to be absurd when one faces this landscape for the first time. This vast "prairie" however occasionally holds true oases in shallow depressions near the dirt roads where the dust, sand, and dryness is replaced by palmtrees and lush green. The centres of those oases are small crystal clear streams which partly form lake-like expansions. And this is also the case in the biotope of *Papiliochromis ramirezi*.

The major distribution area lies south of Puerto Gaitan between the vast Rio Manacacias and the smaller Rio Yacao. There, the fish inhabits oases and small streams up to the villages of La Maria and San Jorge. We found specimens in a lagoon of approximately 100 by 40 metres which was bordered by palmtrees on the property of the Finca La Prima Vera, some 400 metres west of the Rio Manacacias. It was embanked by an almost 100 metres broad strip of peat interspersed with grass. The water in the lagoon was clear and appeared dark. Its ground was sandy to muddy and had a dark grey to black colour.

Aquatic plants were absent and stones could not be found either. It was only for emerse vegetation reaching into the water, leaf-litter, and branchwork that a narrow cover-zone against predators was provided for small fishes. According to a local fisherman, this lagoon would hold a few "*ramirezi*", as they were referred to by him too, only due to the fact that the cover-zone was very small. Water-bodies farther to the south should have more zones of shallow water and vegetated banks and thus would have more dense populations.

The quality of the water was interesting. Total and carbonate hardness were below 1 °dH, the concentration of hydrogen-ions was established to be 5,1, and the conductivity was almost undetectable. It was recorded as approximately 1 micro-Siemens at 28,5 °C. These measurements were taken on 15.3.1982 at 10.00 hrs. The sky was overcast and it was still relatively cool at 31 °C.

Care

Keeping the *P. ramirezi* is not always hassle-free since it is frequently kept under inadequate conditions and exposed to stress. This includes a socialization with inappropriately active or even aggressive fishes, an overpopulation in a too small tank and thus too few zones of tranquillity, and the lack of adequately planted cover-zones.

Furthermore, not only the cleanliness of the water but the chemical quality of it also plays a more important role than commonly thought.

If this species is provided with a sufficiently large and well structured aquarium with just a few matching company fishes, one usually has lasting colourful study objects with an extremely interesting behaviour.

The

breeding

of this fish is not all that easy either. During the past few years especially, an increasing number of reports on unsuccessful rearing could be observed which indicates that not all of this species' secrets have been revealed yet. Although most specimens can be reproduced

easily, it is noteworthy that this success is exclusively based on an artificial rearing. On the other hand, the natural parental care is hardly ever observed any more. The question for the reason is put at increasing frequency.

A few remarks on the natural course of a successful breeding may therefore be useful. These may be the more interesting as they are based on specimens bred in Asia which are generally said to especially lack the abilities for a natural parental care. The reason may be a genetic alteration. In the experiment described here, two pairs were accommodated in an aquarium of 100 cm in length, 30 cm in depth, and 25 cm in height. The specimens were pairs which had formed naturally out of a large group. Each pair subsequently claimed a territory of half the tank. Its decoration was rather spartanic including a few aquatic plants, some smooth flat stones, and a piece of bog-oak. The *P. ramirezi* became very shy after the transfer and in order to provide them with the "enemy factor", two large Guppy females were introduced as company fish. Two days

Wild-caught female specimen of *Papiliochromis ramirezi*

later, all reservation was already forgotten and both pairs faced each other with threatening poses at the frontier of their territories as if one queried the territory of the other. The border-lines were however soon clearly defined and preparations for spawning became more relevant.

Pair No. I created a depression of just under 1 cm in depth and 6 to 7 cm in diameter in the ground by wagging and swimming in circles through the top layer of the substrate or moving gravel with the muzzle. In all cases observed, this depression was situated in the very far corner of the tank. Both pairs never used a stone for spawning. The substrate consisted of gravel with a grain-size of up to 5 mm. Subsequent observations showed that if smaller grain-sizes were provided, e.g. sand, the diameter of the spawning depressions was not enlarged, but usually were dug up to 2,5 cm deep.

Once the spawning pit was excavated to the satisfaction of both partners, the female began laying eggs, with each batch being immediately fertilized by the male. The eggs had a milky-white colour and an average length of 1,5 mm. Occasionally both specimens tried to swim into the depression simultaneously, but mostly one specimen defended the borders of the territory which would occasionally become the cause of heavy battles again. Even the spawning act had to be interrupted every now and then because both partners were required to fight at the front. Nevertheless, the spawning was eventually completed and approximately 250 to 300 eggs rested in the depression neatly arranged covering the entire ground surface.

At almost regular intervals one parental specimen stayed above the clutch fanning fresh water over the eggs continuously by strong movements of the pectoral fins in a slightly bent position of the body with the head down. This prevented particles of dirt and micro-organisms from settling on the eggs. During the time of observation, the water-temperature was kept at 29 °C. At this temperature the conductivity was measured at 240 S and the pH was noted to be 6,3. In comparison with the water-values recorded in the natural habitat in Columbia, these were not necessarily ideal conditions for the breeding of

P. ramirezi. Nevertheless the eggs developed without noticeable losses — maybe the specimens bred in Asia are more tolerant with regard to the chemical quality of the water. Approximately 40 hours after fertilization the embryos broke through the egg-shells. To assist in this process, the parents took them into the mouth and deposited them on an obliquely arranged piece of wood at a distance of 10 cm from the pit.

Even hours after all embryos had been freed from their egg-shells the parents "plucked" the ground of the pit in search of further eggs.

At this stage the larvae had a length of 2,6 to 2,7 mm. The yolk-sac was still very big with small dark spots being visible. The thickening of the head with the eye-sockets and the embryonic stem still appeared to be very delicate, but the end of the gut was clearly recognizable as an anus. The larvae showed at lot of temperament already and lashing the tail could frequently be observed. Probably for the purpose of cleaning, they were often taken into the mouth for a short time. The fry was relocated two to three times a day always changing between the spawning pit and bog-oak root. In between the caring periods, the specimens engaged in more and more vicious fights with the second pair. However, no injuries could be recognized. In order to enable the parents to protect their fry also during the night hours, a very weak illumination was supplied. After 116 hours, i.e. some five days after spawning, the juveniles began to swim.

Once swimming, the young fish form a densely arranged school. At this point of time they measured 3,7 mm in total length which is small compared with other South American Dwarf Cichlids. The freshly hatched Brine Shrimps may therefore be too big for the young Papiliochromis ramirezi and should accordingly be supplemented by smaller food.

The swimming fry is attentively guided by both the parents. To let their efforts become successful one should remove all other fishes from the breeding tank if these are not easily manageable by the parents. Provided with sufficient food and very clean water, the young fish grow rapidly.

Papiliochromis ramirezi ♂, Asian breed

Papiliochromis ramirezi ♂, Golden breed

The Genus Taeniacara
MYERS, 1935

Besides *Apistogrammoides* and *Mazarunia*, *Taeniacara* is the third genus of South American Dwarf Cichlids which contains only one species. Although this species is rarely imported and usually comes in single specimens as side-catch to other fishes, it has become fairly well known amongst the hobbyists due to its very attractive appearance.

Superficially looked at, it quite closely resembles certain representatives of the genus *Apistogramma*. As the latter, they belong to the Geophagines.

The generic features which allow a comparatively easy identification and distinction from other Cichlids include the unusually slender body-shape and the lanceolate caudal fins of the males. Their special systematic position amongst the Cichlids is, amongst others, based on the entire lack of a lateral line.

A first critical examination of the catch

◆ *Taeniacara candidi*
MYERS, 1935

This extremely pretty, but sometimes also very sensitive species has often been referred to as *Apistogramma weisei*. KULLANDER eventually was the first to point out that this is clearly a junior synonym of *T. candidi*.

Males of this species reach total lengths of approximately 55 mm, but one should be aware of the fact that the caudal fin alone accounts for 15 mm. The body of these fish is unusually slender in shape taking almost five times its height. The diameter of the eye is distinctly larger than the length of the snout. The anterior spines of the dorsal fin are not enlarged. The caudal fin receives its lanceolate appearance from the fact that the central rays are enlarged and thread-like. The tips of the ventral fin are also conspicuously filamentous.

Distribution of *Taeniacara candidi*

Taeniacara candidi ♂

A broad black lateral band runs from the hind edge of the eye up onto the base of the caudal fin in male specimens. It is however not permanently displayed and may be completely suppressed in certain moods. The body is coloured brownish above this band whilst the belly region is whitish. The lower part of the head and the gill-covers especially have a greenish golden metallic gleam. The upper lip shimmers light green. A black streak extends from the lower edge of the eye to the lower angle of the gill-cover. The dorsal fin has a glossy blueish colour and is broadly bordered reddish. The black bordered anal fin has a blue central and reddish distal part. The long filamentous tips of the ventral fins are red. Whilst the lower part of the caudal fin is blue, the central portion has a narrow yellowish orange zone followed by a brownish red ground-colour marbled blueish in the top section.

Specific traits

of this species are the absence of a suborbital stripe and the lateral line. The lateral band ranges from the upper lip through the eye up into the caudal fin. Adult male specimens have lanceolate caudal fins whose central section is greatly produced thread-like and very elongated ventral fins. Females have shorter fins and an oval caudal fin which is slightly pointed at its centre portion.

Similar species

Males of *Dicrossus filamentosus* have a different colour-pattern, a lyreate caudal fin and shorter ventral fins.

Dicrossus maculatus mostly has, as the species mentioned afore, a chequered colour-

Taeniacara candidi ♀

pattern, a larger dorsal fin, and a lauceolate caudal fin which only is slightly pointed.

The

natural habitat

The distribution of *Taeniacara candidi* has been indicated as Central Amazon. The collecting site of the three specimens which served for the description of the species, was probably in the vicinity of the Rio Negro. AHL indicated Santarem to the origin of his fish.

Care

Keeping these fish is not always easy and the water-quality plays an especially important role. For an optimal long-term keeping, soft and acidic water is required. Due to the small adult size of this species, it is recommendable to accommodate them in aquaria of their own. These should be decorated with lush groups of creeping plants which leave small unobstructed interspaces, some heaps of rocks, a few caves, and a piece of bog-oak. Fine dark gravel or sand can be recommended as substrate. In order to overcome the initial shyness of the fish, they should be kept together with a few peaceful dither fishes of their size. The species is more hardy than their appearance would suggest, but they react to sudden changes of the water-values very sensitively. A careful balancing of the water-values is thus necessary on occasion of water-exchanges although it may

Although one may think everything has been done, new destinations beckon.

take a couple of hours. The cleanliness of the water and a varying diet are as important factors. Unfortunately, the species is susceptible to intestine parasites.

Taeniacara candidi is peaceful towards other fishes and also leaves aquatic plants untouched. The temperatures should be maintained around 28 °C.

The

breeding

is no matter of effortlessness and usually requires an experienced breeder. Of course, the cleanliness and quality of the water is also a deciding factor in this regard. Karl-Heinz LÖHNDORF of Kiel/Germany, a repudiated breeder of *Apistogramma* species, reported in a personal communication that his experiments revealed that the eggs would develop in very soft, very acidic water with a pH of 4,8. The male might become fairly aggressive towards the female so that the presence of company fishes representing the "enemy-factor" and to which the aggression could wander would therefore be extremely important. The female would move her posterior part of the body up and down with the head directed downwards at an angle of 45 to signal to the male her readiness to spawn. The eggs are laid on the ceiling of a cave and once hatched, the larvae are hung on the side-walls of the cave.

At a water-temperature of 27,5 °C on average the juveniles begin to swim after nearly eight days. It is only the female that cares for the fry; the males defends the breeding territory. At this point of time the "enemy-fishes" become even more important. In the case of their absence, quarrels with the female develop easily and usually end in the loss of the fry.

The rearing of the young fish is also not without problems. Freshly hatched nauplii of the Brine Shrimp and a "food-milk" made up of water from the breeding tank and a small amount of MikroMin powder-food are recommended as first food for the swimming juveniles. Both types of food are carefully injected into the school by means of a syringe. Due to the fact that food is supplied several times a day, special attention must be paid to the cleanliness of the water.

The Genus Teleocichla
Kullander, 1988

is one of the genera of Cichlids which has only very recently been scientifically described. It was suggested by the Swedish ichthyologist KULLANDER in 1988 to accommodate six new species of Dwarf Cichlids of which a few specimens were added to the collections of zoological museums in the early sixties and early eighties. In the meantime, another half a dozen of new species of *Teleocichla* have been discovered which however still await formal description (SCHLIEWEN & STAWIKOWSKI 1989, STAWIKOWSKI & WARZEL 1991). The genus is closely related to the species of *Crenicichla*, and both are allocated to the Crenicichlines. PLOEG (1991) even joined the species of *Teleocichla* with the Dwarf Crenicichla species.

All forms of *Teleocichla* are highly adapted rheophile Cichlids which have found a variety of ways which enable them to live in torrential waters and whose distributions is thus restricted to the vicinity of rapids. They have occupied the same ecological niche as the Cichlids of the genera *Teleogramma* and *Gobiocichla* which occur in Africa and even resemble these in their general appearance. All species are extremely bound to the ground and their ecology is comparable to that of the Gobies and ground-dwelling Cichlids of Lake Tanganyika.

The generic features uniting the species of *Teleocichla* include a very slender body-shape, a small roundish mouth with a short lower jaw, and the special shape of the ventral fin which serve these fishes as supporting organs for their ground-dwelling ecology.

The distribution of the genus extends over the tributaries of the lower Amazon River which either source in the Brazilian Highland or in the highlands of Guyana. Localities are known from the rapids of the Rio Tapajós, Rio Xingú. Rio Tocantins, Rio Araguaia, Rio Jari, and Rio Araguari. Since there are many biotopes of this kind which have not yet been examined it may be expected that further new species will be discovered in the future.

Rapids of the Orinoco near Puerto Ayacucho (Raudales de Atures). Biotopes like this are the home for rheophile Cichlids.

♦ *Teleocichla cinderella*
KULLANDER, 1988

The specimens on which the original description of this species is based originate from the vicinity of the town of Tucuruí. Some of them had been caught in ponds amongst rocks in 1984 which were the remains of the former rapids of the Rio Tocantins after the completion of the coffer-dam. The largest specimen of this series measured only eight centimetres in standard length. STAWIKOWSKI, who was the first to import this species to Germany alive in 1990, however could provide proof that the males may reach a total length of more than 14 centimetres (STAWIKOWSKI & WARZEL 1991). In contrast, female specimens grow a few centimetres smaller.

Teleocichla cinderella has a very slender, elongate body, a conspicuously pointed head, and a small low-set mouth. The dorsal fin is very long, but relatively low. The scientific

Distribution of *Teleocichla cinderella*

name is very obviously derived from the Cinderella of the fairy-tale and refers to the rather drab colouration. Its upper part of the body is

Females of *Teleocichla cinderella* often have shining light green spots.

greyish green and the lower belly region is whitish. Immediately behind the hind edge of the eye there is a small triangular spot. Depending on the fish's mood up to nine dark transversal bars may appear as indications on the upper half of the body which fuse with a row of similar spots at mid-body. These spots form some kind of an ill-defined lateral band.

The dark lateral spots often fade to shining light green markings in female specimens. The dorsal fin, whose soft section is distinctly enlarged in the males and ranges up to the hind edge of the caudal fin in old specimens, is narrowly bordered with white and red. The top edge of the caudal fin has a narrow white submarginal line on a reddish orange ground-colouration. This orange colour is more intense in male specimens.

One of the

specific traits

of *Teleocichla cinderella* which allows to distinguish it from all related representatives of the genus is the conspicuously long dorsal fin which has the unusually high number of 21 to 22 spines.

Amongst the

similar species

with which this Cichlid could be confused all other members of the genus *Teleocichla* need to be indicated. According to the present state of knowledge, these species however have only a maximum number of 21 spines in the dorsal fins.

The

natural habitat

of *Teleocichla cinderella* lies in northern Brazil. Populations have exclusively been recorded from the catchment of the Rio Tocantins and the lower Rio Araguaia. Although the original biotopes in the vicinity of the town of Tucuruí which served as the type locality have been largely destroyed by the erection of the local coffer-dam, this Cichlid does not appear to be an endangered species as it is commonly found in other parts of the river. As is the case in all

other known forms of *Teleocichla*, this fish prefers torrential waters so that its occurrence is limited to rapids. Following observations made by STAWIKOWSKI & WARZEL (1991) it apparently prefers to reside in rocky zones of shallow water where excessive areas of sand alternate with rock surfaces.

Care

Keeping *Teleocichla cinderella* is by no means difficult if the basic ecological requirements of this fish are appropriately met. Since this Cichlid is an adapted ground-dweller it is important to make a ground-surface available to it which is as large as possible whereas the height of the tank is of secondary interest. A few centimetres thick layer of sand should make out the ground. In order to emulate the natural conditions of its biotope, stones and rocks should create an environment with numerous caves and alcoves which can furthermore be used by the fish to define the borders of territories. Since plants are not damaged by the species, the aquarium can also be decorated with some plants.

As may be supposed from the small mouth, this Cichlid is specialized on small prey and should therefore be fed with *Daphnia*, mosquito-larvae, and similar small-sized food-items. The fish learns to also accept frozen food, but flake-food is usually only accepted hesitantly if at all.

So far, nothing has been reported about the

breeding

of this species in captivity. Soft water with pH-values in the acidic zone should however be an adequate basis for a successful reproduction. It is known that not only the female, but the male also participates in caring for the juveniles.

◆ *Teleocichla gephyrogramma*
KULLANDER, 1988

For the scientific description of this species only three specimens were available. They had been collected at the Von Martius Water-falls of the Rio Xingú by the Belgian ichthyologist J.P. GOOSE and King Leopold III of Belgium in 1964. Their standard length only measured between 36 and 45 millimetres although the maximum total length of males may reach approximately 6 cm and that of females some 5 cm. The first data about the colouration and the ecology of these fish was collected by STA-WIKOWSKI and his travel companions in September 1988. They were also the first to import live specimen into Germany and study them in the aquarium (SCHLIEWEN & STAWIKOWSKI 1989).

Compared with other representatives of the genus, the body of *Teleocichla gephyrogramma* appears to be more stout and less elongate.

The snout is short, the mouth small and roundish. The upper half of the body is dark

Distribution of *Teleocichla gephyrogramma*

grey to greyish green, the lower coloured beige. Six very broad dark blotches are usually recognizable on the back region.

Another ten to twelve blackish spots are alternatingly arranged in a row at mid-body.

Male of *Teleocichla gephyrogramma*

Immediately behind the hind edge of the eye there is small black triangular spot. The cheeks are marked with a narrow shining light green streak. The unpairy fins are translucent yellowish; the base of the dorsal fin has four or five small spots of reddish colour.

Due to differences in the colouration, distinguishing between the sexes is easy in adult specimens. The upper half of the caudal fins of the males is bordered with a very conspicuous deep red band which is accompanied by a narrow light blue submarginal line. Furthermore, this fin is marked with a pattern of several vertically arranged rows of small reddish speckles. Females ready to spawn can be recognized by the reddish coloured belly region.

Important
specific traits
of Teleocichla gephyrogramma are the small maximum size, the comparatively stout body-shape, and the colour-pattern.

Amongst the
similar species
which may be confused with this species, especially Teleocichla monogramma needs to be mentioned. This species however has a clearly more slender body-shape. Furthermore, it can be distinguished by the base of the dorsal fin being orange in males as well as in females.

The
natural habitats
of Teleocichla gephyrogramma lie in the north of Brazil where, according to the present state of knowledge, this Cichlid is endemic to the catchment region of the Rio Xingú. Localities have been recorded from the upper as well as from the lower part of this river.

As is the case in other representatives of this genus, this species also is a rheophile Cichlid whose occurrence is limited to rapids.

Interesting details of its ecology were published by SCHLIEWEN & STAWIKOWSKI (1989) who had carefully studied the naturally inhabited biotopes on the rapids above the town of Altamira. According to their observa-

tions the fish are very closely bound to rocky grounds. They are territorial and defend territories whose centres are always characterized by a small hole in the rock which just allows them to fit it. A water-analysis made by these authors on September 25, 1988, at about 14.00 hrs revealed the following data: At an air-temperature of 34,5 °C and water-temperatures between 32,2 and 35 °C were established.

The pH was 6,5 and the carbonate as well as the total hardness were measured at 1 °dH. The iron-content was found to 0,05 mg/l and the conductivity was 120 micro-Siemens.

Care
It should be taken into consideration that this fish is strictly territorial and is adapted to a life on the ground. Outside periods of reproduction the individuals are highly aggressive even towards their breeding partners. This type of behavioural pattern causes the need for an aquarium with a ground-space as large as possible. Its decoration should consist of sand and numerous rocks which are arranged in such a way that they provide ample caves, crevices, and alcoves. It is possible to include plants although it is advisable to arrange them in a way that they do not unnecessarily limited the available ground-space.

The small mouth of this fish indicates that it is specialized on small prey-items. It should therefore be fed with Daphnia and similarly sized live food.

The
breeding
requires soft water with pH-values in the slightly acidic zone to provide a promising basis. Teleocichla gephyrogramma belongs to the specialized cave brooders which preferably lay their eggs in crevices amongst rocks which are as tight as possible. The eggs, larvae, and the juveniles are exclusively cared for by the female. The young fish do not form a school, but tend to leave the breeding territory that is defended by the mother as soon as they can.

◆ *Teleocichla monogramma*
KULLANDER, 1988

The scientific description of this species is based on a single specimen with a standard length of 63,2 mm which was collected by the Belgian ichthyologist GOSSE and King Leopold III of the Belgium in 1964. It was caught on the Von-Martius Rapids in the upper course of the Rio Xingú.

Reaching a total length of approximately six centimetres, this species belongs to the smallest representatives of the genus. Female specimens are considerably smaller than males.

The first information about the appearance of live specimens and their ecological requirements were gathered by STAWIKOWSKI and travel companions in 1989 and published one year later (SCHLIEWEN & STAWIKOWSKI 1989). Live specimens were imported into Germany by the mentioned authors in autumn 1989 for the first time.

Teleocichla monogramma has a relatively pointed head and an extremely slender and elongate body. The roundish mouth is very

Distribution of *Teleocichla monogramma*

small and slightly low-set. The upper part of the body is coloured greyish green to dark grey whilst its ventral side is light grey to whitish.

Behind the hind edge of the eye there is a small black triangular spot. Depending on the

Male of *Teleocichla monogramma*

mood, the flanks may be marked with ten to twelve dark transversal bars which may partly be arranged alternatingly by some bands being more orientated towards the back and others towards the belly. Below the eye there is a horizontal light green shining stripe. The area around the gill-cover may also have a light green gleam. The portion of the dorsal fin immediately above the base of this fin is marked with a narrow brownish orange stripe.

Since the fish have a distinctly developed sexual dichromatism, the identification of the sexes is easy in adult specimens. Males can be recognized by having the anterior spinous section of the dorsal fin coloured deep red. The posterior portion of this fin is narrowly bordered white, and there is a pattern of tiny red dots arranged in four or five vertical rows marking its distal part. Furthermore, the top edge of the caudal fin is conspicuously bordered with a red stripe below which there is a narrow light blue line. In contrast, the dorsal fin of female specimens is more or less uncoloured except for the mentioned orange shade of the base. On reaching maturity the bellies of the females assume a splendid reddish violet colouration.

Specific traits

of *Teleocichla monogramma* are the orange coloured base of the dorsal fin, the mainly red colouration of the dorsal fins of the males, and the reddish violet bellies of females ready to spawn. Furthermore, this species is characterized by having a single lateral line only, by their asymmetrically shaped pectoral fins, and the unusually high number of 89 scales in a longitudinal row.

Amongst the

similar species

which may be erroneously taken for *Teleocichla monogramma*, *Teleocichla gephyrogramma* is the most similar one. The latter mentioned species however has a different colour-pattern, symmetrical pectoral fins, and the scale-count is 75 scales in a longitudinal row at maximum. *Teleocichla cinderella* on the other hand grows distinctly larger and their females do not change the belly-colouration into red.

The

natural habitats

of *Teleocichla monogramma* lie in northern Brazil. The localities discovered to date all lie in the catchment of the upper and lower Rio Xingú. As is the case in all other known representatives of the genus, this species is also a rheophile Cichlid which has highly adapted to a life in the immediate vicinity of rapids and thus all records were made at such locations.

SCHLIEWEN & STAWIKOWSKI (1989) published interesting details on the ecology and biology of this Cichlid based on studies made in the vicinity of the town of Altamira. According to this, the fish was exclusively found in zones of shallow water with a maximum depth of one metre. There, the extremely territorial fish defend territories on the rocky bank-zones which have a crevice amongst rocks or a hollow-laying stone as centre. At the time of low-water, the soft (total and carbonate hardness 1 °dH, conductivity 120 µS/cm), slightly acidic (pH 6,5) water had a surprisingly high temperature of 32 to 35 °C!

Care

For the husbandry of *Teleocichla monogramma* an aquarium with a large ground-space is required since the fish is territorial with a strictly ground-dwelling ecology. This is supplemented by an extreme amount of intraspecific aggression which also includes the breeding partner at times of no breeding activities. Emulating the natural habitat, the aquarium should be decorated with sand as substratum and numerous rocks creating ample niches and crevices.

Due to the small mouth the fish prefer small-sized food like *Daphnia* and larvae of small insects.

On the

breeding

no information has become available to date. Breeding attempts may be based on an emulation of the water-qualities established in the natural habitats.

SELECTED REFERENCES

ARNOLD, J.P. (1912): *Nannacara taenia* REGAN. Ein neuer Zwergcichlide aus dem Amazonenstrom — Aquar. Terrark., 9: 521—524

GÉRY, J. (1983): Le nom de genre de *Apistogramma ramirezi* MYERS & HARRY — Rev. fr. Aquariol, 10 (3): 71—72

— (1991): Wissenschaftliche Beschreibung "aus Versehen" — DATZ, 44 (12): 793—798

KILIAN, B. (1989): *Biotoecus opercularis* gezüchtet — DATZ, 42 (12): 713—714

KOSLOWSKI, I. (1985): Die Buntbarsche der Neuen Welt: Zwergcichliden — Reimar Hobbing, Essen, 192 pp.

— (1985): Descriptions of new species of *Apistogramma* (Teleostei: Cichlidae) from the Rio Mamoré system in Bolivia Bonner Zool. Beitr., 36 (1/2): 145—162

— (1989): Ist *Nannacara taenia* REGAN 1912 doch eine gültige Art? — DATZ, 42 (10): 602

KULLANDER, S.O. (1977): *Papiliochromis* gen. n., a New Genus of South American Cichlid Fish (Teleostei, Perciformis) — Zoologica Scripta, 6: 253—254

— (1979): Species of *Apistogramma* (Teleostei, Cichlidae) from the Orinoco Drainage Basin, South America, with Description of Four New Species — Zoologica Scripta, 8: 69—79

— (1980a): A taxonomical study of the genus *Apistogramma* REGAN, with a revision of Brazilian and Peruvian species (Teleostei: Percoidei: Cichlidae) — Bonner Zool. Monogr., 14: 1—152

— (1980b): A redescription of the South American cichlid fish *Papiliochromis ramirezi* (MYERS & HARRY) — Stud. Neotrop. Fauna Envir., 15: 91—108

— (1982): Cichlid Fishes from the La Plata Basin. Part IV. Review of the *Apistogramma* Species, with Description of a New Species (Teleostei, Cichlidae) — Zoologica Scripta, 11 (4): 307—313

— (1986): Cichlid fishes of the Amazon River Drainage of Peru — Stockholm, 431 pp.

— (1987): A new *Apistogramma* species (Teleostei, Cichlidae) from the Rio Negro in Brazil and Venezuela — Zoologica Scripta, 16 (3): 259—270

— (1988): *Teleocichla*, a New Genus of South American Rheophilic Cichlid Fishes with Six New Species (Telestei: Cichlidae) — Copeia, 1988 (1): 196—230

— (1989): *Biotoecus* EIGENMANN & KENNEDY (Teleostei: Cichlidae): description of a new species from the Orinoco basin and revised generic diagnosis — Jour. Nat. Hist., 23: 225—260

— (1990): *Mazarunia mazarunii* (Teleostei: Cichlidae), a new genus and species from Guyana, South America — Ichthyol. Explor. Freshwaters, 1 (1): 3—14

— et al. (1989): Description of a *New Apistogramma* Species (Teleostei-Cichlidae) from the Morichal River Slong in Venezuela — Acta Biol. Venezuelica, 12 (3-4): 131—139

— & H. NYJSSEN (1989): The Cichlids of Surinam — Brill: Leiden, 256 pp.

— & W. STAECK (1988): Description of a new *Apistogramma* species (Teleostei, Cichlidae) from the Rio Negro in Brazil — Cybium, 12 (3): 189—201

— & W. STAECK (1990): *Crenicara latruncularium* (Teleostei: Cichlidae), a new Cichlid species from Brazil and Bolivia — Cybium, 14 (2): 161—173

LINKE, H. (1986): Der Zwerg aus Peru: *Apistogramma pucallpaensis* — Aquarium heute, 4 (3): 15—16

— (1987): Es ist gelungen: die Vermehrung von *Papiliochromis altispinosa* — Aquarium heute, 5 (1): 12—14

— (1987): Neu- und wieder importierte Zierfische: Raritäten mit Seitenfleck — Aquarium heute, 5 (1): 5—6

— & W. STAECK (1986): Neu im Aquarium: *Apistogramma luelingi* und *Papiliochromis altispinosa* — Aquarium heute, 4 (1): 7—9

Mayland, H. (1990): Aquaristische Neu-heiten und Seltenheiten kurz vorgestellt — Das Aquarium, 24 (3): 52

Meinken, H. (1965): Eine neue *Apisto-gramma*-Art aus Venezuela (Pisces, Percoi-dea, Cichlidae) — Senckenb. Biol., 46 (4): 257—263

Rham, P. de & S.O. Kullander (1983): *Apistogramma nijsseni* Kullander un nou-veau Cichlid nain pour l'aquarium — Rev. fr. Aquariol, 9: 97—104

Ribbink, A.J., B.A. Marsh, A.C. Marsh, A.C. Ribbink & B.J. Sharp (1983): A preliminary survey of the cichlid fishes of rocky habitats in Lake Malawi — S. Africa Jour. Zool., 18: 147—310

Römer, U. (1989): Beobachtungen zum Fortpflanzungsverhalten von *Nannacara* cf. *taenia* — DATZ, 42 (10): 600—601

Schliewen, U. & R. Stawikowski (1989): *Teleocichla* — DATZ, 42 (4): 227—231

Schmettkamp, W. (1982): Die Zwergcichliden Südamerikas. Landbuch-Verlag, Han-nover, 176 pp.

Staeck, W. (1976): Drei wenig bekannte oder neue Zwergcichliden aus den Gattun-gen *Apistogramma*, *Apistogrammoides* und *Taeniacara* — Das Aquarium, 10 (12): 542—546

— (1986a): Ein neuer Zwergbuntbarsch aus Bolivien: Erste Erfahrungen mit *Apisto-gramma luelingi* — Aquarium-Magazin, 20 (7): 267—271

— (1986b): Beiträge zur Kenntnis peruani-scher Zwergcichliden; Teil 1 — DATZ, 39 (9): 288—292

— (1986b): Beiträge zur Kenntnis peruani-scher Zwergcichliden; Teil 2 — DATZ, 39 (12): 546—548

— (1987a): Beiträge zur Kenntnis peruani-scher Zwergcichliden; Teil 3-7 — DATZ, 40 (2): 61—64; DATZ, 40 (4): 153—155; DATZ, 40 (7): 299—302; DATZ, 40 (10): 439—441; DATZ, 40 (12): 543—545

— (1987b): *Papiliochromis altispinosa*. Ein "missing link" in der Evolution der Maul-brutpflege? — DCG-Info, 18 (6): 115—117

— (1987c): Biotope und Lebensansprüche südamerikanischer Zwergcichliden: Zur Ökologie von *Apistogramma*-Arten — Aquarium- Magazin, 21 (1): 10—17

— (1990): *Apistogramma*-Arten Venezuelas: Teil 1 — DATZ, 43 (7): 412—416

— (1990): *Apistogramma*-Arten Venezuelas: Teil 2 — DATZ, 43 (12): 732—734

— (1991a): *Apistogramma*-Arten Venezuelas: Teil 3 — DATZ, 44 (4): 234—237

— (1991a): *Apistogramma*-Arten Venezuelas: Teil 4 — DATZ, 44 (9): 572—574

— (1991b): Eine neue *Apistogramma*-Art (Teleostei: Cichlidae) aus dem peruani-schen Amazonasgebiet — Ichthyol. Explor. Freshwaters, 2 (2): 139—149

Stawikowski, R. (1991a): Cichliden von A bis Z: *Teleocichla gephyrogramma* Kullander 1988 — DCG-Info, 22 (8): unnum.

— (1991b): Cichliden von A bis Z: *Creni-cichla compressiceps* Ploeg 1986 — DCG-Info, 22 (12): unnum.

— & F. Warzel (1991): Jacundá do Tocantins; Teil 1 — DATZ, 44 (8): 517—519

— & F. Warzel (1991): Jacundá do Tocantins; Teil 2 — DATZ, 44 (9): 575—581

Photo Credits

THE AUTORS

HORST LINKE, born in 1938, has had an interest in the aquarium since early childhood. Already quite early the dream of all enthusiastic aquarists to visit the tropical habitats of our aquarium-fishes came true for him. In the year 1963 he undertook a journey throughout Black Africa, and two years later he had opportunity to visit the countries of Panama, Venezuela, Peru, and Bolivia. From the contacts with the aquarium-fishes in the wild, new questions and tasks always developed so that he visited some countries not only once but repeatedly. Beginning in 1973, he undertook collecting and study expeditions to Cameroon, Nigeria, Ghana, Togo, Sierra Leone, Tanzania, Kenya, Thailand, Sumatra, Borneo, Malaysia, Colombia, Peru, and Bolivia in quick succession. During his numerous stays abroad it was always of special interest for him to collect as much information as possible about the life-conditions in the natural biotopes in order to create an optimal environment for the fishes in the aquarium at home. Over the years, his journeys were planned with more and more precisely defined tasks and specific study-goals, may it be to verify doubtful distribution records or to collect material for the work on taxonomical problems.

He made other aquarists profiting from his experiences by lectures, but especially by publications in both national and international periodicals.

WOLFGANG STAECK, born 1939, studied biology and English literatur at the Freie University Berlin, Germany. After his State Diploma he worked as an associate researcher at the Technische University Berlin for several years. In the year 1972 he conferred a degree with the minor subjects Zoology and Botany.

Dr. STAECK is known to a wide public through numerous lectures and the publication of books and papers in journals. Since 1966 he has published a vast number of contributions on Cichlids in German and foreign magazines. Since his major interest is focused on behavioural studies in Cichlids, he is still an aquarist today and familiar with the maintenance and breeding of Cichlids with the experience of many years.

During his numerous study-trips which were primarily intended to learn more about Cichlids in their natural environments and resulted in the discoveries of many new species, subspecies, and colourvarieties, he travelled East Africa especially, but also West Africa and Madagascar. In recent times he undertook journeys to Central and South America to study and collect Cichlids in Mexico, Brazil, Ecuador, Venezuela, Peru, and Bolivia.

A high priority of his research was spent on the Cichlids of the Lakes Malawi and Tanganyika. Not only in these waters but also in rivers of Central and South America, he observed and took photographs of the world of fishes as a diver. Through this he managed to document the ecology and the inhabited biotopes of many Cichlids for the very first time in underwater photographs. As a result of his study-trips he published scientific descriptions of several new species of Cichlids.